Communications in Computer and Information Science 689

Commenced Publication in 2007
Founding and Former Series Editors:
Alfredo Cuzzocrea, Orhun Kara, Dominik Ślęzak, and Xiaokang Yang

More information about this series at http://www.springer.com/series/7899

María José Abásolo · Pedro Almeida
Joaquín Pina Amargós (Eds.)

Applications and Usability of Interactive TV

5th Iberoamerican Conference, jAUTI 2016
La Habana, Cuba, November 21–25, 2016
Revised Selected Papers

 Springer

Editors
María José Abásolo
National University of La Plata
Buenos Aires
Argentina

Pedro Almeida
University of Aveiro
Aveiro
Portugal

Joaquín Pina Amargós
Faculty of Informatics
Higher Polytechnic Institute
Havana
Cuba

ISSN 1865-0929   ISSN 1865-0937 (electronic)
Communications in Computer and Information Science
ISBN 978-3-319-63320-6   ISBN 978-3-319-63321-3 (eBook)
DOI 10.1007/978-3-319-63321-3

Library of Congress Control Number: 2017946690

Printed on acid-free paper

This Springer imprint is published by Springer Nature
The registered company is Springer International Publishing AG
The registered company address is: Gewerbestrasse 11, 6330 Cham, Switzerland

Preface

The 5th Iberoamerican Conference on Applications and Usability of Interactive TV (jAUTI 2016) was part of the III International Congress on Informatics Engineering and Information Systems (CIIISI 2016) within the framework of the 18th Scientific Convention on Engineering and Architecture 2016 (CCIA 18) and the 52th Anniversary of Higher Polytechnic Institute "José Antonio Echevarría" CUJAE. The conference was held during November 21–25, 2016, in La Habana (Cuba).

jAUTI 2016 was the fifth edition of a scientific event organized by the RedAUTI Thematic Network on Applications and Usability of Interactive Digital Television. RedAUTI currently consists of more than 250 researchers from 39 groups — 32 universities and seven companies — from Spain, Portugal, and 11 Latin American countries (Argentina, Brazil, Colombia, Costa Rica, Cuba, Chile, Ecuador, Guatemala, Peru, Uruguay, Venezuela).

These proceedings contain a collection of selected papers originally presented at jAUTI 2016, and later extended and peer reviewed. The papers cover the development and deployment of technologies related to interactive digital TV, second screen applications, audiovisual content production, and user experience studies toward TV-related services and applications.

May 2017

María José Abásolo
Pedro Almeida
Joaquín Pina

Organization

Program Chairs

María José Abásolo   National University of La Plata, Argentina
Pedro Almeida   University of Aveiro, Portugal
Joaquín Pina   Higher Polytechnic Institute José Antonio Echevarría
     CUJAE, Cuba

Program Committee

José Luis Arciniegas-Herrera	University of Cauca, Colombia
Sandra Baldassarri	University of Zaragoza, Spain
Valdecir Becker	Federal University of Paraba, Brazil
Jordi Belda-Valls	Polytechnic University of Valencia, Spain
Antoni Bibiloni	University of Balearic Islands, Spain
Fernando Boronat	Polytechnic University of Valencia, Spain
Sandra Casas	National University of Southern Patagonia, Argentina
Cesar Collazos	University of Cauca, Colombia
Jorge Ferraz de Abreu	University of Aveiro, Portugal
Israel Gonzalez-Carrasco	University Carlos III of Madrid, Spain
Raoni Kulesza	Federal University of Paraíba, Brazil
Mario Montagud	Polytechnic University of Valencia, Spain
Francisco Montero	University of Castilla-La Mancha, Spain
Rita Oliveira	University of Aveiro, Portugal
Cecilia Sanz	National University of La Plata, Argentina
Telmo Silva	University of Aveiro, Portugal

Contents

IDTV Interaction Techniques

IDTV User Experience

IDTV Content Production and Recommendation

System Architecture for Personalized Automatic Audio-Visual Content Generation from Web Feeds to an iTV Platform

Carlos Silva[1] (iD), David Campelo[1] (iD), Telmo Silva[1]([⊠]) (iD),
and Valter Silva[2] (iD)

[1] Digimedia (CIC.DIGITAL), Aveiro University,
Campus Universitário Santiago, 3810-193 Aveiro, Portugal
{cjhs,david.campelo,tsilva}@ua.pt
[2] ESTGAIT, Aveiro University, 3810-193 Aveiro, Portugal
vfs@ua.pt

Abstract. Fulfilling informational needs of seniors is vital for a successful development of active ageing and independent living initiatives, which contribute for an effective provision of welfare benefits tailored for these citizens. This paper aims to propose a system architecture for automated generation of audio-visual contents adapted from Web feeds of information about Assistance Services of General Interest for Elderly (ASGIE). These pieces of high-value generated content are tailored to the seniors' requirements, needs and expectations, for further exhibition on an iTV platform. Also, this paper describes the technical choices leading to a prototype implementation developed in the context of +TV4E project, an ongoing research project of an iTV platform to enrich seniors television experience with the integration of informative content. Future work will involve submitting this prototype and the generated contents to field tests at seniors' home environment.

Keywords: Interactive TV · Audio and video generation · Information needs · Automation · Seniors

1 Introduction

Challenges and opportunities that come with ageing, both at personal and community level, are drawing the attention of several sectors of society. Hence, to promote participation and autonomy in advanced old age, adequate public policies are required in many different areas [3], such as health care, social assistance, finances and housing.

Following the European Commission (EC) guidelines to promote active ageing and independent living initiatives [4] many countries have developed new communication channels to provide information about the services, activities and social pro-grams entrusted to their respective government bodies. Particularly in Portugal, these channels play an important role in enabling citizens with the ability to obtain relevant information about Services of General Interest (formerly referred as "public services" by the EC) through innovative e-government solutions [5]. However, although several web

© Springer International Publishing AG 2017
M.J. Abásolo et al. (Eds.): jAUTI 2016, CCIS 689, pp. 3–17, 2017.
DOI: 10.1007/978-3-319-63321-3_1

sites and institutional portals have been created to broadcast information about such services, their respective information sources typically require direct searches or newsletter registration. In addition, though a lot of investments have been made to promote these informative channels on the Internet, the senior population is still in a position of disadvantage to have proper access to information, regarding the welfare benefits available to them due to the recurrent scenario of info-exclusion [6] and low literacy levels [7] of these citizens. In this sense, with the emergence of specific needs and limitations inherent to the aging process as well as more free time, specially due to retirement, seniors tend to use the TV as the primary medium of both information and entertainment [8]. In the particular case of Portugal, TV is the most popular communication vehicle and 99% of the senior population consumes TV content at least once a week. Hence, considering its penetration and familiarity among the elderly, information regarding public and social services would rather be available on TV. Furthermore, this information should be presented to seniors considering their particularities, needs, requirements and limitations.

This paper proposes the system architecture to generate personalized audio-visual content for the elderly. This study was conducted in the context of the +TV4E project [2] which comes up with an iTV platform for delivering personalized informative contents to senior citizens, featuring the integration of informative content about Assistance Services of General Interest for Elderly (ASGIE) [1] in a personalized way. To this end, the architecture proposed by this study incorporates features for an automated generation of audio-visual contents based on a set of ASGIE Web feeds with support of Web semantic search methods, a Text-to-Speech (TTS) engine and an AV encoding tool. Then, these generated contents will be pushed by the +TV4E platform to the end-users through an iTV application, which is in charge of integrating these contents with the linear broadcasted TV. These, high-value, audio-visual contents aim at informing and are automatically generated in agreement with the senior's specific characteristics and interests in order to better adapt to their preferences, needs and limitations.

The remainder of this paper is structured as follows: The next section briefly presents selected related works, while the methodology used to assess the design requirements of the system architecture is presented in the third section. Platform key features and architecture of audio-visual generation envisioned for the +TV4E Project are described in the fourth section. In the fifth section, details regarding the prototype implementation of the architecture are provided. Finally, the sixth section identifies some practical challenges for the architecture, and the final section highlights technical innovation and business opportunities arising from this study.

2   Theoretical Background

2.1   Seniors' Information Needs

Accessing adequate information regarding services, activities and social programs from which seniors can benefit may be tiresome and frustrating for these citizens. Due to the frequent scenario of info-exclusion [6] and low literacy levels [7], seniors are constantly in an underprivileged situation to obtain information about the ASGIE in a credible, fast and comprehensible way. In addition, such information is often scattered and sometimes difficult to understand, which puts the elderly in a disadvantaged position by not knowing how to access a number of welfare benefits, such as subsidies in medicines, housing complements, social tariffs, etc. Even when the information is available to seniors, a proper understanding of such information may be a complex process due to recurrent usability issues [9], which, in turn, may lead these citizens to social isolation and informational dependence on their formal and informal caregivers [2]. Hence, the development of innovative and adequate technologies plays an important role to enable independency as well as appropriate access to this information from sources other than the caregivers themselves. Particularly in Portugal and despite the important investments that have been done to broadcast information about government-related services, activities and social programs through new e-government interfaces, the level of adoption and penetration of these communication channels with citizens are still very low due to a set of structural factors, such as "low levels of computer skills of the population" [10] and low penetration of Internet access service [11]. In this country, thousands of seniors who have incomes below the supplemental poverty threshold are not able to access the Solidarity Supplement due to lack of knowledge and information on how to access this financial support [12].

2.2   Interactive TV for Seniors

Considering the popularity of TV amongst seniors for information and entertainment purposes [8], a number of innovative solutions to improve seniors' quality of life have been developed to leverage this device usage and experience [13]. Some studies and works in the scientific literature propose Interactive TV (iTV) applications ranging from medical treatment [14] and mental training [15] to socialization [16] and production selling [17]. Thus, this device consists of a valuable medium for broadcasting high-value information in which seniors may be interested. Moreover, in order to pursue higher levels of satisfaction and adoption, an iTV solution aiming at providing such information to seniors should do it according to these citizens' expectations and limitations. Indeed, considering the particularities of TV as a medium for presenting informative content is crucial for enabling a compelling and enriched experience. Contents designed for TV should take into account the target audience's requirements, limitations and particularities. As losses in visual acuity, hearing and mobility are common at age 60 and over [18, 19], all the elements used for building audio-visual contents should be assembled accordingly. A number of studies [19–22] suggest usability guidelines for graphical contents presentation on TV and, considering the context of +TV4E project, below follows some of the most relevant ones: (1) Simpler fonts like Arial or Verdana should be preferred over adorned fonts, such as Gothic, Rosewood or Old English; (2) Graphical interfaces should, preferably, have high contrast (50:1, e.g. black text on white background or yellow or vice-versa); (3) Text movements (e.g. scrolling, animations, etc.) should be avoided as they require a certain level of visual acuity; (4) It is recommended to use paused speech with a ratio of 140 words per minute; (5) Echoes and background sounds should be avoided; (6) Background music should be avoided if another audio track (e.g. voice-over narration) is used. (7) Audio narratives are preferred over text contents on screen as they do not overcharge seniors with an excess of visual con-tent; (8) Voice-over narration should have an adequate speed in order to avoid cognitive overuse; (9) Audio and video contents concurrently should be avoided as it may cause a sense of information overload; (10) Calm and passive narrator voices are mandatory for voice-over narrations; (11) Voice-over narration should draw the attention to visual information; (12) Formal speech should be avoided.

2.3   Automatic Content Generation

Automation consists in using control systems for operating equipment with reduced or even no human intervention. Equipment such as machinery, processes in factories, telephone networks, ships and aircraft navigation may be automatized speeding up production, reducing human errors (especially in repetitive tasks), and thus increasing productivity and profit. For the current study, automation consists in using software applications to control the execution of software and hardware to achieve a predictable outcome. Automation is often used to automate some repetitive but necessary tasks.

Advantages and drawbacks of software automation can be enumerated according to works done by Mosier, Skitka, Heers and Burdick [24], Yakel [25] and Cummings [26]. These works ground reflections and lead to the production of informative videos, or other processes in general, based on automated tasks. Also some drawbacks, majorly socioeconomically must be accounted, such as job loss, ethical and technical issues [27]. As technologies evolve and systems become more intricate, the use of automated procedures becomes more justifiable, most of all in time critical and highly energy consuming tasks. Considering the role played by computer-human interaction is relevant when decision-making comes at play during the process. For instance, it wouldn't be fair to let a machine choose about a person professional career, like his unemployment, without taking any human sensitive approach. So there must exist an equilibrium between automation and human control, having in mind every specific context.

Cummings in [26] depicts the possible automation levels of a certain system according to the depth of its assistance, interaction or dependence upon human intervention. These levels, ranging from 1 to 10, go from a human-dependant system to a fully autonomous one. Higher levels of automation are considered the best for tasks that are very repetitive and with low risk of failure. An instance of a system that does not require any knowledge or judgment is an autopilot system and the approach used for this level of automation (where a human doesn't have any role) is called black box. However, the lack of judgment and decision-power of a machine may lead to some unexpected problems for a more complex task. In addition, having some intermediate level of dependency on a system with partially automated tasks may be negative for the overall performance, leading to loss of skills and situational awareness, and thus severe decision biases [23, 26].

3 Methodology

This study is part of an early stage of the larger ongoing +TV4E project and aims to suggest the system architecture to gather information from a series of predefined Portuguese ASGIE Web feeds to generate audio-visual contents for further exhibition on TV sets. To achieve that, some gerontechnology and iTV research specialists were invited to take part in a focus group which was carried during the +TV4E platform's conceptualization phase.

Before this focus group, and in order to consider the particularities and limitations of seniors as consumers of informative contents presented on TV, the research team decided to invest in a preliminary exploratory approach to gather information about development and implementation of iTV applications tailored for seniors. This approach consisted on a literature survey of research in international databases with the keywords "seniors" and "Interactive TV", which helped to create a preliminary requirements list for the whole +TV4E platform and, particularly, for its content generation (Table 1).

Table 1. High-level design requirements for contents generation of +TV4E platform.

Design requirements	Priority
The system administrator adds an ASGIE Web feed based on their semantic attributes (URL, HTML classes and paths of text contents)	Mandatory
The system searches through the Web feeds periodically for new text contents	Mandatory
Audio-visual contents are generated based on Web feeds' texts	Mandatory
A notification of new informative content is sent to the iTV platforms when the generation process is complete	Mandatory
Audio-visual contents include voice-over narration and text captions	Mandatory
The system administrator is able to include a manually created informative content	Optional
The system administrator is able to include a personalized script to search through Web feeds	Optional

Table 1 lists high-level design requirements related to the audio-visual content generation for the +TV4E platform, including a column indicating the implementation priority. These requirements served as basis for the debates occurring during the focus group with specialists detailed below.

3.1 Focus Group with Gerontechnology and iTV Research Specialists

In the context of +TV4E project, a focus group with research specialists in geronte-chonolgies and iTV played a key role in the conceptual phase of +TV4E platform development and prototyping. Focus group discussions were run in October 2016, and formed by four research experts:

- Gerontechnology researcher experienced in Ambient Assisted Living (AAL) products and services development, and evaluation of human functioning and environmental factors;
- Senior academic researcher whose main areas of interests are new media, cross-platform content, Interactive Television applications;
- Senior researcher and specialist in new media, cross-platform and context-aware content and Interactive Television, with particular interests in multimedia communication systems and pervasive media applied to specific scenarios;
- Senior researcher and specialist in information systems and decision support systems, participating in several national and international projects.

The main purpose of this focus group was discussing the high-level design requirements of +TV4E platform (Table 1). Considering the objectives of this paper, the main contributions of this focus group consisted in a series of insights and suggestions for an automated generation of audio-visual contents. The specialists stated that it is advisable to generate contents automatically, so that human errors are avoided, and personalizing scripts to be run by the system might lead to security faults. The specialists also provided valuable recommendations regarding the graphical elements' presentation to seniors, such as font size, color and use of animations. Findings from this focus group provided valuable contributions for the final design requirements of the platform and, particularly, for its content generation part (Table 2).

Table 2. Final design requirements for audio-visual content generation of +TV4E platform.

Design requirements	
AV producer	Sends a notification of new content available to +TV4E platform
	Maintains ASGIE Web feed based on their semantic attributes (URL, HTML classes and paths of text contents) and Automatically generate videos employing the information sources defined by the administrator
	Controls the web crawling and audio/video production processes
Web crawler	Retrieves structured Web object with classes, tags and url's
	Search for certain keywords in the sources
	Searches content in a recursive way, limiting the number of levels to access
TTS engine	Creates audio files (voice-over narration) based on text contents gathered by the Web Crawler
AV encoder	Uses introductory videos specific to each ASGIE
	Receives content from Web Crawler about sources of information accessed
	Maintains a generic image database for each ASGIE
	Include voice-over narration generated by the TTS engine, as well as captions, both referring to information content

To better accommodate the design requirements of +TV4E platform content generation four modules were envisioned to divide the responsibilities of this process: AV encoder, Text-To-Speech (TTS) engine, Web Crawler and AV Manager. These modules served as basis for the system architecture hereby presented. Table 3 presents these modules as well as their respective requirements. Design requirements concerning the

Table 3. Advantages and drawbacks of Text-To-Speech software solutions.

	Advantages	Drawbacks
Text to Speech **ivona** An Amazon Company	Has a node client library and both genres for all languages; In comparison to the other solutions, it has the best diction; Allows to control parameters such as the rate, the volume, sentence and paragraph breaks;	Although having the best diction it is not perfect in some instances;
ReadSpeaker	Has a good level of diction and both genders for the available languages;	Does not have a node client library;
IBM Watson	Subsists of machine learning, therefore it is constantly evolving;	Does not have the Portuguese language;

inclusion of manually created contents and personalized scripts were removed, while some other requirements regarding the content generation on an automated way were included.

4   Key Features and Platform Architecture

The informational audio-visual contents developed for the project are created based on a single template, with the possibility of more in development. This tem-plate consists on an intro, informative content and an outro. The intro aims to show the project logo and a small animation of ASGIE colour and icon associated. The informative content includes related background images, having a colour mask with an alpha channel, the news title, description and its narration. At last, the outro aims to give an end to the video in a similar way as the intro but without showing the ASGIE icon and colour. It is also intended for the videos to have background music, but this is still being studied with usability and user experience tests among the target audience, and thus hasn't been implemented as of yet. The current structure of the informative videos is subdivided in the following components and will be discussed further in more detail: (i) Intro with Project logo and ASGIE content specific logo; (ii) Informative content with news with respective title and description, that will exist thought-out this component; (iii) Outro with project logo with one of the respective ASGIE background images and the project logo without background.

There are three major steps for achieving the automatic generation of informative contents tailored for seniors and with the above information structure in mind. The generation process is an iterative process where the output of a given step serves as input for the subsequent step in order to build a complete audio-visual informative content. The generation process starts with the Automated Video Producer (AVP), which requests new Web contents from the Web Crawler. In this sense, web feeds are scanned making use of a predefined semantic structure, which may vary from one Web feed to another. If new data is available, it will be retrieved and filtered as plain text contents. In the second step, this plain text is submitted to the Text-To-Speech (TTS) module to create a voice-over narration audio file. At last, the third step consists of encoding and post-production of all inputs retrieved and generated. The architecture proposed by this study applies the 7th level of automation [26], as after receiving all data about the Web feeds the system starts the generation process, with no intervention, and by the end notifies the administrator with logs. Figure 1 shows an overview of the proposed Automated Video Engine (AVE) architecture. This architecture applies two different structures [28]: (a) modular, which allows several areas of functional responsibility; and (b) component-and-connector, which explains how data flows within the structure. In that way, being a modular structure, it is also layered because it stacks the application into different inter-dependent modules and as a component-and-connector structure it also belongs to those who are client-server due to a certain dependency upon client rules that are inputted to a database for the server to access. The layered structure consists of the automated video producer (AVP) along with the Web Crawler, the Text-To-Speech and the Video Encoder modules, while the client-server structure is composed of the Dashboard and the AVP connection to the database and other server-side services.

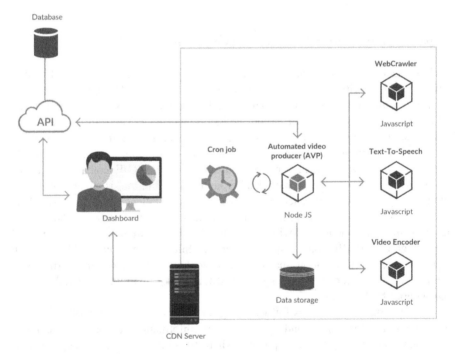

Fig. 1. Automated video engine (AVE) architecture.

The Dashboard is separated from the rest of the system as it offers an interface to set parameters for web crawling and video producing. As it is seen, the Automated Video Producer (AVP), being a component of the engine, contains the main algorithm to control other modules and is called periodically by a time-based job scheduler, and it depends of a constant access to a database, in order to store and read information. A step by step look can describe the architectural modules:

- Web Crawler – Crawling is the process of automatically exploring content within web pages using certain semantic rules. A crawler focuses on collecting content throughout several webpages it finds [29].
- Text-To-Speech – A text-to-speech tries to simulate natural human speaking by combining and formalising digital signals (DSP) with natural language processing (NLP) [30]. Using the content provided by the Web Crawler the synthesizer purpose is to create an adequate voice-over narration for the target audience.
- Audio-visual encoder – An audio-visual encoder has the ability to encode and apply filters to any of the file formats it supports. Amongst its functionalities, being able to use audio, image or video files is one of the most important steps towards generating media following certain rules and definitions regarding usability for seniors, such as font sizes and colours, audio speed, etc.

5   Prototype Implementation

The present study is part of the larger project, which proposes a platform designed in a user-centred approach to increase the info-inclusion of seniors based on the transmission and exhibition of informative contents about ASGIE [1]. Figure 1 shows the prototype implementation schema developed in the context of this project.

The audio-visual content produced by the +TV4E platform is presented and inter-leaved with a HLS stream, which includes the linear TV broadcast. The generated media is distributed as static content to several React applications, being one of them for the elderly, and other for a Dashboard.

Before choosing which technologies should be used for each process it was first necessary to define how they could all be encapsulated with a single programming language. To do so, and in order to simplify the entire process, Node.js was selected as the primary runtime platform. The rationale behind this choice is: (i) Node.js is lightweight and (ii) is supported by a large open source ecosphere of libraries available through its package manager, the Node Package Manager (npm).

The operational system chosen for this prototype implementation was the Ubuntu 16.04, a popular Linux operational system distribution. The informative content creation is started by the system's native time-based job schedule, cron, which periodically starts the Automated Video Producer (AVP). This cron process creates automatically a number of threads for web crawling, speech synthesizing and video en-coding, according to the system's hardware capabilities. After each process ends the generated audio-visual informative content is saved to the machine's hard drive, into a specific folder where all the static contents are available to the Internet through a CDN.

In addition, data about these files may be retrieved from the database through an Application Programming Interface (API).

Some of the content delivery, from the API to the CDN, is made using a secured FTP connection in order to avoid a permanent connection between both servers, which may provide an open route for several attacks [31]. Having several machines focusing on different tasks is a central concern to create a load balance, so one is focused on the API and the applications, and the other on the AVE and the CDN.

Each of the steps for creating an informative video is dependent upon some library, this leads to certain implementation guidelines for each model, for instance, the WebCrawler uses three different Javascript open-source libraries: Cheerio, Re-quest and URL, which are dependent on one another. Request needs a well-formed url, provided by URL, to make a successful http call and return the website body, later on for Cheerio to look for the respective semantic contexts.

Some alternatives were considered when selecting the proper API's and frame-works to use for the text-to-speech and the audio-visual encoder. For the Text-To-Speech one of the most important requirements was having a broad range of sup-ported languages so that it is possible to provide services to several countries, namely Portugal. For the encoder, it was necessary that it was compatible with the technologies in use, therefore having a support node client library was an added value. From all the best open-source alternatives, the following tables describe advantages and drawbacks of the software solutions considered by the research team.

Based on the points in favor of Ivona, this software solution was chosen as a tool for voice synthesizing. It meets all requirements for audio generation, such as having a wide range of languages and is supported by Node.js open source libraries, which enables important speech control parameters (Table 4).

Table 4. Advantages and drawbacks of creating videos APIs.

	Advantages	Drawbacks
FFmpeg	Has a node client library and interfaces for C++, C, Python, Java and MATLAB; Accepts every kind of format;	Becomes a bit complex when demanding the implementation of certain filters Favor their own code while still implementing some of the best free software for libraries, for instance;
OpenCV	Has interfaces for C++, C, Python, Java and MATLAB;	Level of complexity to elevated in regard to the algorithm specifications and the stipulated time to produce;
MLT	Has a node client library and interfaces for C++, C, Python, Java and MATLAB;	Less production stability; Is an abstraction of FFmpeg:

From all of the frameworks available, FFmpeg seems the most adequate alternative, being the simplification, over a Node.js package, of its source code one of the most important benefits for its serviceableness.

The informative content generation depends on several steps, and takes some major aspects into account. Each video is composed of an intro, the informative content, an outro and two audio tracks: the voice-over narration and background music. The intro and the outro clips are small movie clips previously generated and just merged into the final clip in order to avoid any additional system overload. The generation algorithm firstly selects some images to be used as background of the informative content and based on the voice-over narration time length and the text length determines how many clips will be created. The text content for each image clip is changed according to the informative content displayed, doing so eases the algorithmic process and avoids some usability issues from having background images freely changing and disrespecting the integrity of the video, this is also due to the fact that in FFmpeg the text is considered a filter attached to a clip.

6 Validation and Evaluation Scenarios

Providing information to seniors in a personalized way is the main requirement for the platform. However, it is critical to find out an adequate approach for this. Hence, to validate the proposed architecture as well as the implementation choices, seniors will be recruited from nearby cities to take part in rounds of participative design meetings. In these meetings, every design choice implemented for the generated contents will be validated, such as font colours and sizes, sound level, text speed and transitions, etc. In addition, keeping these recruited participants motivated to collaborate is considered vital for the project success.

Findings of later stages in these upcoming participatory design rounds are going to be reported later.

A high-tech world age should be a synonymous of productive, healthy and active ageing, considering the potential this type of technologies can represent to seniors' lives. However, several projects, products and services oriented to the elder do not take into account their specific characteristics and needs, revealing themselves to be less interesting than expected. Stereotyping the elderly as people who suddenly be-come passive and dependent, takes us to develop things to older people rather than to create things with older people [32], therefore the co-creation is one of the most important approaches to design innovative solutions [33].

Defining a high-level architecture to automatically generate informative contents based on information gathered from many ASGIE Web feeds is a cornerstone of the +TV4E project. The conception of this architecture enabled the authors to assess the platform implementation requirements, which unveiled a set of concerns and problems for the upcoming cycles of implementation and validation.

When developing an algorithm to produce informational content, transmitted through a video format, it is mandatory to have a special care about how and where the data is fetched and in which way it will be presented to the public audience, mainly because elderly people have had a lot of visual and auditory perception deterioration.

At age 60 due to losses in visual acuity, hearing, moving and non-communicable diseases, the probability for disability and dead risk arises [18, 34]. So, all the elements must be oriented to cope with these particularities, whether they are audio, semiotic, such as icons or font properties, and the information itself.

About the content that is going to be used, it depends on a source that needs to be somehow connected to automated computer tasks. For this reason, web and RSS feeds are the main source to gather data from. It is a way of staying in focus with updated information while relying on services that already cover important news related to a specific ASGIE. From the entire process the only task requiring human intervention is the selection of sources that match the needs of the +TV4E project, be-cause of the depth and flexibility of the analysis it requires. To simplify the selection process, the dashboard interface aims to control elements related to generated con-tents background images, playback time, music and descriptive data regarding every ASGIE Web feed.

The data retrieved through the process of web crawling is dynamic and unstable, because it depends on the web sources where it is fetched, so if there is any change on the semantic structure of a source, the web crawler won't work has expected. The database holds, for each source, a list of news generated, acting in conformity with the resulting web page output, in that case, new content will only be generated if, after comparing the title of each news from the database with the ones provided by the resulting crawling, there is no duplicate information. The dashboard works as a fast solution for the problem of semantic mismatch, providing an interface to directly change the structure needed for crawling.

Because it isn't known what to expect from the news size, sometimes the resulting crawling process may lead to informative audio-visual content that lasts too much time, let's say, for instance, more than one minute. In cases like this there are two possible solutions, one is to summarize the body of the news text and the other is to let the viewer decide if he, after one minute of video, wants to see the rest. For now, the solution is to let the person decide this, because automatic content summarization is optimized for only certain languages, therefore, the results tend to be unsatisfactory and unpredictable.

The AVE architecture requires, as seen, a machine capable of handling data pro-cessing faster than others, due to the requirements needed to generate a vast number of audio-visual content in the faster time interval as possible. The number of encoding process that can be managed at the same time is controlled directly on the AVE con-figuration files, which sets a proper queue in order not to crash the service. This same machine, at the moment, is also responsible for delivering static content, using NGINX, because it has a load balancer solution that allows for the implementation of multiple machines sharing content through a Network File System (NFS), thus creating a CDN. There is also another machine whose focus is only delivering the API and the web apps.

7   Conclusions

Providing information needed by senior citizens is crucial for this population to "age well and socially included" [33], and an effective delivery of information and public policies is vital for a successful development of countries. Furthermore, full-filling information requirements of elderly using personalized and acceptable methods may give them more independency and autonomy. This paper highlights some of the challenges associated with conceptualization and prototyping of the system architecture of audio-visual content generation for the +TV4E platform. Considering the specific information needs of seniors, several technologies have been created with the purpose of bringing such information to this population. Currently +TV4E project is on a phase of participatory design, considering variables such as the target audience requirements, their interaction with the system and level of satisfaction on different aspects of the platform and the audio-visual content. The co-creation becomes essential in order to establish the best approach for the development of the AVE, this is where the dashboard comes in handy, as well as the other platforms related to this project. The future may hold, in several areas, a space for the automatic production of informative content, being in advertisement, service distribution or public communication and that is why the AVE provides an on growing dynamic solution to aid in a task that until now would be time, effort and monetarily consuming.

Acknowledgements. The research leading to this work has received funding from Project 3599 – Promover a Produção Científica e Desenvolvimento Tecnológico e a Constituição de Redes Temáticas (3599-PPCDT) and European Commission Funding FEDER (through FCT: Fundação para a Ciência e Tecnologia I.P. under grant agreement no. PTDC/IVC-COM/3206/2014).

References

1. Silva, T., Caravau, H., Campelo, D.: Information needs about public and social services of portuguese elderly. In: Proceedings of the International Conference on Information and Communication Technologies for Ageing Well and e-Health, Porto, Portugal (2017)
2. Silva, T., Abreu, J., Antunes, M., Almeida, P., Silva, V., Santinha, G.: +TV4E: Interactive Television as a support to push information about social services to the elderly. In: Conference on Health and Social Care Information Systems and Technologies, CENTERIS, pp 1–6 (2016)
3. Walker, A.: Active ageing: realising its potential. Australas. J. Ageing **34**(1), 2–8 (2015)
4. European Commission, Taking forward the Strategic Implementation Plan of the European Innovation Partnership o Active and Healthy Ageing. Communication from the Commission (2012)
5. National Interoperability Framework Observatory, Portuguese eGovernment Factsheets, Ed. 17.0 (2015). https://joinup.ec.europa.eu/community/nifo/og_page/egovernment-factsheets. Accessed 10 Oct 2016
6. Amaro, F., Gil, H.: The 'Info-(ex/in)-clusion' of the elderly people: remarks for the present and for the future. In: ED-MEDIA 2011–World Conference on Educational Multimedia, Hypermedia and Telecommunications, pp. 1024–1030 (2011)
7. Instituto Nacional de Estatística, Censos 2011: Resultados Definitivos - Portugal, Lisboa, Portugal (2012)
8. Nielsen, Screen Wars - The battle for eye space in a TV-everywhere world (2015)
9. Domenech, S., et al.: Involving older people in the design of an innovative information and communication technologies system promoting active aging: the SAAPHO project. J. Access. Des. All **3**(1), 15 (2013)

10. European Commission, EU eGovernment Report 2015 shows that online public services in Europe are smart but could be smarter (2015). https://ec.europa.eu/digital-single-market/en/news/eu-egovernment-report-2015-shows-online-public-services-europe-are-smart-could-be-smarter

11. ANACOM, Internet access service - 3rd quarter 2016 (2016). https://www.anacom.pt/render.jsp?contentId=1402572#.WJTp9raLRE4. Accessed 01 Jan 2016

12. RTP Notícias, Milhares de idosos poderão beneficiar do CSI, mas não sabem, afirma Vieira da Silva (2016). http://www.rtp.pt/noticias/pais/milhares-de-idosos-poderao-beneficiar-do-csi-mas-nao-sabem-afirma-vieira-da-silva_n960841. Accessed 11 Nov 2016

13. Blackburn, S., Brownsell, S., Hawley, M.S.: A systematic review of digital interactive television systems and their applications in the health and social care fields. J. Telemed. Telecare **17**(4), 168–176 (2011)

14. Stojmenova, E., Debevc, M., Zebec, L., Imperl, B.: Assisted living solutions for the elderly through interactive TV. Multimed. Tools Appl. **66**(1), 115–129 (2013)

15. Miotto, A., Lessiter, J., Freeman, J., Carmichael, R., Ferrari, E.: Cognitive training via interactive television: drivers, barriers and potential users. Univers. Access Inf. Soc. **12**(1), 37–54 (2013)

16. Abreu, J.F., Almeida, P., Silva, T.: iNeighbour TV: a social TV application to promote wellness of senior citizens. Inf. Syst. Technol. Enhancing Heal. Soc. Care **221**, 1–19 (2013)

17. Savvopoulos, A., Virvou, M.: Dynamically extracting and exploiting information about customers for knowledge-based interactive TV-commerce. Stud. Comput. Intell. **142**, 471–480 (2008)

18. Beard, J.R., et al.: The World report on ageing and health: a policy framework for healthy ageing. Lancet **6736**(15), 1–10 (2015). (London, England)

19. Nielsen, J.: Seniors as Web users (2013). https://www.nngroup.com/articles/usability-for-senior-citizens/. Accessed 01 Jan 2017

20. Fisk, A.D., Rogers, W.A., Charness, N., Czaja, S.J., Sharit, J.: Designing for Older Adults: Principles and Creative Human Factors Approaches. CRC Press, Boca Raton (2009)

21. Zaphiris, P., Ghiawadwala, M., Mughal, S.: Age-Centered Research-Based Web Design Guidelines (2005)

22. Hawthorn, D.: Designing Effective Interfaces for Older Users. The University of Waikato (2006)

23. Rifkin, J.: The end of work: the decline of the global labor force and the dawn of the post-market Era. J. Leis. Res. **30**(1), 172 (1998)

24. Mosier, K., Skitka, L., Heers, S.: Automaton bias: decision making and performance in high-tech cockpits. Int. J. Aviat. Psychol. **8**(1), 33–45 (1998)

25. Yakel, E.: Automating Record Services. International Records Management Trust (1999)

26. Cummings, M.: Automation bias in intelligent time critical decision support systems. In: AIAA 1st Intelligent Systems Technical Conference, pp. 1–6, September 2004

27. Ford, M.: Rise of the Robots: Technology and the Threat of a Jobless Future. Basic Books (2015)

28. Bass, L.: Software Architecture in Practice. Pearson Education India (2007)

29. Mirtaheri, S.M., Dinçtürk, M.E., Hooshmand, S., Bochmann, G.V., Jourdan, G.-V., Onut, I. V.: A Brief History of Web Crawlers. In: Proceedings of the 2013 Conference Center Advanced Studies Collaborative Research, pp. 40–54 (2013)

30. Dutoit, T., Ide, N., Veronis, J.: An Introduction to Text-to-Speech Synthesis. In: Text, Speech and Language Technology, vol. 3, p. 285 (1997)

31. Security and NFS. http://www.tldp.org/HOWTO/NFS-HOWTO/security.html. Accessed 10 Feb 2017

32. Coulombe, C.-A., Zhang, J.: Imagine Tomorrow: Report on the 2nd WHO Global Forum on Innovation for Ageing Populations, Kobe, Japan (2015)
33. Rosenberg, P., Ross, A., Garçon, L.: WHO Global Forum on Innovations for Ageing Populations, Kobe, Japan (2013)
34. Nielsen, J.: Usability for Senior Citizens. Seniors as Web Users (2013)

nowUP: A System that Automatically Creates TV Summaries Based on Twitter Activity

Pedro Almeida$^{(\boxtimes)}$ (iD), Jorge Ferraz de Abreu (iD), and Rita Oliveira (iD)

University of Aveiro - Digimedia, Aveiro, Portugal
{almeida, jfa, ritaoliveira}@ua.pt

Abstract. Users post a lot of related TV information on social networks while they are watching TV, mostly in a connected way with the highlight moments of the TV shows. This paper reports on the nowUP project, targeted at the development of a service that automatically creates summaries of TV programs based on the buzz on social networks. The project premise relies on the idea that social media buzz has the potential to be used as an automatic editorial criterion. In this framework, the project goals include the development of a solution that automatically produces TV summaries of popular television programs (like football matches, talent or reality shows) based on the Twitter activity. The solution is based on a data-mining engine that processes the activity of this social network looking for tweets related with TV shows. Based on the program metadata it indexes the twitter activity; correlates tweets; and creates clusters of peaks, being the relevant clusters associated with the TV highlights. With this, a specific developed video engine automatically edits and creates a full video summary (an edited sequence of TV highlights) and publishes it in an online platform. The paper reports on the solution architecture and features and on the results of its preliminary evaluation. The results show that the solution was very successful in achieving the project main goal and the users are willing to have access to this type of social buzz-based video summaries.

Keywords: TV summaries · Highlights · Editing · Twitter · Evaluation

1 Introduction

Globally, personalization technologies have been adapting contents and preparing the most suitable ones to the users, as in the case of news curation. In addition, video contents take an important role in the users' consumption behavior, competing with newspapers, radio, books, games and podcasts among many others [1]. Media corporations therefore need to increase the users' relation with TV shows, providing customizable content. This includes providing shorter video clips like TV summaries of the programs regularly consumed by the viewers, providing a short and quick overview of past TV shows. This is especially relevant in the actual TV ecosystem where catch-up TV [2] actually allow users to quickly review previously broadcasted programs - however without offering an outline/preview of these contents. Though, taking

© Springer International Publishing AG 2017
M.J. Abásolo et al. (Eds.): jAUTI 2016, CCIS 689, pp. 18–31, 2017.
DOI: 10.1007/978-3-319-63321-3_2

in consideration the significant manpower needed to create TV summaries, establishing an automatic alternative for its creation will be a significant outcome.

In this context, the research team was motivated by the opportunity to use the social media buzz as an editorial criterion. Actually, users post a lot of related-TV information on social networks while they are watching TV and, as we observed, the timing of these posts is very close to the most important moments of the TV shows, being it a goal in a football match or an excellent performance of a contestant of a talent show. It was this relationship that the researchers of this project tried to explore aiming to create a system allowing the automatic creation of video summaries of talent shows or sports matches, based on the social activity related to its highlights.

According to Viacom [3], American viewers engage in social networks in an average of ten TV-related activities a week. The extent to which this type of activities is done around premium programs such as Idols, Secret Story and even soccer games and political debates is somehow transversal to many countries. Nielsen Twitter TV Ratings concerning US are quite impressive: in 2014 several TV programs generated millions of tweets resulting in more than a billion impressions each week [4]. In Europe these numbers are also quite expressive. For instance in UK, a study from Kantar Media [5] (about Twitter TV Ratings) shows that in a period of 5 months there were about 40,5 million TV-related tweets, being sport programs the most popular closely followed by entertainment shows. These dynamics strengthen the potential of social networks activity acting as an indicator of the "hot" moments of TV shows. With this in mind a working prototype using Twitter data was developed, combining data mining features with automatic video editing capabilities, to produce summaries for high popularity TV programs like sports or talent shows.

This paper is organized as follows. An initial state-of-the-art concerning solutions for the creation of TV related videos is presented in the next session. Then, in Sect. 3, the nowUP service features are described. Sections 4 and 5 reports on the evaluation process along with the conclusions towards the relevance of such a system and its efficiency when compared to regular editorial manually created summaries. The final section presents the most relevant conclusions.

2   Related Work

2.1   Social Platforms for the Curation of TV Moments

The Twitter Amplify [6] service enables broadcasters to share video content in real time, giving users the opportunity to watch it without leaving Twitter. This solution also manages the distribution and the discovery of that content, allowing for example users to retweet their favorite videos making them available to their own followers, widening the scope of videos in a broader setting [6]. The biggest advantage for content providers is that Twitter Amplify allows them to distribute content as paid information sources by integrating funded sponsors and partners' content [7].

The Wild Moka solution allows ingesting any video stream (including live TV) and, from pre-patented algorithms, enriching the video content in real time, complementing the flow with metadata from any source and in any format [8]. "Canal +"

(French leader in pay-TV services) adopted the WildMoka Moments Share for its use [9]. This social application allows sharing TV moments from streaming content. In this way, the viewer can select a set of pictures or a short video clip and share it with its friends via various social networks (Twitter, Facebook, Google+ or Pinterest) [10]. In addition to this functionality, the shared content may be supplemented with additional information, such as advertisements, promotional messages or #hashtags. Another WildMoka application is the Wild Moments Replay [11]. This solution allows the viewer to review the most appreciated moments of a TV show. The application is especially focused on sports programs due to their own characteristics. Users are able to access their favorite moments through several mechanisms. These moments are automatically generated by video analyzing algorithms.

The Moments Capture application automatically detects TV key moments within a program: TV commercials, the beginning and end of the program, chapters and scenes, key moments as goals in sports events and musical performances in television programs [12]. Despite the automatic selection of key moments these solutions are based exclusively on video analysis and metadata.

With the Tellyo application viewers can capture short TV content into video clips (via a mobile device) and instantly share those moments on social networks with their friends enriched with textual comments. Additionally, users have the ability to navigate through other TV moments shared by friends and other users [13].

TV Timelines [14] is a Twitter feature that has been available since March 2015 and aggregates TV-related content through an interface within the Twitter app. This feature consists of a dedicated page for each TV show, which includes the official TV show and actors' accounts and tweets, tweets featuring video excerpts and other media as well as all tweets about the show.

2.2   Aggregation Platforms for Social Networks TV Related Activities

The Nielsen Social platform [15] identifies, collects and analyses, in real-time, conversations in Twitter for all programs within the most popular television channels, using this data to enhance: (i) the Nielsen Social Guide Intelligence - the component that provides the social commitment towards TV; (ii) Nielsen Twitter TV Ratings - the solution that measures the reach of TV programs in Twitter conversations, and; (iii) Nielsen Twitter TV APIs that provide data to enhance social and second screen applications [16].

The Social EPG application of the Dutch station Veronica enables its viewers to know the activity that is being generated on social networks for a given program while zapping through the EPG. As an example it allows to know that a particular live program is generating a greater number of tweets than others being aired at the same time. Users are able to use that buzz to take decisions on programs they want to watch [17].

2.3   The User Perspective

Creating video summaries implies mechanisms to condense or summarize the original video by analyzing all the contents of the original video sequence. These mechanisms can be based on text descriptions, visual appearances and audio, among others [18]. However, certain actions, facts or opinions are likely to be omitted from these solutions [19]. Alonso & Shiells proposed to create a timeline based on the "peaks" of comments made on Twitter for a live event. The authors verify that the most reported events were not only the goals since users also considered other events important. In this framework, these are important elements that deserve attention during the creation of a football match summary, but are typically omitted from algorithmic solutions. It means that it is possible to track a sports event through Twitter posts without losing relevant events. Thereby creating summaries should be seen as one more tool that can enhance the viewing experience and an entertainment or information activity [1].

Taking into account the increasingly connection between data in social networks and TV content, the hypothesis that a system enabling the user to watch summaries of its favorite TV programs, based on the social networks activity, seems promising. As is shown in the next section, the nowUP project aimed creating a suitable way to integrate the best social network TV related content and deliver it to the viewer.

3   The nowUP Features

As referred, the main goal of nowUP is to automatically create TV highlights of popular television programs (like football matches; talent or reality shows) based on the buzz on social networks, specifically twitter activity. In addition, it was also aimed to integrate the most relevant tweets as oracles of the correspondent TV highlights. Figure 1 presents its system architecture – data flows according the numbers shown in the figure.

3.1   An Overview of the Creation Process

The solution incorporates different modules:

- The metadata analysis module (TV Pulse): this module is responsible for getting information about the shows and related information on social networks. First, it extracts information from the EPG about TV shows (1) (program name and synopsis and time/date of airing) and then searches, through data mining analysis, for activity on Twitter related to these TV shows. Tweets are then analyzed, associated to the related TV show and the most commented moments are identified. In addition, the API extracts the most relevant tweets for later use;
- The video editing module: the following module is responsible for obtaining the TV program video (2). For this, the cloud DVR infrastructure from a telco partner is used. With this information it produces the segmentation and subsequent aggregation of content (video and text) to be used in the final summary. For that an FFmpeg multimedia framework was used. This segmentation uses as reference the

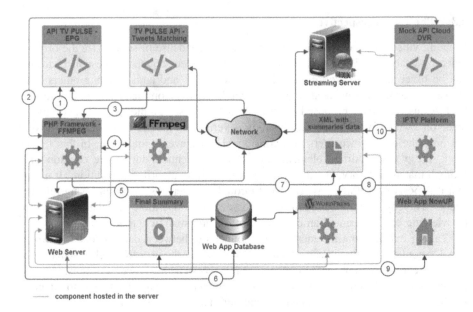

Fig. 1. The nowUP system architecture

peak events detected in the first module, clipping a subset of video for each event (3 and 4).

- The video enhancement module: in order to produce the final summary a visual separator is introduced between each clip (Fig. 2), along with an oracle with the most popular tweet (5) (Fig. 3).

Fig. 2. The events separator included in the summary

The completed clips are presented in a web portal and complementary made available to be viewed when accessing the corresponding catch-up TV program, through the IPTV interface (6 to 10).

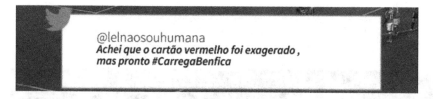

Fig. 3. Oracle with the most relevant tweet related to a specific event.

3.2   Clips Duration

Along with the technical challenges related with data mining, other concerns were taken into consideration. First there was the need to define the length of each clip as part of the highlight. The data-mining module allowed identifying the peak moments but not the duration of such moments. In a preliminary research made by the team (not presented in this paper) an analysis of four TV programs (two football matches and two entertainment shows) was carried to determine the duration of the video segments to be used in the summaries along with the elapsed time between the actual event and the peak on Twitter. The results have shown that the TV genre influences the length of the segments and the reaction to peak events on Twitter. With this information, the segments duration and time correlation with Twitter events were defined for each genre.

3.3   The Meta Information Visual Presentation

The challenges included not only the correct data selection but also building a coherent visual and cinematic approach to the TV summaries. An empirical analysis of different TV programs and highlights was carried and a visual separator was prepared. Graphically, the separator includes the nowUP logo inserted with a visual transition (Fig. 2).

Considering the fact that the most relevant events were detected based on the social activity, there is an additional probability that the most important tweet of an event cluster is closely related with that event. Therefore, on top of each segment, and for a limited period of time, a visual oracle is superimposed. This oracle includes the most relevant tweet correlated with that event, providing a sense of commentary (usually based on audio in traditional TV summaries). With this approach, the team wanted to validate if the oracle had the potential to reinforce the perception of the social related dynamics of the corresponding TV program.

Once all segments are prepared, all the insertions introduced and all the oracles superimposed, the TV summary is ready to be used.

3.4   Delivering It to the Users

To provide access to the TV summaries, a web portal was developed (Fig. 4). It includes the following sections: (i) Homepage - a mosaic of most relevant highlights (based in the social network buzz); (ii) "Search" and "Most Viewed" – alternative ways to find TV summaries; (iii) "Contributors" – the Twitter users are the (subsidiary) editorial staff of

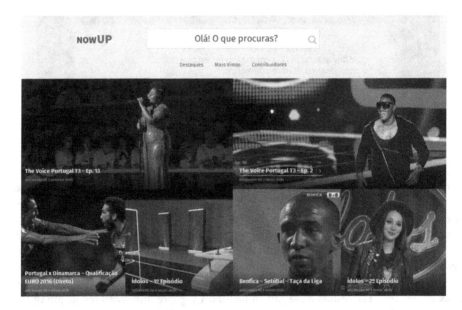

Fig. 4. The web portal home page

nowUP. In that sense, it includes the most important contributors for nowUP (i.e. the ones which tweets were considered as top tweets on an TV event); (iv) "Video details" – for each TV summary the user is presented with detailed information, including: a timeline showing the most relevant events that were detected and used in the video, the number of tweets processed, and other social related statistics.

4 The Evaluation Process

In the scope of the project goals, once the working prototype was concluded an evaluation was prepared.

This evaluation was targeted at: (i) understanding the users' perceptions towards an automatic solution for creating TV summaries using social network activity as the editorial criteria; (ii) comparing the perceived quality of the nowUP summaries versus official (traditional) editorial summaries; (iii) evaluate the user experience related to the nowUP portal, and; (iv) gather the user expectations and motivations towards using this solution in the future.

The tests were carried in the research lab and at the participants' home. In the lab a comfortable and similar to the home environment was prepared. All the tests were made in late afternoon, after the working or studding day. As for the equipment, a computer, a desk and a chair were the needed materials. The characterization of the participants was made through a semi-structured questionnaire [20]. This type of survey was chosen not only to ease the data processing, but also to give interviewees some freedom in their answers. A Google Docs form was used and content analysis was made to interpret the responses from participants. The questionnaire was structured into four main parts, namely: (i) Personal Information; (ii) Television Habits and Preferences; (iii) TV and Social Networks – behaviors towards television consumption and correlated use of social networks; (iv) TV summaries consumption.

4.1   The Evaluation Sessions Structure

The evaluation sessions included the following steps:

- the participants' characterization;
- a small presentation of nowUP, about 7/8 min divided into four main parts: 1- the main design motivation and the context that surrounds it; 2- the correlation between TV content and Twitter generated content; 3- the overall process for the automatic creation of summaries; 4- the overall structure of the website. This presentation was supported by a short set of slides and images;
- the participants' interaction with the nowUP website. For this a script of tasks was handled inviting the users to explore the different sections of the website. The experience was tracked by two data collection techniques, direct observation and a semi-structured survey.

After the hands on session a second survey was delivered to the users. This survey aimed to address the following topics: usefulness of the features; ease of use; satisfaction and future expectation of use; and expectations for the integration of nowUP in an iTV service. Participants were also able to address other topics they found relevant towards the service.

The last part of the tests was focused on the evaluation of the video summaries. For this, participants were invited to watch two types of video summaries: (i) the nowUP summaries concerning a football match (sports genre) and the 'The Voice' talent show (entertainment genre), and; (ii) official and editorial created (by the TV show producers) video summaries for the same TV programs. For the evaluation of emotional reactions transmitted by the nowUP summaries, the research team used the SAM - Self-assessment Manikin [21]. The SAM-Manikin is an assessment method based on 3 sets of simple drawings that directly assess the pleasure, arousal, and dominance associated with the user's affective reactions to some certain stimuli (in this case the TV summaries). This data collection instrument was used immediately after the visualization of each nowUP summary. Just after this, participants had the chance to watch the correspondent official TV summaries and, to conclude, a third semi-structured questionnaire was delivered. This survey was structured into three parts, part 1 about the sports program and part 2 about the entertainment program. Participants had to assign the degree of agreement with four statements concerning the perceived level of: relevance of the content of summaries, extent of information, relevance of the textual (tweets) information; disturbance of the twitter information delivered in nowUP oracles. In the third and final part participants were questioned regarding: their preference between the nowUP summaries and the official editorial summaries; and about their prediction regarding a future use of it via its Web Portal or its integration in an IPTV service.

4.2   The Sample Characterization

With regard to the choice of participants an intentional non-probabilistic sampling was used [22], as participants in the sample were selected by convenience by the research team according to a considered set of criteria, namely their patterns of TV watching and social network behaviors.

Personal information – The sample consisted of 20 participants (10 males and 10 females) with an average age of 28 years old, with different educational and work professional areas. Regarding the complete qualifications, most of participants had a master degree (7), followed by K12 education (6 – bachelor students). Four had completed the bachelor degree and three a technical course. All participants had social network accounts, namely in Facebook and twelve also on Twitter. Finally, the majority of participants (eighteen) subscribed a pay-TV service.

TV habits and preferences – considering the TV viewing habits, most participants watched TV mainly in the afternoon and at night. At night eight participants watched between 1 and 2 h and six less than 1 h. The overall average during workdays was close to 2 h a day. On the other hand, at the weekend participants generally spent more time watching TV (close to 3 h and 30 min per day). Considering the TV genres, participants preferred films and series, with a preference level of 4.0 (in a scale of 1 to 5), followed by entertainment shows with 3.5. Sports and news got a close preference level at 3.4.

Social networks and TV – the majority of participants (12) were used to follow comments about TV shows on social networks with 8 denying this behavior. Considering the moment chosen to track those comments, 4 referred to do it only after the end of the show but 8 said to do it during and after the TV show. Despite 12 participants having an active behavior on tracking social networks, only 4 were used to regularly comment about the TV shows on social networks.

TV summaries consumption – finally, participants were asked to say if they were used to watch TV summaries and if so, where. A total of 14 participants stated having this behavior using official TV related shows websites to do it (10), video sharing web-sites (9) and social networks (9). Concerning the moment when they watched those summaries, 11 said to do it in the day after the broadcast of the TV show, 9 during the following week and 6 just after the show.

5   Results

The evaluation results presented in this section are mainly related to users' perception on the nowUP features, expectations for future use along with the preferences towards nowUP summaries vs official summaries.

5.1   Participants' Emotional Reactions

Participants' emotional reactions towards the two nowUP summaries were assessed through the SAM-Manikin scale, where scores go from 1 to 9. As depicted in Fig. 5, both nowUP summaries got positive values (>5) in the two evaluated emotional dimensions (in this study the SAM "sense of control" dimension was discarded).

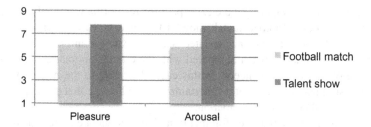

Fig. 5. The participants' emotional reactions to the nowUP summaries.

Despite the fact that the levels of "pleasure" and "arousal" are quite balanced when taking in consideration each type of TV genre; the entertainment summary (The Voice program) scored globally higher than the sports summary (more 28% in the "pleasure" and 31% in the "arousal").

5.2   Characteristics of the nowUP Summaries

After the reported assessment, participants had the chance to watch the correspondent official TV summaries and were then asked to state their level of agreement with a set of sentences comparing the perceived level of the characteristics of nowUP summaries with those of official summaries (Fig. 6). Participants scored their level of agreement with each sentence using a 5-point Likert scale (Totally disagree, Partially disagree, Neutral, Partially agree, Totally agree). However, for a clearer interpretation of the results a (WA) weighted average (−2, −1, 0, 1, 2) was adopted in the graphics.

Regarding the relevance of the content, the gathered answers show that participants found that nowUP summaries provide content with higher significance as compared with official summaries. When the TV genre is considered, it can be seen that the

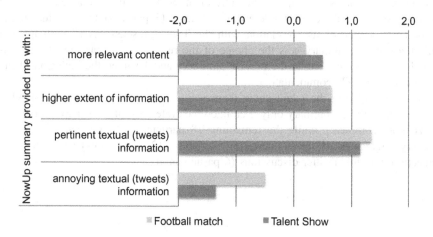

Fig. 6. Participants' perceived opinions of nowUP summaries characteristics (WA).

entertainment nowUP summary got a clearer positive result (the weighted average 25% better than neutral) than football match (nowUP) summary (10% better than neutral).

The answers to the next sentence (related with the extent of information associated with the nowUP summaries when compared with the official summaries) strengthened the relevance of the nowUP concept. In this case, the offset to the neutral value was 33% for both summaries (Sports and Entertainment), indicating that participants found that nowUP gives them more information.

It is important to stress that the aforementioned results may be more linked with the pertinence of the textual information coming from the tweets – those that interleave each TV highlight (see Fig. 3) - than with the video information. The corresponding weighted averages (1,4 – for the football summary and 1,2 for the talent show), with related offsets of 68% and 58% from the neutral value, are clearly a positive indicator of the suitability of the adopted approach to build the video oracles. This is even clear when looking to the level of disagreement that participants showed regarding the potential disturbance of the textual information of those oracles. With offsets to the neutral value of 25% (in the case of the football summary) and 68% (for the talent show), the added value of the information from the tweets is clear.

5.3   Comparison Between nowUP and Official Summaries

In the final part of the test sessions, participants were asked to give their global opinion on the type of summary they most liked (nowUP versus official). They were also asked to freely justify the main reason supporting their choice.

To make a synthesis of the results gathered about each one of the summaries genres (football match versus talent show) a qualitative exploration was made through content analysis. Based on the gathered answers, it was decided to group the answers in a total of 4 categories.

Regarding the football match, as depicted in Fig. 7, it is possible to observe a global split preference (by a total of 10 participants in each case) between the two types of summaries. 10 of the participants preferred the nowUP summary - due to a perceived better aggregation of the most interesting moments (3 participants) and due to the reported importance of its correlation with the Twitter discussions (7 participants); while the official summary was the choice of the remaining 10 participants (9 considered it more complete than the nowUP summary and 1 valued the inclusion of the remarks from the TV commentator).

When considering the talent show there was a clear preference for the nowUP summary: the official summary only accounted the preference of 2 participants (stating it was more complete), while the remaining 18 participants found that the nowUP summary aggregates the most interesting moments (12 participants) and valued its connection with the Twitter discussions (6 participants).

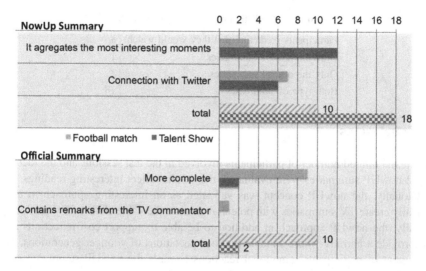

Fig. 7. Reasons for the preference towards a type of summary (nowUP (top) and official (bottom)).

5.4   The nowUP Integration on TV

As participants at this stage of the test sessions had already a significant understanding of the nowUP concept they were asked if they would use the service if integrated in an IPTV platform; how many times a week and how the integration should be made (if integrated in the EPG or in a specific area of the user interface). Table 1 summarizes the gathered answers.

5.5   Prediction of Future Use

Finally, participants were asked about their predictions regarding the type of summaries they would watch if nowUP was available. The gathered answers are summarized in Table 2.

Table 1. Opinions about the nowUP integration on TV

Participants predicting that:	#
Would use the service over an IPTV platform	18
Would use it once a week	10
Would use it more than 3 times a week	8
The service integration should be made inside the EPG	16
The service integration should be made in a specific area	4

Table 2. Prediction of future use of nowUP.

Participants predicting that they would watch:	#
Only the nowUP summaries	1
Only the official summaries	1
Both type of summaries	18

6 Conclusions

Despite the limited number of participants involved in the test sessions and the fact that only 2 nowUP summaries were evaluated, the results reflect interesting readings.

Globally, the nowUP concept was validated as an interesting approach to automatically create TV summaries with potential gains in the value chain of TV producers. Actually, the nowUP approach in addition to be able to support cost reductions may also provide a narrative more suitable to the expectations of younger generations. The assessment of participants' emotional reactions towards the nowUP summaries reinforces this idea.

The nowUP summaries were not only considered as being slightly more relevant than the correspondent official summaries but also providing more information. This seems to be correlated with the inclusion of tweets in the overlaid oracles. This solution as a way to complement the separators, which are automatically inserted between the highlights, seems to be a suitable approach.

When comparing the two TV genres at stake (sports – a football match; and entertainment – a talent show), the evaluation results show that the nowUP strategy may be more suitable when the TV programs lack typical and clearly predicted highlights (easier to find in, as an example, sports TV programs). The usual peak moments for a football match are the goals and referees' polemical decisions, while a talent show presents a higher number of subjective reasons for a moment to be considered relevant or popular. In this scope, the crowd activity seems to be a suitable editorial criterion for this type of TV moments.

As a final remark, this study is not only relevant for its outcomes but also a stimulus for further research, namely further validation with a higher number of participants and a larger diversity of TV genres and also applying the technical approach to other sources of information, namely other Social Networks.

Acknowledgements. The authors would like to acknowledge the remaining partners of the nowUP project (Altice Labs and Telecommunications Institute).

References

1. Forlines, C., Peker, K., Divakaran, A.: Subjective assessment of consumer video summarization. In: SPIE Proceedings - Special Session: Evaluating Video Summarization, Browsing, and Retrieval Techniques, vol. 6073 (2006). doi:10.1117/12.648554

2. Abreu, J., et al.: Survey of Catch-up TV and other time-shift services: a comprehensive analysis and taxonomy of linear and nonlinear television. Telecommun. Syst. **64**, 1–18 (2016). doi:10.1007/s11235-016-0157-3

3. Viacom, When Networks Network - TV Gets Social (2013). http://vimninsights.viacom.com/post/61773538381/when-networks-network-tv-gets-social-in-our. Last accessed 1 Mar 2017

4. Nielsen Social, TV Season in Review: Biggest Moments on Twitter (2015). http://www.nielsensocial.com/tv-season-in-review-biggest-moments-on-twitter/. Last accessed 1 Mar 2017

5. Kantar Media, Who's Tweeting about TV in the UK? (2015). http://www.kantarmedia.com/uk/thinking-resources/latest-thinking/who-is-tweeting-about-tv-in-the-uk. Last accessed 1 Mar 2017

6. Capon, G.: Twitter Amplify will create enormous value for broadcasters and brands (2014). http://www.theguardian.com/media-network/media-network-blog/2014/may/23/twitter-amplify-influence-tv. Last accessed 1 Mar 2017

7. Twitter Amplify, Twitter Amplify Product Video (2014). https://twitter.com/twitteramplify/status/516981620448845825. Last accessed 21 Jan 2016

8. Wildmoka, Platform (2014). http://wildmoka.com/platform/. Last accessed 21 Jan 2016

9. Wildmoka, Press Release – CANAL+ Group selects Moments Share (2014). http://wildmoka.com/press-release-canal-group-selects-moments-share-wildmokas-social-tv-solution/. Last accessed 21 Jan 2016

10. Wildmoka, Moments Share (2014). http://wildmoka.com/solutions/moments-share/. Last accessed 21 Jan 2016

11. Wildmoka, Moments Replay (2014). http://wildmoka.com/solutions/moments-replay/. Last accessed 21 Jan 2016

12. Wildmoka, Moments Capture (2014). http://wildmoka.com/solutions/moments-capture/. Last accessed 21 Jan 2016

13. Tellyo, Tellyo –Media sharing (2017). https://tellyo.com/. Last accessed 1 Mar 2017

14. Ulanoff, L.: Twitter experiments with TV Timelines (2015). http://mashable.com/2015/03/12/twitter-experiment-tv-timelines/#Ip8nGr1eJqq3. Last accessed 21 Jan 2016

15. Nielsen Social, Nielsen Social – Social TV Analytics & Solutions (2017). http://www.nielsensocial.com/. Last accessed 1 Mar 2017

16. Nielsen Social, Products – Nielsen Social (2017). http://www.nielsensocial.com/products/. Last accessed 1 Mar 2017

17. Beuker, I.: The Social EPG: The Next Step Towards Social TV? (2012). http://www.viralblog.com/social-tv/the-social-epg-the-next-step-towards-social-tv/. Last accessed 1 Mar 2017

18. Jiang, W., Cotton, C., Loui, A.C.: Automatic consumer video summarization by audio and visual analysis. In: Proceedings of International Conference on Multimedia and Expo (ICME), pp. 1–6 (2011). doi:10.1109/ICME.2011.6011841

19. Alonso, O., Shiells, K.: Timelines as summaries of popular scheduled events. In: Proceedings of the 22nd International World Wide Web Conference Committee (IW3C2), pp. 1037–1044 (2013). doi:10.1145/2487788.2488114

20. Flick, U.: An Introduction to Qualitative Research, 4th edn. Sage Publications, London (2009)

21. Bradley, M., Lang, P.: Measuring emotion: the self-assessment manikin and the semantic differential. J. Behav. Ther. Exp. Psychiatry **25**(1), 49–59 (1994). http://www.ncbi.nlm.nih.gov/pubmed/7962581

22. Outhwaite, W., Turner, S.: The Sage Handbook of Social Science Methodology, 1st edn. Sage Publications, London (2007)

Automatic Creation of TV Content to Integrate in Seniors Viewing Activities

Liliana Reis⊙, Hilma Caravau$^{(\boxtimes)}$⊙, Telmo Silva⊙,
and Pedro Almeida⊙

Department of Communication and Arts, CIC.DIGITAL/Digimedia,
University of Aveiro, Aveiro, Portugal
{lilianaareis,hilmacaravau,tsilva,almeida}@ua.pt

Abstract. The challenges and opportunities that arise with the increase of older populations are drawing the attention of several sectors of society, as is the case of the technological segment. The development of technical solutions to improve seniors' quality of life and promote their autonomous living is commonly found in the roadmap of research teams and companies. Reports and news show that the elderly feel several limitations and problems concerning the activities of finding and accessing credible information through technical solutions. Statistics and studies also reveal that older people have high levels of daily television consumption, which makes TV one of the ways with a lot of potential to inform seniors. Taking in consideration these two factors, it seems that information broadcast to elderly through television, without requiring a search activity, may be an idea with a lot of potential. In line with this, this paper reveals the process to define audio-visual content for seniors as well as a set of guidelines for the development of iTV platforms for this target group. Seniors' preferences concerning the sound and text elements were gathered in two different moments in two different Senior Universities in Portugal.

Keywords: Automatic · Interactive television · Design · Audio-visual content · Seniors

1 Introduction

The ageing population is one of the most successful human achievements that leads to a significant inversion of the ageing pyramid. Ageing is typically characterized by physical, psychological and social changes that can result in several problems [1, 2], but being old does not necessarily have to be synonymous of illness, disability, dependency, isolation and loneliness. The success of the ageing process is highly determined by intrinsic factors, individual determinants, income, economic security, health status, social services, participation and the surrounding environment [3, 4].

Maintaining social relationships and being alert of disadvantages and inequality situations is essential for a successful ageing process. However, accessing information concerning the world that surrounds us is mainly dependent on a proactive attitude of the individuals and the opportunities that the governments and societies create for them. Many seniors do not have the ability or the resources to search for information

© Springer International Publishing AG 2017
M.J. Abásolo et al. (Eds.): jAUTI 2016, CCIS 689, pp. 32–46, 2017.
DOI: 10.1007/978-3-319-63321-3_3

("pull-oriented" activity) available on sources like newspapers or the Internet, and also, a huge part of this population does not have the required literacy skills to perceive the information. This leads to a high informational dependence on their caregivers' network [5]. But, if the information was delivered in a simple way, with clear language, through a familiar device and without the need for search activities by the user ("push-oriented" activity), it can deeply ease this process and become a relevant solution to inform the elderly. Television is a transversal audio-visual media available in almost all homes, being an excellent information and entertainment medium for elderly people. Concerning this, developing a solution that combines the TV as a delivery medium and the ability to get information in several meaningful areas could represent a solution with great potential to promote seniors' autonomy, wellbeing and quality of life. In this context, the +TV4E project (Interactive Television as a support to information broadcast about social services for seniors) is being developed to promote the info-inclusion of Portuguese seniors through the transmission of video spots with informative content about social and public services. One of the key differentiating factors of +TV4E is the automatic video production based on web news.

In order to create a valuable product, easy-to-use and that fulfils seniors' needs, it is important to gather opinions from potential users through a participative design approach. This process includes, as an example, the definition of the preferred sound and visual elements that will be included in audio-visual content. This paper aims to propose guidelines to audio-visual content for seniors, as well as a set of strategies for developing Interactive Television (iTV) applications for this target group, resulting from participatory design sessions that may represent a support for further studies that involve the definition of digital platforms for seniors.

2   Theoretical Framework

The changes in the ageing pyramid have been greater as a consequence of the increase in the average life expectancy and the decrease in fertility rates [3]. In the 80's there were 378 million people with 60 years old or above all around the world. In 2010 there were 759 million people with 60 years old or above, and 901 million in 2015. It is projected that the percentage of elderly population growth will continue, reaching 1.4 billion in 2030, and nearly 2.1 billion by 2050 [6].

Portugal is not an exception and between 2001 and 2011 the percentage of Portuguese people with 65 years old and above increased from 16% to 19%. In 2015, the number of Portuguese inhabitants aged 65 or more surpassed the number of children and adolescents, which puts Portugal as one of the most aged countries in Europe [7].

The demographic changes require the attention of international organizations, governments and societies. The concept of "active ageing", defined in 2002, was one of the first manifestations showing the concern about the promotion of well-being for individuals in advanced life stages. World Health Organization (WHO) advocates that people living longer must be accompanied by continuous opportunities in 3 pillars: health, participation and security. WHO defines "active ageing" as the process of optimizing opportunities in those 3 pillars, in order to enhance quality of life of older people [4].

Older people should be encouraged to remain active in several life domains, like family, community, political, cultural and social [4]. In the last decades, television (TV) was one of the great discoveries and a change agent for societies. TV is the most used audio-visual media and reaches the podium in the list of preferences of Portuguese individuals [8, 9].

The latest data reveals that in 2010, the average daily consumption of television was 3 h and 29 min per each Portuguese viewer [10]. When analysing data disaggregated by age group, it is possible to see that people with more than 64 years old watch an average of 5 h and 8 min a day [10]. Considering this, TV is the device with greatest potential among elderly population, not only to enhance information acquisition and entertainment, but also to be used as an agent of socialization by promoting conversation between people [11].

Getting proper information may represent a key factor to face daily living challenges which is essential for an autonomous and independent ageing process, although, few recent studies have examined the information needs of the seniors [12]. The conducted surveys show that, in some countries, the needs of elderly citizens are essentially related to financial, housing, health, leisure opportunities, need for informational support on practical daily problems, security, transportation or affective issues [12–17].

Even though none of these studies focused on the informational needs of Portuguese seniors, in an empirical way, it seems to be a transversal trending that the elderly need information about health, finances, pensions and local policies. This information lack is influenced by the low literacy levels of aged Portuguese groups [18], as well as their low knowledge levels in fields such as health and finances [19, 20].

Regarding all these facts, in order to promote info-knowledge within the Portuguese elderly, an iTV platform is being developed by the +TV4E project [5]. This platform aims to disseminate information about public and social services for seniors, by interrupting the visualization of linear TV with audio-visual content about those services.

While developing a technology for seniors it is important to guarantee that the services and products are designed according to the concerns and expectations of the end user. Design iTV services, targeted to older people, granting high levels of accessibility and usability, is very important for the improvement of television "viewing" experience.

In this way, participatory design methodologies are appropriated to this context as they guarantee the commitment and empowerment of users in the definition of technological solutions [21].

The most evident characteristic of senior population is their multidimensional and distinctive way of ageing. As people age they face some degradation regarding visual, hearing and cognitive skills [5, 22] with heterogeneous tendency that enhances the importance of consider them in the design of any application or service oriented to a public with these characteristics. These age-related changes contribute to a decrease of comprehension of the surrounding world, due to the central nervous system becoming slower at processing information captured by the sensorial channels, which causes some loss of information [23]. An interactive system for seniors should be designed taking these factors into account, to become valuable to them [24]. The design of a certain iTV product should consider the target population's perspectives and needs based on their everyday life and how age-related impairments will affect its usage [25–27].

2.1   Hearing Perception Changes

By age 60, there is a 25% loss in ability to process and understand conversational speech due to auditory acuity decreasing [28, 29]. The supporting walls of the external ear canal show signs of atrophy and become weaker in later life, leading to a reduction of the "pre-amplification" effects which causes the seniors to receive sound signals in a relatively lower volume [28]. Czaja and Sharit [30] summarize the age-related changes in hearing: loss of sensibility to pure tones, especially high frequency tones; difficulty in understanding speech; sound localization problems; problems in binaural audition and higher sensibility to loudness. The authors also state that older adults take more time to process audio information [30].

2.2   Visual Perception Changes

Another important change related with the ageing process occurs in the visual abilities, with individuals facing modifications in the eye structure. The decreasing of the pupil diameter limits the amount of light entering the eye and increases the need for luminosity to have a better perception and visual acuity [23, 29, 31, 32]. Older people also experience a decline in adaptability, meaning that the eye's ability to adjust to different viewing distances and places with different lighting levels decreases [30]. Adjusting to near vision also becomes difficult because of the lens rigidity's increase [28, 33]. Also, the loss of contrast sensibility and chromatic distinction, especially violet, blue and green tones [29] and susceptibility to brightness are some of other visual age-related impairments pointed out by the same authors. These are changes that clearly bring some implications in designing an iTV interface as well as presenting information using audio-visual content.

The impairment of hearing and visual abilities profoundly marks the elderly overall performance [28, 33], and consequently affects their interaction with the surrounding environment. In general, for each impairment function there are several studies that define guidelines for the interfaces' design, as will be presented following.

3   Guidelines for Designing Audio-Visual Content

Seniors are willing to use technological systems, however, there are some barriers that can cause resistance, including lack of access, lack of knowledge about its potential benefits, lack of technical support, costs, fear of failure, complexity of the interface or interfaces that were, probably, designed and developed without considering their needs [27, 30].

As previously referred, there are biological and cognitive changes that occur as people experience the ageing process. Considering the goals of this study, visual and hearing impairments were given more focus. In this context, some design guidelines will be approached in this section, based on existent studies on web design and iTV's design for seniors. To simplify the audio-visual content creation process and later implementation of the informative videos, it is important to collect design guidelines and later recommendations already tested and validated in previous studies within this scientific area.

3.1 Typography and Text

According to a BBC study, text is an element that brings challenges when used in the television screen due to, for example, screen resolution, brightness and also because users are not familiar with reading static text blocks on a screen. The exhibition quality of still images on television is poor, thus challenging also the audio-visual content creation [34].

To determine a minimum font size and taking in account that there are different screen sizes and resolutions as well as visual angles and distances from the viewer's side, the tasks reveals to be very challenging. However, the same author recommends that, given the age-related visual impairments in this public, the bigger the font the better [28]. In a more specific level, some authors state that the minimum body text should be around 12 pts [29, 35]. In contrast, Hansen [34] refers that typically body text, in any given circumstance, should be no less than 18 pts and Nunes, Kerwin and Silva [24] tested text's legibility through different sizes and consequently concluded that font size should be presented in a minimum of 40 pts for it to be accessible to the majority of senior users. Although Pereira [36] verifies on his study that most of the participants did not have any difficulties reading text with 15/16 pts size, the author recommends, if possible, a value between 17 and 18 pts since it's a safer option to apply.

Analysing all these standpoints, it is notable the lack of agreement between authors about what font size should be the most suitable or what size should be considered the minimum to be comfortably legible for seniors. Nevertheless, it is important to emphasize that some of these authors, specifically Farage [29], Fisk et al. [35] and Carmichael [28], based their conclusions in design studies for seniors but applicable to a diverse set of contexts of use which includes web, television or printed documents. On the other hand, Hansen [34], Nunes et al. [24] and Pereira [36] define design guidelines to television context. There are some factors like viewing distance, visibility's conditions and cognitive skills associated to sight that lead to a variability of opinions between researchers, which reveals the pertinence and importance in studying and testing this specific element.

In contrast, the font type is a variable with a much bigger confluence between studies. In general, decorative, cursive or serif fonts should be avoided due to being difficult to read and to understand [28–36]. Because of the age-related vision impairments these font types gain imprecise outlines generating blur-type effects that accentuate with the loss of visual acuity [28]. Pereira [36] also recommends avoiding typography that is too light or too thin as well as implementing two different font types at the same time. The recommended criteria can be verified on certain typefaces like Arial, Helvetica or Century Gothic. Authors also advise Tiresias Screenfont as it was specifically developed and designed for television display taking users with visual difficulties into account, including seniors [34, 36].

Beside font size and type, text blocks' distribution and visual configuration are another important element to keep in mind when defining audio-visual informative content for seniors. Pereira [36] highlights that spacing between characters should be around 30% more than the default value and text should be aligned to the left [24, 36]. Morrell e Echt [37] also suggests the use of short line lengths and left justified text. Spaces between text lines cannot be too narrow or else it can break the reading flow, so it is recommended to leave some space between lines and this way the adjacent lines do not interfere with the current line that the user is reading [34, 36]. Another component associated with text blocks, and important to highlight in order to assist the seniors' cognitive skills, is the amount of information displayed on the screen. Carmichael [28] establishes guidelines about the extension and the quantity of text blocks per page. The exhibited text must be as short and succinct as possible, since visual simplicity is fundamental. Confusion and information overload should be avoided so the content should be distributed through various pages if it is necessary [28, 29]. Beside these points, Pereira [36] also adds that a single page should not exceed a maximum of 90 words and recommends dividing the text into small fragments to be easy to read it.

Lastly, on the typography side, contrast is also an important element. The relation between text and the background is an indispensable variable on audio-visual content creation as well as on the information perception. From the analysed literature, the majority of authors do not disagree on their opinions. Generally, a high contrast (50:1) on the screen is advised (for example, white text on black background or vice versa) in order to increase legibility [29, 32]. High levels of contrast turn the interfaces more easily discernible for seniors with colour distinction problems and it compensates the lack of visual acuity, accentuating text legibility [24, 28, 36].

3.2 Iconography

Pereira [36] says that the iconicity's level is crucial for its comprehension. Iconicity's level refers to the relationship of resemblance or similarity between the representation of something and what is being represented, meaning that this is a property that determines the communication's efficiency of an icon. In the case of senior users, due to the age-related decline of cognitive skills like memory and the lack of familiarity with digital systems [37], this is an important variable to study in order to design representative and efficient icons. This information complements with Carmichael's [29] point of view who defends the benefit of figurative icons in contrast with abstract icons.

On the other side, seniors deal better with textual icons instead of pictorial icons as depicted in a study conducted by Rice and Alm and analysed by Pereira [36]. However, textual icons do not necessarily guarantee total efficiency for senior users, and so, the combined use of text and image minimizes possible difficulties related to written language caused by low literacy levels. Therefore, icons should not discard a written mention [38]. Text and image combination results in an understandable icon [24, 39]. Pereira [36] recommends that while designing an interface for an iTV application specifically for seniors, abstract iconography should be avoided as well as graphic associations of recent digital technologies like computers, smartphones, informatics applications or even the Internet. Using figurative iconography with the highest iconicity level possible, not withdrawing either image or text and, finally, an efficient distinction between different icons are other design principles regarding iconography pointed out by the same author [36].

3.3   Colour

Colours play a fundamental role both for aesthetical and communicational purposes. Not only they complement orientation, structure and clarification of different visual elements but also facilitate the comprehension of information.

In general, television screens have a more limited chromatic spectrum and higher luminosity levels (gamma) than computer screens. This results in higher contrast and saturation levels during information/content display [34]. To achieve parity in terms of colour intensity, exhibited images should be darker and less saturated when passed from computer to television screen. Warm tones like intense reds and oranges can cause colour distortion when presented in TV screens.

RGB (the colour system used in televisions) values consist of three channels that vary from 0 to 255; pure white translates into 255/255/255 and pure black into 0/0/0. Hansen [34] recommends avoiding pure whites and blacks and thus the strongest white tone that should be used on television is around 95% or 240/240/240 in RGB. The same thing is recommended in black tones that should be around 5% or 16/16/16 in RGB gamma [34]. Like Hansen [34] and Lu [40] refer, to avoid colour associated distortions on television, these cannot be too bright nor too dark nor too saturated and should not exceed 85% in saturation and luminosity [40].

3.4   Sound

Carmichael [28] defends that using sound could be beneficial for seniors' perception of the information. Yet, as it was already said, natural changes that occur in the ageing process related to hearing lead to a need for considering specific cares when adding an audio layer to video.

Frequencies between 500 and 2000 Hz are preferable, according to Farage et al. [29]. High sound frequencies must be avoided in both speech and non-speech information and sound signals with at least 60 dB are enough to reach senior's ear [29]. Carmichael [28] states that, dealing with senior users, volume should be slightly higher than normal, yet not so loud that it can cause discomfort or annoyance to some users. The ideal is to set sounds in a higher volume than what is established to younger populations, but without causing discomfort to older people [28, 29].

Considering speech and discourse and based on literature, it is possible to argue that verbal information should have a predictable linguistic pattern with expected pauses at grammatical boundaries and a slow but respectful communication pace for an effective informational delivery to the senior [29]. Converging with this idea, clear and independent vocalizations should be used while assuring speech pauses [35]. Sound overlaps like the presence of background music, may interfere with the seniors' ability to hear and distinguish vocalizations. A significant difference between sound and noise is necessary, so the message needs to be at a considerable volume with the background kept at a minimum. Also the volume should be adjustable [29].

Concerning the guidelines previously mentioned, there are several situations in which the authors do not agree. In these cases, the IT developer should choose and define an implementation strategy that can be preceded or followed by tests with the target audience. These tests help to gather opinions that can support the readjustment of the solution. Beside the concerns with the development of a platform that answers seniors' needs (mostly in result of physical impairments) the narration of the information content is also a worry of +TV4E's research team. In line with this, the use of a TTS tool is discussed below.

3.5   Automatic Audio-Visual Creation Supported by TTS Tools

The +TV4E goal of broadcasting informative content about social and public services to older people relies on video creation based on the design guidelines previously referred as well as in the results of participatory design sessions with seniors. However, these videos will be automatically generated by an algorithm that selects content from different web sources and builds audio-visual pieces on its own.

As the study main goal is to reach the best audio-visual approach to informative content, its conclusions will be extracted and used for the algorithm's development that will allow the automatic content generation to be viewed on seniors' televisions. Based on this idea, it is important to analyse some of the existent technological solutions that would contribute for the project's implementation. One of them is the use of a text-to-speech tool, enhancing the autonomous nature of this platform.

A text-to-speech system (TTS) converts written text into human voice. According to Oliveira [41], normal textual language is converted to artificial speech, implying that, before creating the artificial speech, the received text has to be analysed and transformed by the system into a phonetic transcription [41]. This is a tool that appears to be a good option regarding automatic content creation.

Between a diversified list of TTS applications, the research team selected a set as possible options for the +TV4E platform's implementation. Through a comparative analysis between different TTS applications, a selection process for the best and most suitable TTS tool was carried out, without forgetting the target population's needs. Among the tools, three of them were selected to possibly be the most suitable. The list includes Ivona[1] (affiliated to Amazon), ReadSpeaker[2] and Watson[3] (the IBM's solution). After carrying the analysis, Watson was quickly excluded since it did not offer Portuguese language from Portugal, therefore not being suitable for a system targeted to the portuguese senior population. ReadSpeaker and Ivona presented similar advantages and features, but the team concluded into a preference for Ivona. Despite detecting a lack of diction on some words with Ivona, ReadSpeaker's showed other

---

[1] https://www.ivona.com/us/about-us/company/.

[2] http://www.readspeaker.com/pt-pt.

[3] http://www.ibm.com/watson/developercloud/doc/text-to-speech/.

limitations that included lack of rhythm, reading and cadence which could possibly bring comprehension problems to older people. Plus, Ivona's speech sounded much more natural comparing to the other tools. Therefore Ivona was the selected tool due to its natural sounding speech and the offer of both male and female voices. Despite all the data gathered concerning the design guidelines the team decided to enrich it with the target population's opinions and preferences. The project aims to guarantee a positive and comfortable experience to seniors, and therefore having older people participating in collaborative design sessions to analyse and evaluate different audio-visual approaches was thought to be essential.

4   Methodology

To create a valuable service, a participatory design approach with seniors has the potential of contributing to simplify the future integration and use of that service in older people's house. Based on different video content definition ideas, with some auditory and visual elements already pre-defined, participatory design sessions were held in collaboration with a group of senior students from both Senior University of Curia and Senior University of Cacia. The participants were invited to give their opinions about the audio-visual elements proposed and thus contributing to its design's improvement. For the setup of these sessions, a preparatory work was done with a group of four specialists in the technologies and iTV fields to define the functionalities that should be present in the +TV4E platform. The process with the target audience consisted of four key moments: two group sessions that aimed to collect information about sound elements, and another two in order to gather data regarding textual elements. The sessions that analysed the sound elements addressed a total of 22 elements (11 from each University), and the other sessions that evaluated the text component included a total of 19 participants. Details on the participants are presented on Table 1.

The order for the data collection moments was established according to the Universities and students' availability, and resulted on the following alignment: (1) Focus Group (FG) with specialists in iTV (n = 4); (2) group sessions with seniors (Curia) for sound evaluation (n = 11); (3) group sessions with seniors (Cacia) for sound evaluation (n = 11); (4) group sessions with seniors (Cacia) for text evaluation

Table 1. Participants distribution, n (%)

	Sound group session		Text group session	
	SU CURIA	SU CACIA	SU CURIA	SU CACIA
Male	2 (18%)	4 (36,4%)	1 (83.3)	2 (15.4)
Female	9 (82%)	7 (63,6%)	5 (16.7)	11 (84.6)
Total	11	11	6	13

(n = 6); and (5) group sessions with seniors (Curia) for text evaluation (n = 13). The use of two different places for data collection ensured a greater number of opinions and the diversification of the participants considering different influences of the surrounding environment.

4.1   The Evaluation of Sound Elements

The two first moments were focused in testing sound elements, firstly with seniors of Curia and then with seniors of Cacia. Each moment was structured to consider two variables, specifically gender of the voice-over and the use of background music. Firstly, two approaches were presented to seniors: one with a male voice and the second with a female voice, both generated by Ivona's TTS tool. After the participants' contact with the two samples, they were asked about their preferences. Their answers were collected through a method of symbolic voting (raising hands) and consequently registered by the researchers. Secondly, to test the use of background music, seniors were again presented with two different options: one video playing an instrumental background music with a relatively low volume while the voice-over was reading the informative content in a higher volume, and the second example without any music whatsoever, being the voice-over the only sound element. The same method of symbolic voting was used to inquire seniors about which option they thought would be the best.

4.2   The Evaluation of Text Elements

Regarding audio-visual presentation of textual information, font type and font size were selected as the variables to test.

In the first group session, held at the Senior University of Cacia, the participants were presented with three different font faces, previously selected based on the design guidelines gathered in literature review: Arial, Helvetica and Tiresias Screenfont. Each font was complemented with short sentences applied in both dark and bright backgrounds as well as coloured background. This time, they were inquired through individual questionnaires (supported in paper) asking them to choose one font type concerning the reading difficulty, its appropriateness to the video's context and finally, they were asked to choose the best font type globally. The same method was used in order to collect data about font size.

In the literature review there was little convergence between authors in establishing a minimum font size, concluding that this depended on contexts of use, different viewing distances or visibility's conditions. So, the font size was considered important to test in the project's context. The participants were presented with five different font sizes, on a range between 40 and 60 pts [24], so that they could choose on the questionnaire which one was easiest to read and which one was most suitable to the video context.

Despite the data collection approach used at University of Cacia, this proved not to be as effective as the previous method used in the sound testing sessions, the voting by symbolic process. There was some difficulty for the participants to answer the questionnaires individually without monitoring. Plus, right after the answering process, when asked for an opinion, a lack of coherence between opinions was noted.

Fig. 1. Group session for text elements evaluation

In line with this, the research team decided that in the second moment regarding font type and size held at the Senior University of Curia (see Fig. 1), the data collection should be done with the voting by symbolic process.

This fourth and last moment in collaboration with Curia's senior students, the same options presented in Cacia were presented to them regarding font size and type. Still this time, the three different font types (Arial, Helvetica and Tiresias Screenfont) were followed by an example sentence on a single coloured background only. Regarding font type, and unlike in Cacia, the participants were only asked which one was the easiest for them to read. The font size, instead of the questions made in Cacia, they were only asked the minimum size they could read without making any effort.

5   Results and Discussion

In this section, will be presented the achieved results as well as will be discussed the outcomes.

5.1   Sound Elements

A total of 22 individuals participated in the group session that analysed the sound elements, namely the voice-over gender and background music. Regarding the voice-over gender, the individuals were invited to answer the question "Which voice gender did you find most appealing?". Most of the individuals (n = 15), around 68.2%, chose the female voice. No references were found in the literature concerning this topic, which makes this decision dependent on the sensitivity and preference for each one.

The background music in the informational video spot was the second sound element targeted. The video spot's exhibition without background music was the chosen scenario by the majority of the inquired seniors (63.6%). Two of the total respondents (9.1%) had not been able to define a position concerning this feature. These results corroborate the design guidelines defined by Farage and colleagues [28] who suggest that the use of overlapping sounds can interfere with the seniors' speech comprehension. Despite seniors' preference to eliminate the background music on video spots, this element seemed to lend credibility to the voice-over. Concerning this, and considering the design guidelines in literature [29], the research team decided to maintain the background music in the minimum volume and increase the volume of the main message voice (to create a more appealing video).

5.2   Text Elements

The evaluation of text elements was focused on the font type and size. As referred, the analysis of this feature was followed using different methodologies (through inquired and symbolic voting process). Nevertheless, it was guaranteed the match between the questions presented to the participants.

Tiresias was the preferred font type, with 52.6% of the votes, in a sample of 19 participants. Helvetica collected five votes (26.3%), followed by Arial with only four (21.1%). These results are congruent with the guidelines found in literature that suggested the use of sans-serif fonts. The results are in line with the argued by the authors that referred Tiresias as one of the most suitable font types to people with visual impairments [34, 38].

The opinions concerning font size were sparse. It should be noted that in Cacia's University the seniors answered two questions "The easiest-to-read font size was..." and "The font size that best fit the video was...". In Curia's University, the seniors were invited to answer the question "What is the smallest font size you are able to read without effort?". With 5 votes each were 40, 50 and 55 pts, followed by 45 pts with 4 votes. Taking all participant's comments into account as well as their reactions pointed out in the fieldwork, the research team decided to implement 55 pts to the font size in the video spots. This option will be later tested in real context with seniors.

6   Conclusions and Future Work

The co-creation process enhances the possibility that a technological solution in development process answers the needs and expectations of end-users. It is very important to promote the engagement of possible end users since the initial stages of a product's development, namely in the definition of technical requirements, available functionalities and in the design (which includes, for example, sound and graphic elements). To assure a positive and comfortable experience when receiving information about social and public services through iTV, participatory design sessions were held, with a sample of Portuguese seniors.

From the four moments that aimed to define the preferred sound and text elements' use it was possible to get the following results: preference for a female voice, for an instrumental background music with a relatively low volume while the voice-over is reading the informative content in a higher volume and use of Tiresias Screenfont at 55 pts. After the definition of these elements, other variables will be further tested in order to set the complete group of guidelines for building audio-visual content to +TV4E project context. Concerning this, tests are planned to analyse the use of a background image, use of colour to distinguish the different informational main areas (for example, social, health, finances, etc.), iconography and speech speed. Afterwards, in the +TV4E platform development's context, the next step will be testing and evaluating the developed prototype with seniors, in real context. Therefore, a set-top-box with the +TV4E application will be installed in the seniors' home, but allowing them to watch television without disturbances in their usual routines. This platform will provide the six TV channels available in the Digital Terrestrial Television system in Portugal. This process will not involve any financial costs for the participants.

One interesting conclusion that resulted from this work was the need to adapt the data collection approach used with seniors. It was notorious that what the researchers considered to be the most adequate method, based on the literature, was not the most efficient with the population. Thus, changing from the questionnaire approach to the method of symbolic voting was one of the adaptations required. It is not possible to predict the reaction of the participants to different methods of data collection, however the ability to adapt the process in order to obtain data with quality in the simplest way is desirable.

It has also been observed that older participants show increased difficulties in focusing attention on the subject under analysis and are easily distracted by unimportant information and get tired quickly. In this way, it is essential to prepare fast and concise sessions for data collection. The researcher promoting the evaluation must also be able to adapt and manage the dynamics effectively, without losing the purpose of the session.

The reduced sample is one of the limitations of this study. This is due to the difficulties in recruiting elderly individuals to participate in the study mainly regarding to limitations in time frame of the project. It is assumed that this fact inevitably affects the achieved results, however it is expected that this will be attenuated with the planned future work.

As future steps, the research team intends to test the videos (created considering the audio-visual elements detailed in this study) delivering it through the +TV4E platform. These tests will allow refining video elements according to the seniors' inputs. Afterwards, cultural probes will be held with potential final users, recruited in another context, during a certain period of time (further defined). The inputs gathered in this phase will be essential to readjust the studied aspects (text and sound) in the final informational videos format.

Acknowledgements. The research leading to this work has received funding from Project 3599 – Promover a Produção Científica e Desenvolvimento Tecnológico e a Constituição de Redes Temáticas (3599-PPCDT) and European Commission Funding FEDER (through FCT: Fundação para a Ciência e Tecnologia I.P. under grant agreement no. PTDC/IVC-COM/3206/2014).

References

1. Schneider, R.H., Irigaray, T.Q.: O envelhecimento na atualidade: aspectos cronológicos, biológicos, psicológicos e sociais. Estud Psicol **25**, 585–593 (2008)
2. Schroots, J., Birren, J.A.: Psychological point of view toward human aging and adaptability. In: Adaptability and Aging, Proceedings of the 9th International Conference of Social Gerontology, Quebeque, pp. 43–54 (1980)
3. Scobie, J., Amos, S., Beales, S., Dobbing, C., Gillam, S., Knox-Vydmanov, C., Mihnovits, A., Mikkonen-Jeanneret, E.: Global AgeWatch Index Global AgeWatch Index 2015: Insight report (2012). doi:10.2196/jmir.2306
4. Kalache, A., Gatti, A.: Active Ageing: a policy framework (2002)
5. Silva, T., Abreu, J., Antunes, M., Almeida, P., Silva, V., Santinha, G.: +TV4E: interactive television as a support to push information about social services to the elderly. In: Conference on Health Social Care Information Systems and Technologies, CENTERIS, pp. 1–6 (2016)
6. United Nations: World Population Ageing 2015, New York, USA (2015)
7. PORDATA: População residente: total e por grupo etário - Portugal (2016)
8. Nielsen: Screen Wars-The battle for eye space in a TV-everywhere world (2015)
9. Entidade Reguladora para a Comunicação Social: As novas dinâmicas do consumo audiovisual em Portugal 2016, Lisboa (2016)
10. Marktest Group: Portugueses viram cerca de 3h30 m de Tv em 2010 (2011). http://www.marktest.com/wap/a/n/id ~ 16e0.aspx. Accessed 20 Oct 2016
11. Abreu, J., Almeida, P., Silva, T.: iNeighbour TV: A Social TV Application to Promote Wellness of Senior Citizens. Information Systems and Technologies for Enhancing Health and Social Care. IGI Global, pp. 1–19 (2013). https://doi.org/10.4018/978-1-4666-3667-5.ch001
12. Edewor, N., Ijiekhuamhen, O.P., Emeka-ukwu, U.P.: Elderly people and their information needs (2016)
13. Bruce, H.: Personal, anticipated information need. Inf. Res. **10**(3), 1–15 (2005)
14. Troup, G.: Information and older people in Scotland (needs and strategies) (1985)
15. Barrett, J.: Support and information needs of older and disabled older people in the UK. Appl. Ergon. **36**, 177–183 (2005)
16. Zou, C., Zhou, P.: Analyzing information needs of elderly people: a survey in Chinese rural community. Open J. Soc. Sci. **2**, 109–115 (2014)
17. Everingham, J.-A., Petriwskyj, A., Warburton, J., Cuthill, M., Bartlett, H.: Information provision for an Age-friendly community. Ageing Int. **34**, 79–98 (2009)
18. Instituto Nacional de Estatística: Censos 2011: Resultados Definitivos - Portugal (2012)
19. Espanha, R., Mendes, R.V., Fernandes, J.: Literacia em Saúde em Portugal - Relatório Síntese. Lisbon (2016)
20. Banco de Portugal: Release of the results of the Second Survey on the Financial Literacy of the Portuguese Population (2016). https://www.bportugal.pt/en-US/OBancoeoEurosistema/Cooperacaoinstitucional/ConselhoNacionalSupervisoresFinanceiros/Pages/PNFF_20161021.aspx#_ftn1. Accessed 9 Nov 2016
21. Swallow, D., Petrie, H., Power, C., Lewis, A., Edwards, A.D.: Involving older adults in the technology design process: A case study on mobility and wellbeing in the built environment. Stud. Health Technol. Inform. **229**, 615–623 (2016)
22. Cancela, D.M.G.: O processo de envelhecimento. O Portal dos Psicólogos, pp. 1–15 (2007)

23. Tye-Murray, N., Sommers, M., Spehar, B., Myerson, J., Hale, S., Rose, N.S.: Auditory-visual discourse comprehension by older and young adults in favorable and unfavorable conditions. Int. J. Audiol. **47**(Suppl 2), S31–S37 (2008)
24. Nunes, F., Kerwin, M., Silva, P.A.: Design recommendations for TV user interfaces for older adults: findings from the eCAALYX Project. In: Proceedings of 14th International ACM SIGACCESS Conference Comput Access – ASSETS 2012, p. 41 (2012)
25. Orso, V., Spagnolli, A., Gamberini, L., Ibañez, F., Fabregat, M.E.: Involving older adults in designing interactive technology: the case of seniorchannel. In: ACM International Conference Proceeding Series (2015)
26. Stojmenova, E., Debevc, M., Zebec, L., Imperl, B.: Assisted living solutions for the elderly through interactive TV. Multimed. Tools Appl. **66**, 115–129 (2013)
27. Silva, T., Abreu, J., Pacheco, O. Identificação de utilizadores: a chave para a personalização de aplicações de TV interativa para seniores? Commun. Stud. **14**, 137–156 (2013)
28. Carmichael, A.: A style guide for the design of interactive television services for elderly viewers. Indep. Telev. Comm. Winchester **129**, 2865 (1999)
29. Farage, M.A., Miller, K.W., Ajayi, F., Hutchins, D.: Design principles to accommodate older adults. Glob. J. Health Sci. **4**, 2–25 (2012)
30. Czaja, S.J., Sharit, J.: Designing Training and Instructional Programs for Older Adults (Human Factors & Aging). Taylor & Francis Group, LLC, Boca Raton (2013)
31. Fonseca, I., Amado, P., Costa, L.: Desenho de interfaces para seniores: desafios e oportunidades no projeto SEDUCE. Rev. Prism. 0 (2014)
32. Caldas, A.C.S.: Tutoriais audiovisuais para o uso das TIC pelo cidadão sénior. Universidade de Aveiro (2014)
33. Hawthorn, D.: Designing Effective Interfaces for Older Users. The University of Waikato (2006)
34. Hansen, V.: Designing for interactive television. 1–40. (2006)
35. Fisk, A.D., Rogers, W.A., Charness, N., Czaja, S.J., Sharit, J.: Designing for Older Adults: Principles and Creative Human Factors Approaches. CRC Press, Boca Raton (2009)
36. Pereira, L.: Princípios orientadores de design de interfaces para aplicações ITV orientadas para seniores portugueses. Universidade do Porto (2013)
37. Morrell, Q.W., Echt, K.V.: Designing written instructions for older adults learning to use computers. In: Handbook of Human Factors and the Older Adult (1997)
38. Pereira, L., Brandão, D., Martins, N.: Designa 2014. In: O Des. ícones no quadro das especificidades do indivíduo sénior. Covilhã, pp. 501–79 (2014)
39. Koutsourelakis, C., Chorianopoulos, K.: Icons in mobile phones. Inf. Des. J. **18**, 22–35 (2010)
40. Lu, K.Y.: Interaction Design Principles for Interactive Television. Georgia Institute of Technology (2005)
41. Oliveira, R.A.S.: Acessibilidade na Web 2.0: criação de uma interface de apoio à leitura de tag clouds por utilizadores com deficiência visual. Universidade de Aveiro (2009)

A Semantic Recommender System for iDTV Based on Educational Competencies

Diego Duran[1]([⊠]) ⓘ, Gabriel Chanchí[2] ⓘ, Jose Luis Arciniegas[1] ⓘ,
and Sandra Baldassarri[3] ⓘ

[1] Universidad del Cauca, Cll. 5 #4-70, Popayan, Colombia
{dduran,jlarci}@unicauca.edu.co
[2] Institución Universitaria Colegio Mayor del Cauca,
Cra. 7 #2-34, Popayan, Colombia
gchanchi@unimayor.edu.co
[3] Universidad de Zaragoza, María de Luna 1, 50018 Saragossa, Spain
sandra@unizar.es

Abstract. Interactive Digital Television (iDTV) provides a large amount of educational programs useful for supporting students' learning and teaching processes. Nevertheless, despite the continuous growth of the number of available contents, it is hard to find those which can be useful for a specific educational purpose. In order to provide a solution to this issue, in this paper we propose a model of a semantic Recommender System for educational iDTV programs, in which, the concept of competency and its features have been integrated as contextual information to enhance both the user and program information. Thus, we can establish filtering strategies in accordance with educational requirements. Furthermore, this proposal incorporates ontology-based filtering to enhance the inference capacity of another approaches, such as, content-based, collaborative, and syntactic matching.

Keywords: Educational competency · Metadata · Recommender system · Semantics · Interactive digital television

1 Introduction

The educational teaching process involves mutual interaction among teachers, students, the object of knowledge and the contact environment, with the goal of developing competencies [1]. Educational competencies define criteria for establishing the basic levels of educational quality.

Interactive Digital TV (iDTV) offers a huge amount of video programs that can be used to support competency-based learning (e.g., educational TV shows and learning contents) [2], being these a pedagogic and didactic instruments in teaching and learning processes that take advantage of the student's multisensory capacity [3]. There are many benefits of using video in education, e.g., facilitating thinking and solving problems, assisting with mastery learning, and increasing student motivation [4]. Nevertheless, finding contents adapted to student's needs is a challenge due to the large amount of them available on iDTV. For this reason, one of the current major challenges

© Springer International Publishing AG 2017
M.J. Abásolo et al. (Eds.): jAUTI 2016, CCIS 689, pp. 47–61, 2017.
DOI: 10.1007/978-3-319-63321-3_4

is to facilitate access to resources that meet the persons' needs in an easy and simple way [5, 6]. Thus, the Recommender Systems (RSs) arose as tools focused on assisting users in the selection of contents. For every context in which these systems have been applied, the goal is to reduce the number of choices available to user so they could see only those contents which are relevant to their interests and preferences in a high degree [7]. Although the utility of RSs is evident, we have found some lacks in the models:

- Different methods found in the literature [8–10] are capable of recommending TV programs, tourist experiences and learning resources. However, these do not include mechanisms to address educational requirements. RSs usually base their operation on viewing, searching and ranking records, which could not be pertinent and meaningful information in an educational context.
- There are RSs capable of assisting teachers and students to find interesting contents, however, no evidence has been found of models that consider the competencies to recommend iDTV programs.

In order to address the aforementioned issues, in this paper we propose a general model of a semantic-based RS for iDTV video programs based on educational competencies. For this, the model considers: *(i)* the properties of the programs that are related to competencies; *(ii)* the logical relations among different competencies; *(iii)* the proficiency level as a criterion used to recommend programs; *(iv)* a set of filtering strategies used to recommend the programs in accordance with such proficiency level.

This paper is organized as follows: Sect. 2 introduces some concepts and previous works related to this research while Sect. 3 defines and justifies a set of core features, such as the approach, and the type and filtering strategies of the RS. In Sect. 4 we describe the model of the RS, which comprises a set of techniques in regard to the RS approach, type and filtering strategies, and then, the components of such model. In Sect. 5 the possibility of extending the scope of our proposal is discussed. A Conclusions and future work section is finally presented.

2 Background

Firstly, in Subsects. 2.1 and 2.2 we explain theoretically an approach to two core concepts for this work: competency and competency-based education. Secondly, in Subsect. 2.3 we describe a set of previous works on RSs.

2.1 An Approach to the Concept of Competency

The term "Competency" has been the core of debate and confusion between researchers. In [11] it states that competency is a "fuzzy term" that may share different natures, opinions and scopes. Competency is a term created for the people to represent something that is not evident, and it is used to evaluate some human aspects and features, hence, defining the term competency is a difficult task.

The debate and confusion are greater if the term competency is analyzed from the English language. According to [11], the words competency and competence are commonly used as synonyms, but some researchers and competency practitioners apply differences between the two terms. For instance, in Oxford English Learner's Dictionary [12], competence is "the ability to do something well and efficiently." While about Competency in [11] it says "means the same things, but is more frequently used in educational argot, in which means 'the various skills that pupils are to be taught and teachers are to be prepared to teach.'" In order to address these confusions in Web education area, metadata standards have been developed. For instance, the standard Reusable Definition of Competency or Educational Objective (RDCEO) [13] and the IEEE Reusable Competency Definition (RCD) standards [14] are intended to provide an extensible form for formalizing any aspect related to competency and its relations, such as knowledge, skill, attitude, or educational objective. These standards are important in this study because they provide a "bridge" between pedagogic aspects and technologic possibilities. They define four elements to take into consideration in regard to any application: (1) generic definition (e.g., identifier, title and description); (2) the context of the competency (e.g., primary or secondary education); (3) evidences of the competency; and (4) dimensions, which are transverse variables to the other elements (e.g., skills, knowledge and topics).

On the other hand, competencies can be structured in competency maps, which establish both broader and narrower relations among them. From a pedagogical point of view, a competency map is a reference guide for reaching general competencies through specific competencies. In this regard, the Simple Reusable Competency Map (SRCM) [15] draft standard provides a set of metadata elements used to describe the structure of competency maps. Figure 1 presents an example of competency map, in which the relations between a broader competency (C1) and its narrower competencies (C2, C3 and C4) have a weight value between zero and one. In this case, C3 is more important to C1 than C2 and C4.

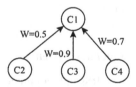

Fig. 1. Example of a competency map using the structure of SRCM

2.2   An Approach to the Competency-Based Education

Based on [16, 17], Fig. 2 shows an approach to the dynamics of competency-based education, in which some features that may influence the design of RSs are represented. The dynamic has two main actors: the teacher and the student, each one with requirements related somehow. The teacher determines and directs the offered courses, and defines the learning goals and assessment activities (e.g., verbal and written tests). Both the goals and the evaluations are defined by the teacher, considering educational competencies.

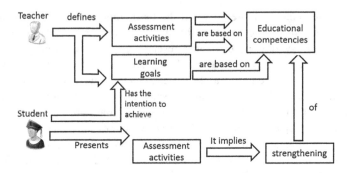

Fig. 2. An approach to the dynamic of competency-based education

On the other hand, the student begins the courses with the aim of obtaining a performance framed by the learning goals defined by the teacher. Similarly, the student answers to proposed Assessment Activities (AAs) in order to measure his proficiency level. The results allow the teacher to determine whether the student must strengthen his/her knowledge.

This dynamic allows us to conclude about a set of student's needs that may be taken into account in the design of this proposal: (1) teachers and student can use iDTV programs to support competencies based in the results achieved in AAs; (2) the student can use iDTV programs before the evaluation activities; (3) the student can strengthen his/her learning by using iDTV programs.

According to [2], the types of educational iDTV program are: (i) educational TV shows, which are TV programs of "Educational" genre, although it also could be classified as "TV programs" (e.g., Jeopardy); (ii) courses, such as t-learning applications related to TV programs (e.g., an English language course is recommended because of the user is a Spanish man watching an English movie); (iii) learning contents, which are video learning objects (e.g., a video related to certain documentary watched by the user is recommended.

2.3 Previous Works on Recommender Systems

It is important to emphasize that most RSs in literature are based on syntactic matching techniques, which relate items by means of common attributes (or keywords) in their metadata. In the case of competencies, from the pedagogical point of view it is not correct to affirm that two competencies are related (i.e., they are complementary to each other, or one supports the other) only because they are similar. Then, introducing a semantic analysis may be convenient.

Issues in contexts in which semantics plays an important role are usually addressed by applying techniques of the Semantic Web. As regards research on recommender systems, many authors have introduced mechanisms of automatic reasoning over semantic descriptions (e.g., descriptions formalized in ontologies or taxonomies) in the filtering strategies, in order to find items that best match the user needs. According to experimental results, the quality of semantic-based recommendations was improved in comparison to syntactic techniques.

In the iDTV context, an ontology-based RS for TV programs is proposed in [8]. Following an item-based approach, the recommendations are obtained by adapting measures of semantic similarity to filtering strategies over the ontology, which formalizes the concepts defined in TV-Anytime standard. In [7], a semantic RS for iDTV is proposed, in which a set of demographic information is used to obtain program recommendations while the cold-start problem is addressed. The demographic information is included to the semantic model proposed in [8]. These works are based on TV-anytime standard, which lacks a description of educational features of programs, hence the formalized ontologies have the same lack. Specially, competencies are not included in programs descriptions, thus the models are unable to recommend according to real life educational goals. In addition, the filtering strategies follow an item-based approach, which uses the persons' past preferences to obtain recommendations. This type of information may not be related to educational processes, thus the filtering strategies may not be in accordance with students' needs.

A RS in a collaborative learning environment based on influence diagrams is proposed in [10]. The system analyzes student tracking and collaboration assessments in the context of collaborative learning in an e-learning environment to identify the student circumstances and then propose personal recommendations. Once the circumstances are known, the collaboration problem identified, and the decision resolved, the student circumstances support and explain the recommendation. In this work the competencies and the iDTV programs are not considered to establish the recommendation strategies.

In the area of semantic-based RSs, there are works in another contexts such as tourism, market and health. Usually, the semantic models follow an item-based approach, thus the filtering techniques cannot be used or adapted to educational context due to these are based on past user experiences. For example, a recommended system for touristic packages is described in [9]. The system uses the consumer's experience point of view in order to apply fuzzy logic techniques to relating customer and hotel characteristics, represented by means of domain ontologies and affect grids. After receiving a recommendation, customers provide valuations of it based on his/her experience. Based on these valuations, the rules of the system are updated in order to adjust the new recommendations to past user experiences. A RS for products is described in [18], in which these are formalized in a taxonomy. This system is based on a modified product taxonomy and customer classification to identify customers' shopping behavior: product addictive, brand addictive or a hybrid addictive. By analyzing each customer's preferred brand or product, the system can recommend products to customers. A health-aware RS for medical products is proposed in [19], in which the properties of items are formalized in an ontology. The system introduces a filtering strategy centered on the properties that characterize the items and the users, which in turn serves to present the recommendations in a much more enticing manner.

3   Core Features of the Recommender System

In order to address the issues to find educational iDTV programs, in this paper we propose a RS that includes the concept of Competency in its model.

We have included in the core features of the RSs some aspects related to competency-based education and the utility provided by the iDTV programs in the teaching and learning processes (mentioned above in Sect. 2). These features are represented in Fig. 3: its approach, and its type and filtering techniques.

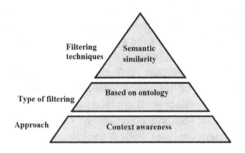

Fig. 3. Core features of the Recommender System

RS approach: context-aware. Traditionally, RSs are based on approaches that recommend items by using individual preferences. This is the case of the content-based and the collaborative approaches, which select similar contents and users using visualization and ranking records. Thus, these approaches are focused on two types of entities: the user and the item. After the analysis of the dynamics of a competency-based education, considering only users and items may be insufficient. In order to address this issue, we have decided to use information related to educational competencies to incorporate students' needs in the filtering process. Thus, the recommendations are meaningful within the learning process.

Filtering type: Ontology-based. Competencies in education involve a set of concepts useful to describe them in an appropriate way. (i.e., those mentioned in Sect. 2: definition, context, evidence and dimensions). This fact indicates that there is a semantic knowledge that can be formalized to infer relations between competencies and iDTV programs. In this paper, we propose to formalize such information using ontologies, which may allow: *(i)* to describe such knowledge in a natural way, and *(ii)* to use mature Web semantic techniques to find direct and indirect relations through the concepts of the semantic knowledge.

Filtering techniques: semantic similarities. The filtering techniques define how the semantic Web techniques are used in order to obtain recommendations. This proposal consists of setting filtering strategies related to educational context, and then define how to adapt the semantic similarities to them. For instance, if the purpose is to recommend iDTV programs to support the competencies in which the student has difficulties, a filtering strategy is the recommendation of programs directly related to such competencies within the ontology. In this case, the semantic similarity is applied measuring how much a specific program is related to each competency through the formalized concepts within the ontology. A second strategy is to recommend programs that share more Semantic Sequences (SSs) with the competencies in which the student presents difficulties. This fact supposes more complexity at the computational level. In this case, it is necessary to infer all the SSs between competencies and programs, considering the competency with difficulties as starting point. The SSs are built across the concepts formalized in the ontology by using the measure of semantic similarity.

4 Our Model of the Recommender System Based in Educational Competencies

The proposed model is shown in Fig. 4. The features of its components are explained in detail below.

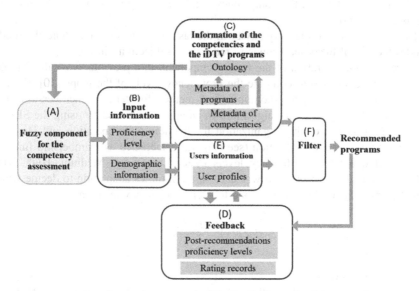

Fig. 4. Model of the Recommender System

(A) Fuzzy component for the competency assessment
Given the need to supply useful information about the students' requirements, the model includes a Fuzzy component for the assessment of competencies based on the features of the competency maps, which computes the proficiency levels of the competencies with the inherent precision of techniques of qualitative analysis.

For example, Fig. 5 shows an example of competency map, in which some Assessment Activities (AAs) (e.g., test and workshops) and their weights have been included at the lowest level of the map. In this case, the student has a qualitative proficiency level for each AA (that have been assigned by the teacher of a course).

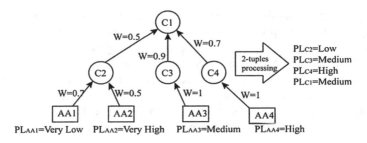

Fig. 5. Example of a Competency Map

The goal of the fuzzy component is to compute the proficiency levels of the competencies by using those of the AAs. Then, a general view of the students' capacities is offered.

All the computed proficiency levels are used in the model to obtain recommendations in accordance with students' needs. In the example in Fig. 5, the student may have learning problems in the competency C2. Then, the goal of her/him recommendations is to support C2.

Taking into account the subjectivity in the task of evaluating a student, the model includes the use of fuzzy techniques to reduce the subjectivity in data.

As regards the operation of the fuzzy component, in a previous work the 2-tuples techniques were adapted to compute the proficiency levels of the maps [20]. Furthermore, in [21], we developed a computational method for defining membership functions based on Fuzzy C-Means algorithm. In an application case by using the SERCE dataset (i.e., a dataset of the Organization for Economic Co-operation and Development), the normalized *sinc* function (see (1)) was established as membership function for different qualitative proficiency levels (Very Low, Low, Medium, High, Very High). This membership function was used in the 2-tuples adaptation to decide which qualitative proficiency level is assigned to each competency in the map.

$$sinc_N(x) = \frac{\sin(\pi x)}{\pi x} \tag{1}$$

(B) Input information
This is the minimal user information necessary to generate suggestions of iDTV programs. In order to obtain user profiles as complete as possible, the input information is composed of the proficiency levels (obtained by the **Fuzzy component for the competency assessment**) and the demographic information related to educational curriculum (e.g., age, languages, educational cycle or level) in a complementary way. Hence, the filtering strategies can be led to obtain recommendations by considering student's educational requirements and his/her individual features.

(C) Information of the competencies and the iDTV programs
This component contains the information of both the contents and the competencies (and any other type of information that is related to them), as well as the structures for their formalization. From a logical point of view, this information establishes relations between contents and competencies. In order to conceive it, we propose:

1. The use of metadata to describe the context entities and their relations: between iDTV services (i.e., program location) and programs, and between educational competencies and competency maps. There are currently metadata schemes that enables the development of application profiles that may be useful. For instance, TV-Anytime standard [22] is used to describe programs from the iDTV service point of view and Learning Object Metadata (LOM) standard [23] from the educational point of view, IEEE RCD is used to describe competencies; and SRCM to describe competency maps. In a previous work [24], we proposed a metadata application profile of TV-Anytime, which include IEEE LOM and RCD for describing VoD contents. Here, that work has been extended for considering any iDTV program.
2. The use of an ontology that relates the TV programs and the competencies by adapting the above mentioned metadata to the structure of the ontology (i.e., hierarchies of classes, instances of those classes and interrelations among the instances).

As regards metadata, it enables to establish relations between the context entities through their descriptions, as shown in Fig. 6. **Competency** and **Competency map** are entities that have been integrated to the TV-Anytime Content Description model. the **Program location** entity represents the iDTV service, the **Program** entity represents the iDTV programs, the **Video Fragment** entity represents the video fragment associated to the iDTV programs, the **Competency** entity represent the competencies, which are associated to video fragments, and the **Competency map** entity represents the competency maps, which are associated to the competencies.

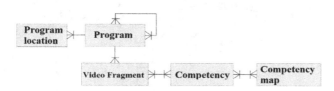

Fig. 6. Metadata description model

The ontology is the result of an alignment process of several domain ontologies, one of them for each metadata scheme. The ontology formalizes the metadata entities and their relations as concepts and properties respectively (i.e., data and object properties), as shown in Fig. 7. The entities are related among them through both direct relations (e.g., Has and isRelated relations) and indirect relations (i.e., through properties).

Through the ontology, SSs that link the concepts can be obtained. For example, if certain student has a Low proficiency level in the competency C1, it is important to find iDTV programs semantically related to C1.

Figure 8 presents a fragment of the ontology, in which C1 has relations with another competencies (C2 and C3) through their attributes (P1, P2 and P3). Also, competency C3 has relations with the video fragment VF1 through the attribute P5, and so on. Then, filtering strategies and measures of semantic similarity are applied over the semantic relations of C1 in order to find the programs that can be recommended.

Competency map and competency

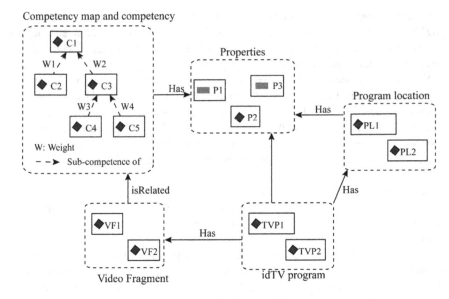

Fig. 7. Model of the ontology

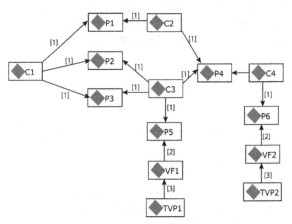

[1]: relation between a competency and an attribute
[2]: relation between a video fragment and an attribute
[3]: relation between a TV program and a video fragment

Fig. 8. Fragment of the ontology that indicates semantic sequences among concepts

(D) Feedback

This information allows the system to update and to adjust the recommendations based on changes of the educational requirements. In the model, we define two types of information:

1. The proficiency level, which is given by the **Fuzzy component for the competency assessment** after the recommendations. If the proficiency level of a competency

changes in time (better or worse), then the recommendations must change because the student's needs have changed as well.
2. Ranking records given by teachers and students that are used to measure the quality of the contents.

(E) Users information

This component contains useful students' information, which is organized in profiles. Basically, the model specifies two types of user information:

1. The records of the proficiency levels attained by all the students for the competency maps. This information allows the system to continuously adjust the recommendations. Taking into account the example in Fig. 5, the user profile is formalized in a table as the one shown in Table 1.

Table 1. Example of a user profile composed of proficiency levels

Elements of the map	Proficiency level
AA1	Very low
AA2	Very high
AA3	Medium
AA4	High
C1	Medium
C2	Low
C3	Medium
C4	High

2. Demographic information related to the learning process, for instance, information about the curriculum (current educative level, area, topic).

(F) Filter

This component is in charge of inferring recommendations by using both the user information and the ontology. For this purpose, it adapts measures of semantic similarities of the semantic Web on the ontology to find contents that may help to support the student's needs. In this work, we propose to define filtering strategies (such as the mentioned in Sect. 3) before adapting the measures of semantic similarity, which can be deducted from the work of teachers. For instance, a strategy is to recommend contents directly related to the competencies in which the student has difficulties. Another strategy is to recommend contents that develop the greatest number of competencies in which the student has difficulties. A final strategy is to find direct and indirect relations between competencies and then recommend the contents that share the greatest number of SSs as possible. For each strategy, the measures of semantic similarity are adapted to obtain the final recommendations.

For example, considering the fragment of the ontology presented in Fig. 8, recommendations based on the latter strategy can be obtained by adapting the methodology described in [8], as it is described in the next phases:

1. The construction of SSs, starting in the competencies with low proficiency level and finishing in the TV programs. The SSs are constructed by measuring the semantic intensity through the attributes of the competencies, the video fragments and the TV programs. In order to measure the semantic intensity, it is necessary to adapt metrics such as: the sequence length, the semantic relevance and the hierarchical similarity. If the semantic intensity exceeds a certain threshold level, the attribute, the competency, the video fragment or the TV program is added to the sequence. The sequence finishes with the last TV program that exceeds this level. From Fig. 8, we can infer the SSs as follows:

> SS1: C1, P1, C2, P4, C4, P6, VF2, TVP2.
> SS2: C1, P2, C3, P4, C4, P6, VF2, TVP2.
> SS3: C1, P3, C3, P4, C4, P6, VF2, TVP2.
> SS4: C1, P2, C3, P5, VF1, TVP1.
> SS4: C1, P3, C3, P5, VF1, TVP1.

2. The establishment of the most relevant sequences. The most relevant sequences are those that share more elements. For this, ρ-path and ρ-join associations are useful [25]. From the above mentioned SSs, we can see that all of them are relevant.
3. The extraction of the contents from the most relevant semantic sequences. In this phase, the most adequate contents are extracted from the most relevant SSs (e.g. the contents most related to several competencies with low proficiency level at same time). For this, the Branch and Bound (BNB) algorithm is used.
4. The obtaining of the list of recommendations. This list is composed of contents that exceed certain level of semantic intensity.

5   Extending the Scope of Our Model

This work proposes a RS focused on iDTV programs. However, its model can be applied to OTT platforms that provide video contents such as Youtube.com and Learner.org. Since the metadata models of these platforms cannot be modified, a solution is to relate them to the **Competency** and **Competency map** entities (see Fig. 6) in a logical way. This process can be carried out by linking the descriptions of the contents in each platform to the model of the RS by means of metadata elements. Therefore, the changes must be applied in the component C (**Information of the competencies and the iDTV programs**) of the proposal, while the others do not require modifications. This situation involves a new dynamic for the end-user to be adapted to the features of the video-sharing platforms. For example, any student with internet access can obtain recommendations at any time, and any person can produce and upload contents that may be recommended if these contents have educational features.

Finally, there are several possibilities to present the list of recommendations. In the iDTV, an application can be deployed on the TV screen in parallel with the TV programs seen by the user (the scheduled programs) in certain moment. Such an application may show the recommendations, indicating which can be seen in that moment (because it is a VoD program or because it is presented in certain channel) or which will be presented in another moment (in accordance to the scheduling of the TV service). In the case of OTT platforms, a Web application can be developed, which can be accessed by the users at any time. The contents can be played embedded or accessed by means of a link to the platform. In both cases, the notifications may be useful.

6 Conclusions and Future Work

In this work we present a RS for iDTV programs, focused in educational competencies. In practice, the objective of the RS is to support learning processes by suggesting programs that may be useful to overcome students' requirements.

The model follows the context-aware approach and it incorporates the competencies as an additional entity (i.e., in addition to the traditionally used user and content), which may have a positive effect on the accuracy of the recommendations. In order to establish logic relations between the system entities (i.e., user, contents and competencies), we propose the use of an ontology as an information structure. Considering the ontology, measures of semantic similarity are adapted in accordance with filtering strategies. Since the concept of competency is abstract, the metadata schemes have an important role in this work because they define a standard point about the competency concept and how to use it to describe an educational resource. For this reason, the metadata is the basis to formalize relations between programs and competencies within the ontology.

Other models of RSs usually use explicit and implicit information as input and relevance feedback. After the analysis of the dynamics of competency-based education, we conclude that this type of information does not allow an accurate description of the proficiency levels. Therefore, in this work we propose the integration of a fuzzy component to maintain a qualitative and updated record of the proficiency level. This information is an important part of the student profile, because allows the RS to focus the recommendations to the support of the competencies in which the student has low proficiency levels.

In the near future we will develop an application by using Java and a set of experiments to measure the effectiveness of the proposed model in approximately 3 and 6 months, respectively. For this purpose, a set of contents will be described and then recommended in accordance with real data related to competency maps and student profiles provided by teachers. The recommendations will be analyzed by a group of experts, verifying if the programs may be relevant for each student. Hence, measures of evaluation metrics, such as precision and recall, will be obtained. Additionally, we will study a way of making semi-automatic and automatic descriptions of TV programs related to competencies within approximately 1 year. For this purpose, we will implement a mechanism to relate features of the programs (which are collected by mean of audio analysis techniques) and semantic sequences over the ontology.

Acknowledgements. This work is supported by the National Doctorates program, call with reference number 617-2013 of Colciencias, the UsabiliTV project supported by Colciencias with ID 1103 521 2846 and the Asociación Universitaria Iberoamericana de Postgrado (AUIP). Also, this work is partially supported by the Government of Spain, contract TIN2015-67149-C3-1R and the RedAUTI project (Red temática en Aplicaciones y Usabilidad de la Television Digital Interactiva), CYTED 512RT0461.

References

1. van der Klink, M., Boon, J.: Competencies: the triumph of a Fuzzy Concept. Int. J. Hum. Resour. Dev. Manage. **3**(2), 125–137 (2003)
2. Véras, D., Prota, T., Prudêncio, R., Ferraz, C.: A literature review of recommender systems in the television domain. Expert Syst. Appl. **42**(12), 9046–9076 (2015)
3. UNESCO ICT Competency Standards for Teachers, http://unesdoc.unesco.org/images/0023/002348/234822E.pdf, last accessed April 04 2017
4. The University of Queensland: Pedagogical benefits, http://www.uq.edu.au/teach/video-teach-learn/ped-benefits.html, last accessed April 02 2017
5. Deuk, H., Kyeong Kim, H., Young Choi, I., Kyeong Kim, J.: A literature review and classification of recommender systems research. Expert Syst. Appl. **39**(11), 10059–10072 (2012)
6. Bobadilla, J., Ortega, F., Hernando, A., Gutíerrez, A.: Recommender systems survey. Knowl.-Based Syst. **46**, 109–132 (2013)
7. Ávila, J., Palacio, X., Espinoza, M., Saquicela, V.: Semantic recommender system for digital TV: from demographic stereotyping to personalized recommendations. In: Asia-Pacific Conference on Computer Aided System Engineering on Proceedings. IEEE, Quito (2015)
8. Blanco-Fernández, Y., Pazos-Arias, J., Gil-Solla, A., Ramos-Cabrer, M.: AVATAR: an improved solution for personalized TV based on semantic inference. IEEE Trans. Consum. Electron. **52**(1), 223–231 (2006)
9. García-Crespo, Á., López-Cuadrado, J., Colomo-Palacios, R., González-Carrasco, I., Ruiz-Mezcua, B.: Sem-Fit: A semantic based expert system to provide recommendations in the tourism domain. Expert Syst. Appl. **38**(10), 13310–13319 (2011)
10. Anaya, A., Luque, M.: Recommender system in collaborative learning environment. Expert Syst. Appl. **40**, 7193–7202 (2014)
11. Lundqvist, K., Baker, K., Williams, S.: Ontology supported competency system. Int. J. Knowl. Learn. **7**, 197–219 (2011)
12. Oxford University Press, English Oxford Living Dictionaries, https://en.oxforddictionaries.com/definition/competence, last accessed April 02 2017
13. IMS Global Learning Consortium, Reusable Definition of Competency or Educational Objective, https://www.imsglobal.org/competencies/rdceov1p0/imsrdceo_infov1p0.html, last accessed April 02 2017
14. IEEE Computer Society: IEEE Standard for Learning Technology—Data Model for Reusable Competency Definitions - 1484.20.1-2007, New York (2007)
15. Simple Reusable Competency Map, http://www.ostyn.com/standardswork/competency/ReusableCompMapProp.pdf, last accessed April 02 2017
16. Argüelles, A., Gonczi, A.: Competency based education and training. Limusa, Mexico (2000)
17. Montenegro, I.: Aprendizaje y Desarrollo de las Competencias. Magisterio, Bogotá (2003). (in Spanish)

18. Hung, L.: Personalized recommendation system based on product taxonomy for one-to-one marketing online. Expert Syst. Appl. **29**, 383–392 (2005)
19. López-Nores, M., Blanco-Fernández, Y., Pazos-Arias, J., Gil-Solla, A.: Property-based collaborative filtering for health-aware recommender systems. Expert Syst. Appl. **39**, 7451–7457 (2012)
20. Guerrero, F., Otero, P.D., Duran, J.L.: Arciniegas: Método basado en el procesamiento de información cualitativa para la evaluación individual y grupal de competencias educativas. Thesis. Popayán: Universidad del Cauca (2016) (in Spanish)
21. Guerrero, F., Otero, P.D., Duran, J.L.: Arciniegas: Método computacional para la identificación de funciones de pertenencia en entornos de lógica difusa. In: 11th Colombian Computing Conference (CCC) on Proceedings, IEEE, Popayán (2016) (in Spanish)
22. European Telecommunications Standards Institute: ETSI TS 102 822-3-1 V1.7.1, Sophia Antípolis (2011)
23. IEEE Working Group: IEEE 1484.12.1 (2002)
24. Guzman, D., Chinchajoa, J., Duran, D., Chanchí, G., Arciniegas, J.L.: A metadata scheme for vod educational contents: an educational competency-based approach. Revista Científica **1**(28), 42–59 (2017)
25. Martín-Vicente, M., Gill, A., Ramos, M., Pazos, J., Blanco, Y., López, M.: A semantic approach to improve neighborhood formation in collaborative recommender systems. Expert Syst. Appl. **41**(17), 7776–7788 (2014)

Video Consumption and Preservation

Online Educational Videos: The Teenagers' Preferences

Carolina Almeida[⊠] and Pedro Almeida

University of Aveiro - Digimedia, Aveiro, Portugal
`{carol,almeida}@ua.pt`

Abstract. Young people are strongly engaged with the activity of watching online videos, especially in social platforms like Youtube or Facebook. The most popular viewed genres include musical and other entertainment genres. Educational videos struggle to occupy a relevant place in the young viewing habits. Nevertheless, this amount of time spent watching on demand or streamed content opens attractive opportunities for educational content to try to grab a part of that time, if designed to be appealing and engaging. In this context, this research focuses on collecting the teenagers' opinions and preferences regarding online video, namely educational videos and their opinions on the possibility of including this genre of videos in their daily video consumption habits. The study adopted a qualitative approach and 16 teenagers were involved in the data collection procedures that included watching different videos, answering a questionnaire and discussing the opinions in a focus group. The results show that teenagers prefer relaxed or comic approaches in educational videos. Videos should have short duration, fast editing and include infographics. Participants also referred that they would be interested in integrating educational videos in their consumption habits but in moderate way.

Keywords: Online video · Teenagers · Informal learning

1 Introduction

Nowadays teenagers spend several hours a week or even a day watching online videos. Studies are focused mainly in users with 16 years old or more, but the results point to an increasing trend that may be even stronger in younger audiences. According to the key findings of the international study "TV and media 2016" [1] (carried out in 22 countries including the USA, several European countries like Germany, Greece, Italy, The Netherlands, Poland, Romania, Russia, Spain, Sweden, UK and Portugal, South America countries, Australia, North Korea, and other Asian countries), that analysed media consumption habits, since 2012 the total time spent watching online video has increased in 4 h and the amount of time spent watching linear TV has decreased 2,5 h. And even the behaviours of the traditional TV viewing have been changing and have been enriched with multitasking activities, including searching for TV program related information or following social networks activity, that allowed for the cohabitation of traditional watching behaviours with complementary activities in the mobile devices [2]. The TV and media 2016 study [1] also provides detailed data about the consumption habits of

© Springer International Publishing AG 2017
M.J. Abásolo et al. (Eds.): jAUTI 2016, CCIS 689, pp. 65–76, 2017.
DOI: 10.1007/978-3-319-63321-3_5

younger populations (from 16 to 24 years old). This generation watches a weekly average of 3,7 h of on demand streamed user generated content (UGC), 2,9 h of streamed on demand series, 2,3 h of streamed on demand movies, 1,4 h of other video content and 1 h of on demand educational or instructional videos. It is clear that the educational content is not by far the teenagers' top choice in online video. Nevertheless, the increasing amount of time spent watching on demand or streamed content opens the possibility for the creation of new educational content, designed to be appealing and engaging with the purpose of capturing a part of the time youngsters spend in this viewing activities.

This research focuses in the analysis of teenagers' preferences about online video gathering their expectations about new educational video content. The final main goal will be to define guidelines for the creation of appealing educational videos, namely natural sciences videos, able to be relevant in informal learning situations.

2   State of the Art

2.1   Viewing Habits

Teenagers start using technologies since young age being one of its main uses watching (online) videos, especially on their mobile devices [3, 4]. In a study carried out in 20 countries including Portugal, results show that teenagers (from 16 to 34 years old) get more than half of the videos they watch in their mobile devices and the average weekly time spent in that activity has shown an increase in three hours from 2012 to 2015 [4]. Another study [5] conducted among the UK population (18-34) compared the viewing habits in desktops and mobile devices and found that the later got a daily average of 69,9 min of online video consumption as compared with 45,8 min in desktops.

According to data collected in 2013 by the YouTube® platform, regarding the preferred genres of North American teenagers and young adults (from 16 to 24 years old), both male and female individuals prefer to watch, above all, music videos [6, 7]. Female individuals also watch comedy, movies and animations, and health and beauty videos [6]. Male individuals watch, besides music videos, gaming videos, followed by comedy, movies and animations [7]. Educational videos don't play a relevant role in their consumption habits. According to the same study, educational videos are on the 5th position in the routines of female [6] and on the 7th of male individuals [7], far behind the other entertainment genres.

Despite the lower relevance of the educational genre, actually the viewing habits are changing and it is important to explore the opportunities that this mass consumption of videos may offer to educational videos in this informal viewing moments.

2.2   Motivations of Online Viewers

As referred, young people are strongly engaged in watching online videos. In this scope, Khan carried a study aiming to identify the motivation factors that drive viewers to online video, both in passive and active ways (e.g. by commenting the videos), with analysis of users sense of gratification associated to those practices [8]. This research concluded that, besides seeking relaxation and entertainment (3,49 in a scale from 1 to

5, being 5 the highest score), the motivation to learn new things was also an important driver with 3,03 [8]. As Mayer [9] assumes, if a video is meaningful, learning will take place. This power of video over other media, like textual media, has also been high-lighted in other areas, like for scientific communication [10].

It is also important to identify which features in the videos may be correlated to its success. Gupta et al [11] analysed beauty (video) commercials in what relates with its sound dimensions, visual effects, content, message and appeal to emotions. According to this research videos whose messages have social and youth appeal have higher number of views. Concerning to visual aspects, slow motion ads have the higher number of views. Sound saturation, background music and loud music are the audio characteristics related to the most viewed adds. Unexpected formats or surprise end-ings are the content characteristics of most viewed ads [11].

In line with these results, Douglas et al [12] studied the inspirations that were taken in consideration in the development of new videos (like whiteboard videos) to the Massive Online Open Courses (MOOCs) and Physics courses of Georgia Institute of Technology. The authors concluded that the videos were mostly influenced by other (non-educational) informal and entertainment videos [12] and were a more engaging and expressive way of presenting content to students. Despite the presented studies drawing conclusions applied to marketing strategies, [11], or clearly defined to be used in formal educational environments, [12], its conclusions could be useful to the development of a framework to support the creation of new educational videos about natural sciences.

3   General Objectives

This study comprises two stages: the first, targeted at carrying a survey about the online video consumption habits of Portuguese teenagers, aged between 12 and 16 years old, and; the second, including the preparation, production and publication of natural sci-ences videos in popular online platforms. These videos will be produced taking in consideration the literature review and the preferences gathered on the first stage, that are presented here. It is the aim of the study that the new videos may reveal its potential to be integrated in teenagers informal learning practices.

Therefore, the following sections present the survey carried to teenagers, trying to understand which characteristics of the videos can be applied on the production and publishing of new natural sciences contents to achieve higher levels of attractiveness and interest from teenagers and that fulfil the goal of being integrated in its informal viewing sessions.

4   Methodology

In order to accomplish the first objective, an evaluation model of the habits and viewing preferences of teenagers was designed. This model aimed to evaluate the technical, aesthetics, and discourse features of online (educational related) videos, namely to get the preferences of the sample. This model also aimed to understand the level of interest of teenagers to integrate the proposed new content in their usual consumption habits.

A non-probabilistic sample of 16 participants was chosen: teenagers between 12 and 16 years old, students in the 3rd cycle of the Portuguese public educational system. The sample was balanced with 8 males and 8 females. The participants from a central location in Portugal, lived nearby the researcher area and voluntarily agreed to participate after being invited to.

To prepare the evaluation phase there was the need to select and prepare different sample videos. This content was extracted among a selection of Youtube channels and videos that were previously analysed by the researcher, in its state of the art review of the most popular educational online videos.

After this selection, two complete videos, one with 11 min and another with 2 min, were prepared and targeted the evaluation of different characteristics: length, editing, rhythm, infographics, music and sound effects, and the content organization.

For the analysis of the preferred type of scenarios, a video with 4 segments extracted from popular videos, one for each type of scenario (virtual scenario, studio, real but neutral scenario, real scenario contextualized with the thematic of the video) was used. To evaluate the communication style, a 3 segment video was prepared (a relaxed style, a comic style and, a more formal style). Finally, another video explored 3 types of animation: 2D, 3D and stop motion. These videos showed each segment preceded by simple black frames identifying the segment (A, B, C or D) (see Fig. 1). These videos had an average duration of 3 min each.

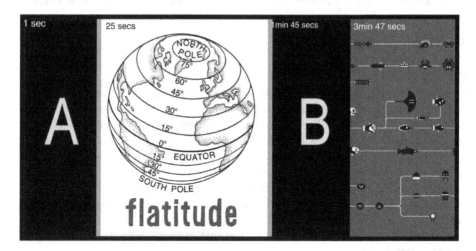

Fig. 1. Frame examples of the style video. Screenshots (visible in the picture) from Vsauce (https://www.youtube.com/watch?v=IJhgZBn-LHg) and from Kurzgesagt – In a Nutshell (https://www.youtube.com/watch?v=hOfRN0KihOU).

The evaluation phase was structured in three moments: (i) the first stage allowed the evaluators to watch the selected and pre-prepared videos; (ii) next the evaluators answered a questionnaire to allow us to get their characterization and they evaluated the viewed contents; (iii) the final stage consisted of a focus group, to clarify preferences and expectations about new video contents. This last phase was relevant because this type of data collection allows "participants to engage in meaningful conversations about the topics that researchers wish to understand" [5].

4.1 The Evaluation Stages

According to the participants' agendas, the evaluation was carried in two dates, the first with 12 participants and the second with the remaining 4 participants (in this group there were 4 in the first stages and 3 in the focus group).

As referred, each evaluation included the 3 stages. In the first stage participants watched the five prepared videos followed by the second stage, the completion of the questionnaire. These parts took an average of 1 h. The last stage explored a guided discussion (focus group) about participants' video consumption habits, preferred video characteristics and about the possibility of integration new educational videos in their viewing habits. It took an average of 30 min. To support the focus group two additional videos were prepared to be used in case of need to clarify some characteristics, namely the editing rhythm. These videos were shown during the first focus group session to clarify the concept of rhythm. In the second focus group session, there was no need to do it since the participants were clear on what editing rhythm meant.

In both sessions the order of the clips was the same: the first video was the complete video with 11 min, followed by a complete 2 min long video, the scenarios clip was next followed by the communication styles clip and finished with the clip that contained the different types of animation. The videos were presented in a 32" flat screen TV.

The evaluation was carried in a regular home scenario, aiming to act as an informal place, since the greatest percentage of the video consumption (around 80%) occurs at home [13]. Knowing this, going to a lab was not a viable option. The regular home was used as the scenario, as seen in Fig. 2.

Fig. 2. Participants engaged in the evaluation procedures.

The different evaluation stages allowed to get qualitative (e.g. from the group discussion) data and quantitative (from the questionnaire).

5 Results

In this section both quantitative and qualitative results will be presented. Quantitative and qualitative data from the questionnaire, along with qualitative data from the focus group session was gathered. The following section is organized accordingly to the analysis dimensions defined to be evaluated. Each dimension is presented in a different sub-section.

5.1 Sample Characterization and Viewing Habits

According to the questionnaire, we found that 43,8% of the participants watch online video less than an hour a day, 25% watch more than five hours, 18,8% watch between one and two hours and 12,5% say watching three to four hours daily. The average hours spent watching online video, for this sample, is approximately 2,6 h daily.

The number of participants stating to watch more than five hours daily were all boys (4). They said to have strong gaming habits and therefore they watched videos to improve their performance. They also mentioned watching videos about curiosities, from natural sciences videos to social phenomena like dictatorial regimes. On the focus group they enounced several curiosities and gamming channels or youtubers. In these videos they value the editing style and the length of videos as key factors when choosing what to watch.

Girls expressed shorter viewing periods (mostly less than two hours a day) and their preferences went towards makeup, being that a central part of their daily routines. They referred to try to choose a different makeup style everyday which lead them to search for tutorial videos on that subject.

Based on the focus group results, and considering all participants, watching online videos is a way of developing cooking skills (20%), informatics skills (20%), sport skills (13%), and other practices like makeup (7%), or dancing (7%). We found that watching Do It Yourself (DIY) videos is a common practice among participants.

Almost all participants considered that they not only learn new things, but also learn in a more comprehensive way while they watch online videos. Despite this, they are not used to clarify school doubts through videos, only through written content or by means of online searches (60%). When they need to find information for school projects, 20% state to use online video and written sources, classifying both with equal levels of credibility. The same participants state that using videos in project presentations is a strategy to captivate their audience.

Since many of the videos being evaluated were English spoken, it was relevant to get the participants English comprehension level (presented in Graph 1). Participants classified their English oral comprehension as bad (12,5%), reasonable (31,3%) and the remaining (56,2%) as good.

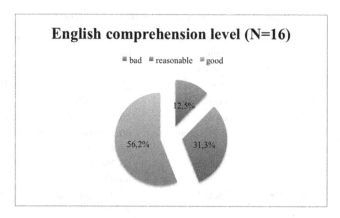

Graph 1. English comprehension level of the participants (N = 16)

5.2 Preferences About Technical Characteristics

Considering the preferences towards the type of host, participants preferred participant hosts. Arguments shared in group discussions sustained the host participation as a pleasant element of the video, since one of the most referred add-ons to watch a video was its host reputation.

Focusing on the editing rhythm of videos, it was clear in oral discussions that the fastest edited ones were the preferred ones. Participants characterized two videos with different editing types as appropriate (video 1 with a slower editing than video 2). Video 2 was rated as suitable by 86,7% of the participants (see Table 1).

According to the majority of participants of the two work sessions the videos should be short. Both responses to the questionnaire (see Table 1) and group discussion statements stand towards short videos. A video with a time length of 3 min is rated as appropriate.

Finally, music and sound effects were also referred as positive characteristics. Comments like "Cool sound effects!" were also registered during the group discussion moments.

The following table presents a synthesis of the preferences about the 3 studied dimensions.

5.3 Preferences About the Speech Dimension

To evaluate the speech dimension participants watched the two main videos: the longer one (11 min) with a detailed description on the evolutionary theory and a shorter one (about 2 min) with a time-lapse explaining the evolution of life on Earth, comparing the geologic time scale to a 24-hour interval. The two complete videos approached contents with some scientific terms like "Mutation" or "Eukaryotic cells", but one of the videos clearly explained each scientific concept and the other don't. It was not clear, only with data from the questionnaire, if participants prefer a more scientific and detailed language or a more colloquial speech: 50% were neutral about language

Table 1. Preferences about studied dimensions.

Dimensions	Sub-dimensions	Instructions to include in new videos	Data support (participants' preferences)
Technical	Host	Participant and present host	27,7% appreciated absent host and 50% didn't. [*1]
	Edition rhythm	Fast	86,7% considers appropriated[*3]
	Duration	2 to 3 min	66,7% considers this interval appropriated. [*3]
	Music	Include	65,2% appreciated and 20,9% didn't.[*1]
	Sound effects	Include	42,9% appreciated and 16,7% didn't.[*2]
Speech	Language complexity	Plain language	Supported by qualitative data.
	Level of detail in explanations	General or detailed explanation.	Data from Graph 3
	Speech style	Comic or relaxed	Top choice is comic presenters (66,7%); 2nd choice is relaxed presenters (60%).
Aesthetical	Scenario	Virtual	56,7% prefers virtual scenarios.
	Infography	Include	79,1% appreciated.[*1]
	Animation	2D	43,8% prefers 2D animation.

[*1] Averages from assessment of complete videos;
[*2] Preferences related to video 1;
[*3] Preferences related to video 2.

complexity of the video that explained clearly each scientific concept; 31,3% were also neutral about the complexity of language from video 2 (which didn't explain clearly concepts like eukaryotic cell), and 50% stated that the language used wasn't complex. The summarized data is presented in Graph 2.

When considering the depth how the content is explored in each video, 56% of the participants stated to like the way the contents were explained in Video 1 (the more detailed one) and 6% didn't. On the other end 75% liked the general way to approach the concepts presented on Video 2 but 13% didn't like it (see data presented in Graph 3).

In line with this results, data from the focus group discussion show that the participants prefer videos with colloquial approaches to scientific concepts (e.g. "The host should use plain language" – free translation).

Considering the speech style, the comic style was stated to be the favourite by 66,7% of the participants followed by the relaxed style to 60% of the participants. Therefore, if there is a presenter, his speech should not be too fast and his style should be comic.

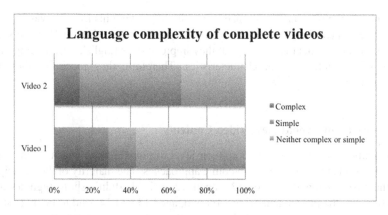

Graph 2. Language complexity of complete videos (N = 16)

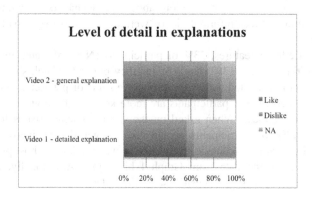

Graph 3. Level of detail of scientific concepts' explanations (N = 16)

5.4   Preferences About Aesthetical Dimensions

Focusing on the type of preferred scenario, a clear tendency from this group puts the virtual scenario has the favourite (56,7% of the participants) (see Table 1).

Concerning to the type of animation, it was found that 2D Animations were the favourite for 43,8% of the participants.

They valued infographics that allow a better comprehension of the oral speech, especially when an English spoken host is presenting it.

The participants who classified their English oral comprehension as bad or as reasonable expressed that the understanding of the topics was possible by means of the infographics and animations. Nevertheless, they said to prefer to watch content in Portuguese. They verbalized sentences like "*I understood the topic because of the images, for me it could be in Japanese that I would understand the same!*" (a free translation from Portuguese).

For the ones who considered their English oral comprehension as good (56,2%), watching online content in English makes them improve their English comprehension.

In the first session one participant made clear that improving his English was a concern and watching entertainment videos was a strategy to achieve that goal. In the second session two participants made clear that they improve their English by watching videos because of the entertainment characteristics. Therefore, they recognize they learn without noticing.

5.5   Expectations About New Video Contents

Finally, participants were asked about their level of motivation to watch, in the future, videos about science topics but with comic approaches. The majority of the participants from the first session (9 out of 12), aged 12 and 13, didn't show high levels of motivation, but the participants of session two, aged 13 and 14, said to be interested in integrating this type of videos in their daily online video viewing routines, especially if the videos were published with a low frequency, like once a week and not daily.

During the Focus Group, some opinions about what teenagers expect, in the future, to watch in natural sciences informal videos were discussed between participants and the researcher.

Focusing on editing features, 33% of participants (N = 15) stated its preferences towards fast editing videos, 13% clearly stated they prefer to watch short segments.

According to the collected data, we can observe some dispersion about the interest in new science videos. Older participants are more keen on these videos and younger participants more sceptical. When asked on the specific characteristics for these scientific videos, 47% of participants would like to get those videos with comic approaches and the same percentage would like to watch a known host presenting the scientific contents, as the data from Graph 4 highlights. Additionally, 20% of the participants would like to watch musical scientific videos.

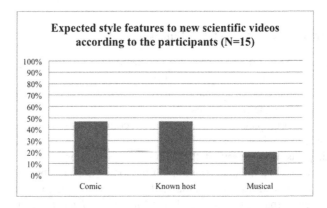

Graph 4. Expected style features to new scientific videos according to the participants (N = 15)

6 Conclusions

Based on the results of the study, and using this exploratory methodology, it was possible to perceive some of the features and elements that should be included in future informal educational videos. Considering this sample, it was clear that the comic videos are the favourite ones. Therefore, such an approach will be used in the creation of the new contents.

Videos with infographics, fast editing and short duration are the ones already available in their daily routines and these characteristics will be included in the new videos to be developed.

The sample shows preferences for a real and participant host, the use of virtual scenarios and 2D animations. Music and sound effects were also appreciated by this sample of participants. The language and the scientific depth of the contents should be light and simple.

The amount of time spent watching online video seems to be larger than the data gathered from previous studies [1]. This could be justified by the fact that this sample included younger users than the ones of previous studies. In addition, although the participants refer to watch DIY videos, they don't search for educational content, showing an even higher gap for this type of videos than what could be observed in the results of previous studies.

As stated in previous works, the video features can motivate or may not favour the motivation to watch a video [8]. The selected videos were not originally designed to this research, and therefore it was not possible to control all the variables in order to guarantee a generalization.

Additionally, these results were not conclusive enough to determine clearly all the dimensions of the new videos but some relevant insights will be useful as a starting point to the production of new videos.

Further research with wider and representative samples should be implemented in order to validate the presented conclusions as representative of the online video consumption of Portuguese teenagers and their preferences in new informal educational content. Nevertheless, the future stages of this project, namely the online publication of the new to be produced videos and the related data gathering its publication strategies should allow to further validate these expectations and results.

The researchers expect to find a balanced way to create videos that may allow a deep and meaningful learning maintaining high levels of interest and motivation from the viewers.

Acknowledgments. This paper reports on a research developed within the PhD Program Technology Enhanced Learning and Societal Challenges, funded by Fundação para a Ciência e Tecnologia, FCT I. P. – Portugal, under contract # PD/00173/2014 and # PD/BI.

PD†F **FCT PhD PROGRAMMES**

References

1. Ericsson ConsumerLab: Tv and Media 2016 (2016)
2. Abreu, J., Almeida, P., Teles, B., Reis, M.: Viewer behaviors and practices in the (new) television environment. In: Proceedings of the 11th European Conference on Interactive TV Video - EuroITV 2013, pp. 5–12 (2013). doi:10.1145/2465958.2465970
3. Deloitte Development: Millennials and the Mainstreaming of Digital 2015 (2015)
4. Ericsson ConsumerLab: Tv and Media 2015 (2015)
5. Comscore Inc.: The Global Mobile Report: How Multiplatform Audiences and Engagement Compare in the US, Canada, UK, and Beyond (2015)
6. Statista: Most popular YouTube video categories based on female Millennial user engagement as of December 2013 (2015). http://bit.ly/1STPvMW. Accessed 27 Apr 2016
7. Statista: Most popular YouTube video categories based on male Millennial user engagement as of December 2013 (2015). http://bit.ly/1VVBFKQ. Accessed 27 Apr 2016
8. Khan, M.L.: Social media engagement: What motivates user participation and consumption on YouTube? Comput. Human Behav. 66, 236–247 (2017). doi:10.1016/j.chb.2016.09.024
9. Mayer, R.E.: The promise of multimedia learning: using the same instructional design methods across different media. Learn. Instr. 13, 125–139 (2003). doi:10.1016/S0959-4752(02)00016-6
10. Moura, M., Almeida, P., Geerts, D.: A video is worth a million words? comparing a documentary with a scientific paper to communicate design research. Proc. Comput. Sci. 100, 747–754 (2016). doi:10.1016/j.procs.2016.09.220
11. Gupta, H., Singh, S., Sinha, P.: Multimedia tool as a predictor for social media advertising- a YouTube way. Multimed. Tools Appl. (2016). doi:10.1007/s11042-016-4249-6
12. Douglas, S.S., Aiken, J.M., Greco, E., et al.: Do-It-yourself whiteboard-style physics video lectures. Phys. Teach. 55, 22–24 (2017). doi:10.1119/1.4972492
13. Ericsson Consumer Lab: TV and Media 2014 (2014)

We Need to Talk About Digital Preservation of Audiovisual Collections: Strategies for Building National Networks

Rostand Costa[1](✉), Guido Lemos de Souza Filho[1](✉),
Valdecir Becker[1](✉), and Alvaro Malaguti[2]

[1] Digital Video Applications Lab (LAVID),
Federal University of Paraíba (UFPB), João Pessoa, Brazil
{rostand,guido,valdecir}@lavid.ufpb.br
[2] Rede Nacional de Pesquisa (RNP),
Ministry of Science and Technology (MCTI), Rio de Janeiro, Brazil
alvaro.malaguti@rnp.br

Abstract. This paper is about the relevance of creating national networks to digital preservation of audiovisual collections, from both film and television industry. The proposal arises from the perception that, in the same proportion that the audiovisual production is being created in digital formats, it is expected the preservation of such information to be based on appropriate techniques and technologies also digital. It is similarly considered that the concern of digitization and preservation of collections are present in several initiatives guiding public policy in many countries. Based on the experiments already undergoing in the world, especially in the most advanced countries in the area, it is possible to predict that the building of a national network for the promotion of audiovisual digital preservation, with range and broad scope, can significantly contribute to the development of the national expertise in the area, to consolidate partnerships and to leverage the emergence of solutions adapted to the context of each country. Steps in this direction could include, among other actions, the promotion of two complementary strands of initiatives: (a) the organization of a consortium of public and private organizations interested in digital preservation; and (b) assembling a "backbone" of national repositories for large-scale digital preservation.

Keywords: Digital preservation · National networks · Digital repositories · Audiovisual collections · Preservation management

1 Introduction

This article aims to encourage debate on the relevance of creating national networks for audiovisual collections digital preservation. The proposal was triggered by the emerging perception that, as a considerable part of the artifacts related to audiovisual production is being created in digital formats, it is expected that preservation practices related to such information should also be based on digital techniques and appropriate technologies.

© Springer International Publishing AG 2017
M.J. Abásolo et al. (Eds.): jAUTI 2016, CCIS 689, pp. 77–90, 2017.
DOI: 10.1007/978-3-319-63321-3_6

It is also considered that the digitalization and preservation of collections are present directives in several initiatives guiding public policies in many countries[1].

For a quick contextualization, digital preservation can be understood as "the set of processes responsible for ensuring continued access to digital information over long periods of time, i.e. periods greater than the technological environment life expectancy necessary for interpretation and/or reproduction of information" [1]. In a further definition, digital preservation "is concerned with the continued ability to maintain authentic digital content, interpretable and accessible, even when used on a different technological platform than the one initially used at the time of its creation" [2].

When compared with the preservation of physical collections, preservation for digital content brings in itself an association, almost confrontational, between great risk potential and great protection potential [3]. The risk potential is represented by digital storage transience that can be irretrievably lost because of technical or human failure much more easily and quickly than traditional not digital media The protection potential, in turn, is anchored in the fact that digital collections can be indefinitely reproduced and stored with complete fidelity and integrity. Thus, the perfect continuity for digital collections depends largely on seeking a balance in implementing measures. This balance should take full advantage of the potential for protection to the point of neutralizing its inherent risk potential.

Furthermore, digital preservation involves essentially different challenges from those found in more traditional media storage content. From a more traditional point of view, the act of preserving is translated into the act of keeping unchanged and intact. In a digital environment, however, preserve the action can also refer to change, rebuild and renew it. Where renew can mean change formats, update media and/or replace hardware and software. In short: if on the one hand, we want to keep the content exactly as it was created, intact; on the other hand, we want to continue to access it through modern platforms. This is the "digital preservation paradox" as described by Sayão [4].

A growing number of organizations (including the ones gathered in MetaArchive Initiative [5]) bet that the most effective efforts for digital preservation occur in practice, when a strategy to keep multiple copies of digital content in different locations is adopted [6]. This strategy usually involves matrix repository fitting, capable of storing digital collections in a pre-established methodology, including replicas loss identification mechanisms to quickly reconstruct the minimum amount of necessary copies integrity and timing [2].

Assembling such a framework for distributed digital preservation, usually requires the adoption of strategies involving storage units' geographic distribution and a strong security implementation in each individual unit. All that in a combination of approaches that seeks to ensure content survival [3]. Thus, maximizing the physical and logical security measures implemented in each storage unit reduces the probability that they compromise. In turn, replication prevents that any individual copy loss lead into a total loss of the preserved contents.

---

[1] In Brazil, we can mention the National Culture Plan (PNC) and other documents produced by the Ministry of Culture.

However, it is unlikely that a single culture memory organization has the ability to set up and operate properly several geographically distributed computational infrastructures. In this sense, collaboration between institutions is essential, and such collaboration requires technical and organizational investments. It is not the case of having only a suitable technological solution, but also long-term robust inter-institutional agreements need to be established, or there will not be enough commitment for a tuned performance over time. In this sense, the challenge may represent more a political problem than a technical one. Because in particular, for digital preservation in various segments, such as academic, artistic and/or cultural, to name a few, it depends on public and private institutions to undergo changes in direction, mission and lasting sources of funding [7].

The preservation for long-term audiovisual digital content, in turn, also brings its own and very particular challenges. One of the most emblematic is related to the scale that such content may involve. Whereas a single copy digital video master, without compression and depending on its duration and its resolution can reach a significant size (2.9 TB/h to 4K resolution at 24 frames), an average repository could easily reach a Peta bytes magnitude.

Storage for large files, besides being expensive, is also quite susceptible to the phenomenon known as "data degradation" (or bit rot), in which silent failures occur in bit-level systems based on arrays, even in high-end ones. When one considers that the current discs have bit failure rate around 1 in 10^{14} and 1 TB requires about 10^{13} bits of storage space, it can be inferred that the losses are not only expected but almost inevitable [8].

Thus, it is essential to understand how damage can occur and what impact it does on audiovisual digital content preserved, especially when it is involved some compression technique [9]. In this sense, investigation of specific mechanisms that are efficient, scalable and can be applied to detect corruption and recovery of this content is very welcome and represents an open and active area of research.

The rest of this paper is organized as follows. Section 2 contextualizes the challenges of preservation of audiovisual collections in television segment and as the migration to digital preservation will produce significant impacts. Section 3 discusses the non-technological aspects of management, especially the organizational and methodological obstacles involved. Section 4 discusses the importance of national networking of digital preservation for national coverage, both for the consolidation of conservation infrastructure on a large scale and for the emergence of a technical and methodological tool that meets the uniqueness of each nation. Section 5 provides a development and creation of collective initiatives political and strategic vision for national scope and raises the question of sectoral and thematic organization role for national networks promotion. Finally, Sect. 6 contains our concluding remarks.

2   The Challenges of Preserving Television Audiovisual Collections

Collections preservation is also a recurring theme in television industry, where broadcasters keep raw materials and edited files for future use. Despite cultural aspect not being the focus of preservation, broadcasters collections[2], help to tell political, economic and cultural history in the World.

Broadcasters collections proper preservation is critical for two reasons: reprise and reuse. In the first case, materials such as films and soap operas, are reprised with some frequency. Whereas reuse is more important for television news, where archival material is constantly used to cover text made by the reporter based on existing images, reducing the costs of new recordings. In addition, excerpts for news and reporting ever conveyed can run again placed in new programs.

Historically, the files consist of films, with the material from the beginning of TV history, quadruplex tapes (two inches), VPR (one inch), U-Matic (3/4 in.), SVHS (Super Video Home System) and analog Betamax with recorded material both PAL-M (Phase Alternating Line – Modified) and NTSC (National Television System Committee) format (up to the 1980s the PAL-M recorders were common, but fell out of favor due to high costs, compared to NTSC technology). With the evolution of formats, broadcasters have come to include other media in the collection, such as digital Beta tape, used till now. It is noteworthy that up to half of the 2000s, every file is in SD (Standard Definition) format, i.e. with 4×3 resolution.

As digital technologies emerged, also did the first preservation systems television archives in file format. The first format used was MPEG-2 (Moving Picture Experts Group) for both SD and for the first recording HD (High Definition). Compatibility issues also emerged. Broadcasters that scanned the files in MPEG-2 format face compatibility problems with the workflow of digital TV, all based on the MPEG-4 format.

The same questioning is done now considering the possibility of high definition migration to 4K resolution. Questions about MPEG-4 future, evolution for their profiles and the adoption of common formats and codecs in movies such as Motion JPEG-2000 (Joint Photographic Experts Group) or RAW format, hinder strategic definitions of archives preservation technologies adoption.

It is necessary to differentiate collections preservation made by private broadcasters, which rely on proprietary solutions provided by specialized companies in the area, from public/state televisions, which often face difficulties to preserve the collection. It is not rare to find public or state broadcaster without file, or with miniature collection due to costs.

This scenario affects content exchange, essential for closing program schedules in public and state televisions. What broadcasters do not store properly cannot be shared. To resolve this issue, it is necessary to consider local, regional, national and international strategies content exchange.

---

[2] Like the ones from TV Record (www.r7.com) and TV Cultura (www.tvcultura.com.br), to name just two in Brazil.

Based on this context, can be highlighted three challenges for digital preservation of television archives, which can be overcome by the creation of a national preservation network:

- Cost reduction, so that the technology is accessible to small broadcasters, especially public, state and community;
- Adequate compression, coding and indexing technology, to minimize the risks of new technologies turn acquis obsolete and inaccessible;
- Content exchange in appropriate formats (or simple transcoding formats and codec solutions), so that access is facilitated.

3   Preservation Management: A Look Beyond Technological Aspects

It can be said that digital preservation area is in its early stages of formation and technological, methodological and political apparatus to preserve digital information is still being built. Much of the knowledge accumulated in recent decades in preservation and access to digital resources is beginning to consolidate into a set of strategies, technological approaches, methodologies and formal recommendations [10].

Some of these practices start to become collectively known as digital curation. Still an evolving concept, the digital curation is described by Sayão as "active management and preservation of digital resources throughout its cycle of interest, with the perspective long-term challenge of meeting the needs of current and future generations of users" [4].

As one of the most relevant search results on that front, the Digital Curation Centre[3] (DCC) brought a high-level model based on a series of stages to effectively manage curation and digital preservation [11]. In DCC management model arranged in rings as shown in Fig. 1, we highlight the following main groups of processes (inside out):

1. Actions on data, comprising the treatment of objects or databases in any digital format;
2. All Life Cycle Actions, which deals with the description and information representation, planning preservation and participation of the actors involved definition;
3. Sequential Actions, that cover conceptualizing, creating and/or receiving data, evaluating and selecting, archiving, accessing, using and reusing and transforming; and
4. Occasional Actions, involving disposal, reassessment and migration activities.

While proposition of the ideal model, the necessary steps to digital curation, in theory, are available, but this does not imply that all organizations must fulfill the full cycle. In fact, the operation of the stages will depend on the actual needs of

---

[3] The Digital Curation Centre (DCC) is an internationally-recognised centre of expertise in digital curation with a focus on building capability and skills for research data management. (http://www.dcc.ac.uk).

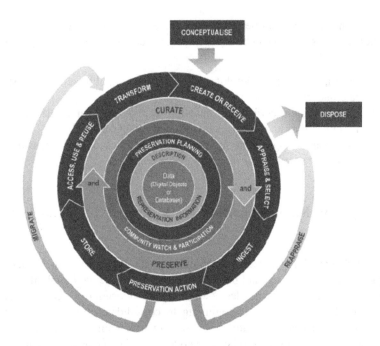

Fig. 1. DCC model lifecycle (Image Font: Higgins, S. (2008) *The DCC Curation Lifecycle Model* [11])

each organization [4]. In this sense, the first stage of the model, Conceptualize, includes the development of a Data Management Plan (DMP). This plan is of utmost importance because it will define the actual life cycle of the curatorship and also the preservation requirements for all used digital artifacts and/or produced in the scope under discussion [12]. These requirements are essential for, among other things, guide the exploration and selection of technological tools to be used in the assembly of a repository of digital preservation adhering to identified needs.

The very understanding of the figure of the digital preservation repository, in turn, has also matured. Several categorizations of this type of structure are emerging. One of them is related to the type of access that the objects of the preserved collection may (or may not) have. From this viewpoint, the preservation repository may be Dark, Open or Dim types.

There are subtle variations in the definitions used by several authors [5, 13, 14], but in a simplified way, we can consider that a dark archive as a digital preservation repository where access to content is limited to organizational custodians while an open archive is a digital preservation repository where access is open to a wide community of users. With a hybrid behavior, dim archive incorporates elements of the other two models: restricted access for some objects to internal employees while access to other items in the collection can be accessible to the public.

There is still no consensus on the best approach to be adopted, but in a recent survey Arellano [10] verified that most preservation repositories cited in the literature records like the dual access function and preservation (open archives) and few can be considered dark archives, with sole purpose to preserve [15].

Besides access function, a number of other repository characteristics need to be planned and defined. The adoption of good practices and recommendations is essential. A methodological basis recognized is the OAIS[4] (Open Archival Information System) reference model [16, 17]. The OAIS is a conceptual model that aims to identify the functional components that should be part of an information system dedicated to digital preservation, as well as its internal and external interfaces and the information objects exchanged inside.

Although it has arisen within an initiative aiming to develop a set of standards that regulate the long-term storage of digital information produced in the context for space missions, one of the supplementary contributions of the model was the emergence of a specific terminology that would facilitate communication between the various actors involved in digital preservation processes. Figure 2 illustrates the various factors provided for in OAIS reference model.

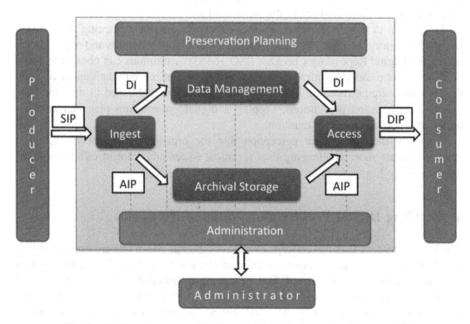

Fig. 2. OAIS reference model (Open Archival Information System) [16]

The Producer is the entity outside the repository responsible for submitting digital content to the system. Submission Information Package (SIP) represents such material. During the submission process, called Ingest, the system is responsible for verifying the physical, logic and semantics integrity of the received content. In this step, all the Descriptive Information (DI) that accompanies the digital representation of archived

---

[4] This model was approved as an International Standard in 2003 (ISO Standard 14721:2003).

content and that will support its location and recovery is validated. In case the Producer does not submit this information it should be generated in the system. Also in the context of ingestion, all the operations necessary to turn a SIP into an Archival Information Package (AIP) is made. The AIP is a logical structure that can unify all constituents of the digital representation. It is this structure that will be the preserving target by an adherent system to OAIS model.

The DI or metadata, as it is commonly called, can be provided by the producer or can be generated by the system. This information is stored and managed by the functional component Data Management. In addition, this component should save descriptive information, allow to establish relationships between metadata and the preserved content (AIP), ensure the location of digital content and allow to obtain reports and statistics on repository contents.

In turn, the material to be preserved (AIP) is stored in the Archival Storage. In addition to storing the digital representations, this component is responsible for managing the entire storage structure, to ensure that the representations are not degenerated by malfunction of the media, perform health checks and provide features of safeguard and data recovery in disaster situations.

In addition to the OAIS model, another concept is also strengthening, the Trusted Digital Repository, or TDR [18]. Through compliance with standards and requirements of Trusted Digital Repository Checklist (ISO 16363), institutions can obtain the status of TDR for its preserving infrastructure, which is recognized internationally. In practice, a trusted digital repository must meet the standards established in its principles, policies, streams and preventions, keeping a digital preservation plan and also the necessary documentation for curation.

Currently there is a clear perception that the organizational aspects of digital preservation are more challenging than technical issues and a lot of effort and community energy begins to focus on these aspects [10, 19–22].

4   Building Digital Preservation National Networks

It is in this context that the concept of network digital preservation becomes meaningful. The approach is not new and there is already a number of initiatives in this direction in progress in the world. One of the most advanced is the National Digital Information Infrastructure and Preservation Program (NDIIPP), created in 2000 by the United States Congress Library. The NDIIPP has several areas of operation, among them there is the development of better standards and conservation practices; identifying digital information classes eligible for maintenance; in addition to the digital content storage in a national collection. One of the most significant technical partnership program is the one involving Stanford University, through investments in LOCKSS[5]/CLOCKSS platform (Controlled Lots of Copies Keep Stuff Safe).

There is also movement in this direction in Brazil. The Cariniana Network, for example, is a pioneering initiative of the Brazilian Institute for Information in Science

---

[5] https://www.lockss.org.

and Technology (IBICT) focused on digital preservation of electronic documents services. Initially, storage of electronic journals was structured with open access for the eight partner institutions of the project, based on OJS[6] (Open Journal Systems)/SEER[7] (Electronic Journal Publishing System) and LOCKSS platforms.

Another initiative is the German Network of Expertise in long-term STOrage of digital Resources (NESTOR[8]), that began in June 2003 as a cooperative effort of 6 partners representing different players within the field of long-term preservation. The network was sponsored by the German Ministry of Education and Research with funding of 800.000 EURO.

Based on such experiences, it is possible to envisage that the assembly of a particular national network for the promotion of audiovisual digital preservation, broad range and scope, can significantly contribute to the development of national expertise in the area for the consolidation of partnerships and leverage the emergence of solutions best adapted to the context of each country.

Steps in this direction could include, among other actions, the promotion of two complementary axis initiatives:

(a) organizing a consortium of public and private organizations interested in digital preservation; and
(b) assembling a national "backbone" of repositories for large-scale digital preservation.

The first axis would focus on the discussion of political, regulatory and methodological aspects of digital preservation, with emphasis on meeting the general and specific demands of the different segments represented. An example that can serve as inspiration is the Digital Preservation Coalition (DPC) [23], established since 2001 in UK.

The second axis, in turn, could focus on more technological and operational aspects, including architectures, service models and protocols, and mechanisms for integration/cooperation. An interesting reference is the Digital Preservation Network (DPN) [24], which integrates more than 60 digital preservation ecosystems in the United States, especially universities.

More specific initiatives or themes, new or in progress, could be integrated into such axis in different ways. For example, the creation of a wide cooperation network, involving various actors who work in the production and audiovisual preservation, could be backed by one or more anchor, large-scale and high reliability infrastructure, belonging to the national backbone. The needs of each segment, in turn, could be defended by an adequate representation in the consortium.

Within the audiovisual preservation network itself is important to ensure that actors with different profiles can participate and contribute in different ways, with different responsibilities and resources. A possible topology would be the organization of audiovisual preservation infrastructure in hierarchical rings, where each node of each

---

[6] http://openjournalsystems.com.

[7] http://seer.ibict.br.

[8] http://www.langzeitarchivierung.de/Subsites/nestor/EN/Home/home_node.html.

ring would have a specific role. Network management and preservation management, however, would be responsibility of the institutions that make up the core-ring, including those that would integrate the conservation of backbone.

5 Promoting and Connecting Networks: The Role of Sector Organizations

A strategic institution in the context of development and testing technologies to audiovisual preservation is the RNP - National Network of Education and Research[9]. Deserving highlight two R & D initiatives supported by this institution: Working Group on Network Storage and Working Group on Digital Preservation with Distributed Storage.

The Working Group on Network Storage[10] was developed in partnership with Federal University of São Paulo (USP), Federal University of Paraíba (UFPB), Federal University of Campina Grande (UFCG), University of Tennessee and CESNET (e-Infrastructure for Science, Research and Education) in 2005. The aim of the implemented project was to provide new functionality for RNP community and explore the impact of advanced technologies in network storage by deploying a temporary storage infrastructure data with interfaces for both users (via browser) and for applications (via API) for cloud storage. This is a key technology for distributed audiovisual preservation and networking.

The Working Group on Digital Preservation with Distributed Storage[11] was carried out in partnership with Federal University of Paraná (UFPR) and Federal University of Ceará (UFC) in 2010. The aim of the project was to develop technology for long term preservation of digital content through distributed storage of low cost and highly reliable system based on Peer-to-Peer (P2P) networks concepts.

These are two examples of RNP initiatives that contribute to the audiovisual preservation area. In partnership with the Programadora Brazil Audiovisual Reference Center, which operates at the Brazilian Cinematheque, RNP has produced an audiovisual preservation demand survey which mapped a total 294 collections in public and private TVs, community TVs, university TVs, public institutions of all levels of government, foundations, private companies, independent producers and cultural collective. The study identified a total of 3,740,382 units of content, with 173,296.5 h stored in 30,185 media.

In Brazil the top notch professionals involved in the preservation of audiovisual content are members of ABPA (Audiovisual Preservation Brazilian Association), a private, non-profit, cultural, technical and scientific civil association whose purposes stimulate awareness and promote public interest in safeguarding and access to Brazilian audiovisual heritage as a cultural artistic, educational, economic and historical source. The mission of ABPA is "to contribute to the development and technical, scientific and

---

[9] https://www.rnp.br/.

[10] http://www1.rnp.br/_arquivo/gt/2005/GT_Armazenamento_em_Rede.pdf.

[11] https://memoria.rnp.br/_arquivo/gt/2010/GT-DigitalPreservation_fase1.pdf.

cultural improvement of professionals working in the field of audiovisual preservation, promoting recovery, improvement and dissemination of audiovisual preservation work through various actions and initiatives. Organization of forums and seminars for the discussion of issues related to the world of audiovisual preservation, the defense of higher education institutionalization aimed at training professionals to work in the field, and editing of specialized publications are examples of such initiatives"[12].

The National Audiovisual Preservation Plan was approved in the Association of Audiovisual Preservation Annual General Meeting in June 2016. The plan is part of a diagnosis of the problems in the area and proposes a set of actions aimed at implementing a National Preservation Audiovisual Policy. Among the proposed actions should be highlighted:

- To establish shared governance principles for the National Policy for Audiovisual Preservation, with the definition of joint responsibilities between public authorities and society in order to promote synergy between the actions taken by municipal authorities, state and federal, as well as coordinate the work of public and private institutions;
- To promote the progress of a decentralized process of audiovisual preservation in the country, promoting and supporting regional film archives and audiovisual archives;
- To establish a network of audiovisual preservation institutions throughout Brazil;
- To improve the infrastructure of institutions that hold audiovisual collections across the country considering a balanced regional distribution of goods and resources; and
- To develop institutional preservation of coordinated policies for public and private audiovisual collections.

This plan, if accepted and adopted by the institutions responsible for audiovisual preservation in Brazil creates conditions for organizational and technical solutions based on decentralized structures and networked.

6 Conclusions

The management of audiovisual preservation involves the creation of inclusive digital objects policies, storage and retrieval of and the definition of specific requirements for each type of content to be preserved. However, the challenge of ensuring the continuity of digital collections can represent much more a social and institutional issue than a purely technological nature of problem because, in particular for digital preservation of audiovisual collections held by public organizations, it depends on, institutions that undergo changes in direction, mission, management and funding sources.

In order to seek the sum of efforts to address collaboratively both the technical aspects and organizational aspects involved in the management of preservation,

---

[12] http://www.abpreservacaoaudiovisual.org/site/abpa/missao.html.

we defend the thesis that the assembly collaborative national network for audiovisual digital preservation can contribute significantly to the emergence of integrated repositories. It can serve also for large-scale preservation, based on modern technologies and methodologies, as well as foster the development of expertise in the area, contributing to the emergence of well-adapted solutions to each context.

Preliminary actions in this direction can be inspired by the focal points that the German initiative NESTOR [25] has adopted:

- Continuous effort to raise cultural memory organizations awareness on the needs of actions related to digital collections long-term preservation;
- Technical, organizational, legal bases information organization to spread available knowledge and projects, research and case studies dissemination;
- Cooperation between national and international institutions through the establishment of strategic alliances between cultural organizations, industry and academia to jointly find solutions to mutual challenges;
- Creation of interdisciplinary forums for the development and coordination of strategies, services, technologies and standards for digital preservation of audiovisual collections; and
- Development of a lasting and sustainable organizational model for long term digital preservation repositories.

The creation of audiovisual preservation national networks can also be strategic for other reasons, including the promotion of integration of collections and the interoperability of metadata. In this sense, an important consequence of digitization is the emergence of numerous new opportunities, which are possible only when the content is in electronic means. One of the first is the radical expansion of the description of possibilities of content and the resulting interoperability that this can generate. Digitalization both the actual content, the databases of memorials institutions before being a technological fetish, it is one of the essential conditions to enable the flow of information between the institutions and the networking and collaboration between them. When associated with the use of the Internet, digitalization also offers enormous possibilities for memorials institutions (film libraries, archives, libraries, documentation centers and others) to expand and redefine the services they provide to their respective user communities.

Pragmatically, some of these features could, for example, be incorporated into tools such as ICD [26], a platform for managing and sharing digital content developed by LAVID[13] (Digital Video Applications Lab) in partnership with RNP. The incorporation would be done through a specific module that allows the integration, more transparently and automatically, of the bases of digital assets repositories belonging to the audiovisual preservation network.

---

[13] www.lavid.ufpb.br.

References

1. Webb, C.: Guidelines for the Preservation of Digital Heritage. United Nations Educational Scientific and Cultural Organization - Information Society Division (2003)
2. Ferreira, M., Saraiva, R., Rodrigues, E.: Estado da Arte em Preservação Digital. RCAAP. Fevereiro (2012)
3. Skinner, K., Schultz, M. (eds.): A Guide to Distributed Digital Preservation (2010). http://open.bu.edu/bitstream/handle/2144/1351/GDDP_Educopia.pdf?sequence=1
4. Sayão, L.F., Sales, L.F.: Curadoria digital: um novo patamar para preservação de dados digitais de pesquisa. Informação & Sociedade: Estudos 22(3), 179–191 (2012)
5. MetaArchive. MetaArchive Cooperative (2013). www.metaarchive.org
6. Ruusalepp, R., Dobreva, M., Kultuuriministeerium, E.V., Wetenschapsbeleid, F., Minisztérium, N.E.: Digital Preservation Services: State of the Art Analysis. Technical report, DC-NET (2012)
7. Márdero Arellano, M.Á.: Critérios para a preservação digital da informação científica. Tese de Doutorado. Universidade de Brasília (2008)
8. Addis, M., Lowe, R., Middleton, L., Salvo, N.: Reliable Audiovisual Archiving Using Unreliable Storage Technology and Services. IT Innovation Centre, UK (2009)
9. Schallaue, P., et al.: State of the Art Report on Damage Prevention and Repair of Digital AV Media. DAVID consortium (2013)
10. Márdero Arellano, M.Á., Oliveira, A.F.: Gestão de repositórios de preservação digital. RDBCI: Revista Digital de Biblioteconomia e Ciência da Informação, Campinas, SP, vol. 14 (3), pp. 465–483 (2016). doi:10.20396/rdbci.v14i3.8646346, ISSN: 1678-765X
11. Higgins, S.: The DCC curation lifecycle model. Int. J. Digital Curation. 3(1), 134–140 (2008). ISSN: 1746-8256
12. Ferreira, M.: Introdução a preservação digital - Conceitos, estratégias e actuais consensos. Escola de Engenharia da Universidade do Minho, Guimarães, Portugal (2006)
13. Lavoie, B., Dempsey, L.: Thirteen ways of looking at... digital preservation. D-Lib Mag. 10 (7/8), 20 (2004)
14. Mullen, L.: Dark Archive, 152 p. University of California Press, Berkeley (2011). ISBN: 9780520268869
15. Portico. Digital Preservation Service by ITHAKA (2016). http://www.portico.org/digital-preservation/the-archive-content-access
16. Lavoie, B.: The Open Archival Information System Reference Model: Introductory Guide. DPC Technology Watch Report (2005). www.dpconline.org/docs/lavoie_OAIS.pdf
17. ISO. ISO 14721: Space data and information transfer systems - Open archival information system - Reference model (2003). http://www.iso.org/iso/catalogue_detail.htm?csnumber=24683
18. ISO 16363/TDR, Trusted Digital Repository (2011). https://www.crl.edu/archiving-preservation/digital-archives/metrics-assessing-and-certifying/iso16363
19. Pickton, M., Morris, D., Meece, S., Coles, S., Hitchcock, S.: Preserving repository content: practical tools for repository managers. J. Digital Inf. 12, 1–14 (2011)
20. Ruusalepp, R., Dobreva, M.: Digital Preservation Services: State of the Art Analysis (2012)
21. Skinner, K., Schultz, M.: A Guide to Distributed Digital Preservation (2010). http://www.metaarchive.org/sites/default/files/GDDP_Educopia.pdf
22. Subotic, I., Schuldt, H., Rosenthaler, L.: The DISTARNET approach to reliable autonomic long-term digital preservation. In: Yu, J.X., Kim, M.H., Unland, R. (eds.) DASFAA 2011, Part II. LNCS, vol. 6588, pp. 93–103. Springer, Heidelberg (2011). doi:10.1007/978-3-642-20152-3_8

23. DPC. Digital Preservation Coalition (2002). http://www.dpconline.org
24. DPN. The Digital Preservation Network (2016). http://www.dpn.org
25. Dobratz, S., Neuroth, H.: Network of expertise in long-term STOrage of digital resources - a digital preservation initiative for Germany. D-Lib Mag. **10**(4) (2004). http://www.dlib.org/dlib/april04/dobratz/0dobratz.html
26. Mariz, D., Pessoa, D., Pires, A., et al.: Plataforma de Intercâmbio de Conteúdo Digitais. Escola Superior de Redes. RNP (2014)

Social TV

Beyond the TV Borders: Second Screen as a Tool for Audience Engagement

David Campelo$^{(\boxtimes)}$ ⓘ, Telmo Silva$^{(\boxtimes)}$ ⓘ,
and Jorge Ferraz de Abreu$^{(\boxtimes)}$ ⓘ

Digimedia (CIC.DIGITAL), Aveiro University, Campus Universitário Santiago,
Aveiro, Portugal
{david.campelo,tsilva,jfa}@ua.pt

Abstract. The growing popularity of mobile connected devices has transformed the way TV content is conceived and consumed. Interacting with these devices while watching TV is a trending behaviour that represents a challenge for the TV industry as this interaction often distracts viewers from the TV content. Consumers use the second screen to retrieve further information about narratives, characters, purchasing goods and researching on products and services advertised. In a scenario of systematic live and linear TV audience erosion and ad-skipping broadcasters, marketers and producers are continuously looking for new ways to leverage different media strategies to keep TV viewers engaged with the primary content, promoting consumers' loyalty and generating more revenue flows. In this paper, a set of second screen cases was selected to ground a reflection on how second screen solutions may be applied to foster the viewer and consumer engagement.

Keywords: Second screen · Audience engagement · Interactive TV · Participatory culture · Crossmedia strategies · Social TV

1 Introduction

In the end of the 20th century takes place the information technology revolution as an economic, social and technological trend which goes beyond the Industrial Revolution [6]. Years later, at the dawn of the 21st century, mainly with the popularity of the PC and the Internet, arises the media convergence, a "phenomenon involving the interconnection of information and communications technologies, computer networks, and media content" [9]. More than a technological process, media convergence also covers economic, cultural and social aspects as a result of development and integration of different media forms and platforms based on consumer needs. In a media convergence scenario consumers are motivated to explore, create and share information, forming a participatory development culture built upon information consumption, generation and sharing through dispersed media platforms [15]. The integration of the various forms of media takes place with support and cooperation of the media industries, which now seek new ways and structures to finance their business [26] and the combination of broadcast and broadband networks can be leveraged for delivering a wide range of personalized TV services [13].

© Springer International Publishing AG 2017
M.J. Abásolo et al. (Eds.): jAUTI 2016, CCIS 689, pp. 93–104, 2017.
DOI: 10.1007/978-3-319-63321-3_7

Linear and live television viewing [2] used to be a relationship experience between the viewer and the TV program only. The appearance of new media like the Web followed by smart multimedia mobile devices has been transforming the way this old medium is consumed. The term "hypertelevision" was coined by Scolari [26] to describe the contemporary phase of television in a world of fragmented content and non-sequential viewing where the television itself stimulates interactions in a set of audiovisual resources tailored for more sophisticated and active consumers.

Interacting with a second screen is a trending behavior that has been evolving over the past few years with the growing usage of smartphones and tablets. The emergence of extra screens turned the act of watching TV into a communal, richer experience, and soon the television industry realized the potential of delivering contents to the audience through these often-connected devices, via program specific apps or social media campaigns, such as Twitter temporary hashtags or social media fictional profiles. According to a Nielsen report [22], 84% of U.S. smartphone and tablet owners use these devices as companion screens while watching TV. However, they are not always used for browsing things related to the TV content. Dealing with this new, multi-tasking way of consuming broadcasted media comprises a new challenge to the television industry in order to keep the audience engaged with the broadcasted content instead of distracting them from it [11, 12, 14].

In this paper, a set of second screen cases with different purposes like advertisement (using a crossmedia mobile application), entertainment (using transmedia strategies) and interaction (through social media networks) was selected to ground a reflection on how companion devices may be applied to foster the viewer and consumer engagement. These cases were selected due to their remarkable popularity and number of active users. Strategies to keep viewers linked to the main broadcasted content are highlighted and criticized on how they could be improved for more compelling, profitable and interesting experiences.

2   Second Screen as an Engagement Tool

Since the beginning, television has been a collective and social experience, with people talking about the TV programs during the broadcasting with people nearby, at home. The popularity of the companion devices [1] has influenced the TV viewing experience in a way that people do not need to wait until the next day to expose their thoughts on TV contents also to physically distant friends, since they are able to do this during the TV show or right after its end by using these connected devices. Based on information exchanged in social media networks, viewers may influence other viewers' opinions about shows, get tips of new interesting series, and talk about the latest gossip on the artists life. A huge amount of this interaction now takes place during the TV broadcast, allowing television advertisers and producers to receive live feedbacks about their programming, with interaction among viewers generating hints for the TV producers on how to develop the shows and creating opportunities for advertisers. The novelty of user-TV interactions in second screen devices has a positive contributing effect to the user experiences. However, some features and approaches should be reviewed in order to enhance content navigation and user experience [19].

2.1   Shazam Second Screen Experience

An example of second screen experience offering exclusive content is implemented by the Shazam mobile application, which has evolved from a song identification service to an interactive advertising provider in a form of a portal to second screen experiences in partnership with TV shows and events. This cooperation of broadcasters, producers, advertisers and mobile software developers was materialized as a flow of content between television and mobile devices representing a classical cross media strategy [15].

Officially launched in 2011, Shazam "Resonate" TV platform [29] provides advertisers with mechanisms of message supervision, brand management and revenue control through live connected screen experiences. In addition, the mobile application users are provided with additional information regarding the show they are watching, including what music is being played, news related to the cast or guests among others. This initiative enables marketers with a new channel of advertising opportunities. In addition, Shazam also developed a rating tool oriented to help broadcasters and advertisers in measuring the impact of their campaigns, providing data regarding where and when ads are resonating with their target audience.

As the user activates the app, the program being watched is recognized based on audio recognition technologies, and users can receive further information. Hence, viewers of some of the biggest events broadcasted live mainly in the United States (e.g. Super Bowl, Olympic games and Grammys) are encouraged to access additional information during the commercial breaks, using their mobile phones and tablets to access exclusive contents, such as complementary videos, behind-the-scene interviews, casting, gossip, photos or any related social media activity, etc. (Fig. 1).

Fig. 1. Shazam extra content presented during big live TV shows. Source: www.shazam.com

Exclusive discounts, special consumer offers and coupons are also available for the viewers who activated this application during the advertisements broadcast. With the purposes of decreasing ad-skipping and time-delayed views, only people watching the show at prime time could access these exclusive contents. Additionally, the Shazam application has been used in several other countries [30], in TV commercials integrated with call-to-action logos on TV screen corners, prompting viewers to access extra contents by activating the mobile application.

In 2012, while announcing its plans to work anytime of day, Shazam generated enthusiasm on TV platforms and channels suffering from systematic live and linear TV audience erosion and ad-skipping [24]. Huge investments of cross-platform, rich-media projects with interactive and social networking features have taken place. Also in 2012 Shazam generated $300 million USD from selling digital goods through affiliate partners [7]. Higher ad and brand recalls [28] endorse the benefits and the efficacy of the Shazam's crossmedia strategy for TV advertising and confirming that it engages viewers and improves brand recall, with the majority of the application users bookmarking ads and exclusive contents for future interaction. According to reports by Frank N. Magid Associates [10], viewers who activated the application for pulling up extra contents had more interest in further engagement with brands, talked more about the brand with others and revealed future intent to take action.

Bookmarking information for future interaction proved to be a key feature in the application as it increases brand or product exposition from a few seconds ad to several minutes of engagement, which represents a significant lift in campaigns' effectiveness. However, requiring activation for receiving content may exclude some users from taking part in ad campaigns. Studies conducted by Almeida et al. [3] on notification mechanisms used in second screen applications concluded that the most suitable strategy for delivering notifications to the second screen applications, in order to provide a balanced user experience, should be based on a combination of a visual notification (on TV screen) along with visual notifications on the second screen. A better approach for pushing contents to viewers' second screens may result in positive outcomes in revenue flows without affecting the overall user experience.

2.2 'The Walking Dead' Transmedia Experiences

Considering the current scenario of content fragmentation and segmentation of the audience [27], an efficient alternative to bring the viewers back to linear TV transmission is the transmedia storytelling strategy. Jumping through different media platforms provides deeper experiences, motivates participation and is inductive to more content consumption [15].

A well-applied transmedia case has distinct media platforms telling complementary self-contained stories around a central narrative, which is usually available on TV. It is exactly what "The Walking Dead" [4] series has been doing to reach its millions of viewers and fans around the world. Based on the comic book series of the same name by Robert Kirkman, the show follows a group of survivors living in an apocalyptic earth full of undead, lethal creatures. In addition to the TV show a set of short video clips that reveal a brief storyline was developed as "webisodes". Usually launched during season breaks, they keep viewers attached to the central narrative even when no episodes are being aired on TV. These videos work as short autonomous series and expand the overall narrative considering different point of views of early outbreaks of the undead apocalypse. New characters are introduced specially for each set of webisodes, forming spin-off stories in a complex fictional world of networked events around a central narrative flow.

As stated by Jenkins [15], people are choosing to "invest deeply in a limited number of franchises rather than dip shallowly into a larger number". Thus, to embrace other media platforms as well as other audiences, Twitter profiles, Facebook pages and social games are available for the fans too. These mediums allow users to post and check live comments on the episodes, respond to surveys and interact with other fellow fans via chat systems too. Another transmedia strategy to offer fans a new social way to engage with the series is a companion application to be used during the main show exhibition on television only (Fig. 2).

Fig. 2. The walking dead Story sync second screen app. Source: www.amc.com

By activating the Story sync application (Fig. 2) at the time of the televised premiere, a practical inclusion is perceived by the audience, engaging the viewers while not distracting them from the main content, which is synchronized with the application via digital audio recognition technologies [5]. This second screen application provides polls, trivia and ads for viewers as they watch new episodes of the show in a strategy considered less intrusive than traditional visual advertising as it provides supplementary information on what viewers are already viewing. It is worth noticing that this second screen application avoids disturbing the user if the scene presented on television goes faster than the usual (e.g. on action scenes), while the supplemental content is pushed during commercials and calm scenes. This balance between engagement by providing extended content and distraction by a second screen application plays a crucial role for an enriched live TV viewing experience [11], driving viewers to the TV screen and making appointment (linear) TV viewing relevant again.

In addition to comic books, TV shows and second screen experiences, a live zombie obstacle event was created to expose fans to an immersive experience into the fictional apocalyptic world, transcending the original technological media platforms and taking the relationship between the viewers and the narratives to another level, improving the sense of immersion in the franchising. Providing various levels of experience stimulates and sustains audience loyalty [15].

Many other live events have taken place worldwide, most of them promoted by fans themselves, which turns these fans into prosumers, who proactively take control of their viewing experience and create new independent experiences around the main narrative. These fans find on the Internet a place for sharing thoughts and insights about the series and transmedia strategies, which are considered by producers, advertisers and screenwriters on their next moves.

"The Walking dead" franchising is one of the most remarkable cases of transmedia ever produced, with all the TV shows, webisodes, games, mobile applications and live events converging to the same story. Surely, transmedia strategies are accountable for the success of this franchising as the diversity of media helps to reach people of many different places, with different interests and tastes for TV series, games and stories, which leads to higher amounts of dedicated fans and creates more potential revenue flows. Having a diverse audience may look like an opportunity for producers at first sight. However, it may rather be an issue for marketers and advertisers, as the more diverse is the audience the harder is to tackle a possibly wider variety of viewer interests and habits. Finally, personalization based on viewers' interests and habits is crucial for higher levels of audience engagement. Focusing on personalized contents may lead producers to more efficient and profitable transmedia cases.

2.3 The Social TV Experience

With the advent of online social networks, status updates and social interactions turned to be frequent and, with the increasing usage of connected phone devices, they became instantaneous. A study about Twitter users' behavior and responses to television [20] showed that 85% of them usually tweet about TV programs, with 72% of this amount tweeting while watching TV. Therefore, producers are willing to extend their relationships with the audiences by adding attractive interactive components of social media networks to live transmission, creating a new concept of Social TV [8].

Social networks often have an advantage over other third-party entities in the second screen environment as they already have a pre-existing engaged audience. Social TV viewers typically use Facebook, YouTube and Twitter to check in to the program, watch program related videos, check program-related updates, see program-related photos, and find out what other people think and talk about the program [16]. Particularly in the case of Twitter, step by step broadcasters have been taking it into account as a mechanism to drive people back to prime time, which is very attractive for revenue purposes [11]. Temporary on screen hashtags as closed captions, celebrities tweeting during live events, live polls by tweets, tweets used as part of TV shows and so on are commonly integrated tools applied by TV producers [17]. According to Twitter Playbook [31], TV shows increase the amount of tweets by 20% right after the on-air appearance of the hashtags. Likewise, 50% of Twitter users keep browsing what people are saying about the show during primetime hours and hashtags help them to find the desired content. Though watching less traditional linear TV seems

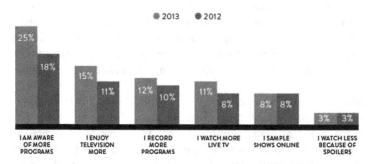

Fig. 3. Impact of social media on TV viewing. Source: Nielsen State of Social Media Report Q4 2012–2013.

to be a trend, many people still watch linear TV programming content if it has a social media link [23], and due to social media people are becoming more aware about TV programming (Fig. 3).

Globally, 53% of people like to keep up with shows so they can join conversations on social media networks [23]. This new Social TV concept has been increasingly used as a tool for real-time inter-audience feedback retrieval, checking viewers' enthusiasm during the live broadcast. Broadcasters, producers and marketers have been leveraging the social TV to keep viewers far from time-shifting devices and PCs, rewarding people for watching live and linear transmissions and interacting with sponsors. Exclusive contents such as live-tweets from actors/casts, posts from the official show among others have been proving that social TV promotes a direct and almost immediate increase of TV viewers' engagement [31]. As an effective example of social TV employment, actors of American television series tweeted at prime time, encouraging fans to tune in for the original live transmission.

Years ago, Rupert Murdoch said, "Technology is shifting power away from the editors, the publishers, the establishment, the media elite. Now it is the people who are taking control" [25]. A higher level of engagement with the content entices the audience to generate more content. Extensions, parodies, spoilers, mashups (remixes) and adaptations are some of the content generated proactively by the fans [27]. Moreover, these viewers create their own parallel narratives on Twitter, "reinvigorating live TV viewing and creating new forms of audience interaction" [17].

Social TV initiatives are complementary for building relationships with the audience, driving viewers' conversations about TV programs, seeking deeper brand engagement, and increasing TV shows ratings. The rise of this new concept of social TV based on real time social networking interactions enables a positive opportunity to foster viewer engagement with TV programs and their advertisers [20]. Currently, finding out why certain TV shows compel viewers to share impressions with others, while other programs do not, seems to be the immediate task for TV broadcasters and second screen developers [21].

Twitter and other social networks have an advantage over standalone dedicated second screen applications due to the wider use of its mobile applications. Indeed, social networking mobile applications work as default gateways for social TV interactions, decreasing costs of implementation and easing the production of value-added social TV experiences. However, these applications may not be suitable for proactively feeding viewers with contents and building up personalized relationships with the audience.

Dedicated standalone second screen applications may be tailored to viewers' expectations and habits, establishing exclusive channels, which enable broadcasters and advertisers to extent brand exposition from few seconds to several minutes of interaction. Of course, discoverability is an important issue to be tackled when creating dedicated second screen applications. According to Geerts et al. [11], announcing the application onscreen, letting the audience know it is there, and providing a very low threshold for accessing it are necessary steps to deploy a financially viable application. In addition, having a dedicated second screen application helps minimizing audience distraction from the main broadcasted content as TV broadcaster and advertisers may control the interactive experience.

3 Discussion

The cases presented in this article endorse some second screen experiences as valuable promotional strategies for broadcasters, producers and advertisers, actively engaging viewers in several activities around their contents. Taking in consideration this well-established value chain, one observe that a multiple approach to storytelling in various narratives and media provides a more complex and immersive experience along the potential to attract different market segments, seducing a more diverse audience with different narratives and contents in different media. In a time where viewers increasingly avoid advertising messages and are changing their viewing habits, the TV industry is constantly seeking options to strengthen the audience engagement, namely by leveraging the combination of the viewing experience with social interaction features and techniques with a clear focus on viewers' involvement rather than on passive consumption. In addition, the second-screen experience provides opportunities for broadcasters, marketers and content producers to connect the target audience via relevant messaging and notifications, even when the main content is not being aired on TV.

In their recent national wide study with 300 U.S. TV viewers, Lin and her colleagues [16] empirically analyzed the effect of social TV on the dynamics of the engagement between viewers and programs. The authors examined how viewers' participation on social networks and social TV applications may be related to, mostly, satisfaction, commitment with the content and emotional consequences after a program relationship breakup. Findings show that interactions via social TV networks and applications with programs and other viewers work as extensions of TV viewing experience. Also, results indicated that the more viewers engage in social TV activities, the greater their satisfaction and investment toward their favorite programs. Finally, as broadcasters often actively bring social media contents into their programming, viewers may also be indirectly encouraged to search for information and become involved in other activities regarding alternative programs.

It is vital to leverage the momentum of second screens applications to foster interaction, to create more compelling and immersive viewing experiences, and thus, enhance satisfaction and strengthen relationship investments [16, 20]. According to Nagy and Midha [20], there is a great potential for broadcasters and advertisers in the "'earned audiences' (users exposed to Tweets about television programs and their sponsors)" as these viewers frequently take actions related to viewing content as well as engage with brand sponsors. However, it is also important to notice that the more second screens are developed, the greater is the challenge of "how to appropriately balance the timeliness of information delivery with the cost of interrupting user tasks" [14].

Though nowadays adopting a second screen strategy seem to be a must-do for many broadcasters and content producers, it is still hard to overcome some technical details to properly implement it. Many different second screen frameworks and technical solutions were developed, such as the IRT's FIcontent Second Screen framework[1] and the Active Loop framework[2]. Some of them imply installing extra smartphone/tablet apps, such as "The Walking dead" app; while other would mash up many different contents in a single app, such as the Shazam app. Both have advantages and drawbacks, as installing a new app for every different show may be tiresome and using the same app may rather be confusing.

After adopting (or developing from scratch) a technical solution for second screens, one must also create a plan for coordinating user access to the different media in second screens. Considering that timing is crucial in the TV world [11], synchronizing access these media contents is a key challenge for content producers and TV broadcasters, as the second screen content may draw attention away from the main content that appears on TV screen. A good timing for TV comprehends selecting the precise moment for presenting media contents to provide an optimum effect. On this regard, Geerts and his colleagues [11] present valuable recommendations for designing second screen apps, namely related to ease of use, timing and added value. Finding the right balance between engagement and distraction in the second screen strategy play a crucial role to engage viewers with the show and not distract them so they cannot follow the plot anymore. Moreover, content updates and notifications should not be too long and closely matched with the pacing of the show itself [1, 3].

In addition to the traditional smartphone/tablet app solutions, some TV manufacturers have allied themselves with broadcasters to work on hybrid TV solutions, which would enable Smart TVs with content-aware apps. In order to tackle the many diverse initiatives already created with this end, in Europe, it was established a technical standard for combining two or more screens called Hybrid Broadcast Broadband TV (HbbTV) [18], which defines an open standards-based framework that enables bi-directional communication between web applications for TV and second-screen devices [32]. Initially demonstrated in France in 2009, HbbTV is a standard for hybrid

---

[1] http://lab.mediafi.org/discover-secondscreenframework-overview.html.

[2] http://www.active-loop.com/products/.

digital TV to harmonize broadcast transmission and interactive media contents, which may be delivered through the broadcast signal itself or through internet connection, for presentation on Smart TVs and set-top boxes. This standard has merged with a similar industry initiatives, namely the Open TV and the Smart TV Initiative, which in turn involves heavy-weight TV manufacturer brands such as Samsung and LG. These various organizations take in many of the worldwide TV manufacturers and comprehend general technical solutions ranging from broadband application download to content synchronization with connected devices. Finally, considering their latter releases, these standards and initiatives may also be regarded by TV content producers as the forthcoming technical pattern for second screen solutions, easing the development of innovative and richer viewing experiences.

4   Conclusion

The growing usage of mobile connected devices has unveiled opportunities for media consumption never seen before. Consumer viewing habits involving much more than the traditional linear broadcasting services become a trend, including new interactive displays, time-shifting viewing and real-time collaborative discussions. Television has become more interactive and viewer's interests are influenced by information made available online.

Be it through broadcaster initiatives of personalized services, advertising campaigns or via social media networks, second screens usage represents a big challenge for TV broadcasters and producers. While the majority of viewers already split their attention between the TV and another screen, the average gaze on the TV decreases drastically [12]. Besides, there is still a lack of evidences regarding what works and what does not work when developing and using second screen solutions [3, 11]. Notifications mechanisms, personalized transmedia approaches and high value-added dedicated second screen apps are important aspects for building up successful second screen cases.

In a scenario of systematic audience erosion, ad-skipping and illegally accessed content, broadcasted television has changed enormously along with its viewers. Some may say the TV as we know does not exist anymore; some may say TV will die. Among all predictions and facts, a must-do for broadcasters, marketers and producers is to better understand the viewers' requirements and habits so strategies involving second screen are more efficient and profitable, promoting viewers' loyalty and generating more revenue flows.

Acknowledgements. This study is funded by the Brazilian National Council for Scientific and Technological Development – CNPq (grant 204935/2014-8) and supervised by Prof. Dr. Jorge Ferraz Abreu and Prof. Dr. Telmo Silva at the University of Aveiro, Portugal.

References

1. Abreu, J.F., Almeida, P., Silva, T.: A UX evaluation approach for second-screen applications. In: Abásolo, M.J., Perales, F.J., Bibiloni, A. (eds.) jAUTI/CTVDI -2015. CCIS, vol. 605, pp. 105–120. Springer, Cham (2016). doi:10.1007/978-3-319-38907-3_9
2. Abreu, J., Nogueira, J., Becker, V., Cardoso, B.: Survey of Catch-up TV and other time-shift services: a comprehensive analysis and taxonomy of linear and nonlinear television. Telecommun. Syst. **64**(1), 57–74 (2017). doi:10.1007/s11235-016-0157-3
3. Almeida, P., Abreu, J., Silva, T., Duro, L., Aresta, M., Oliveira, R.: Notification mechanisms in second-screen scenarios towards a balanced user experience. In: 7th International Conference on Intelligent Technologies for Interactive Entertainment (INTETAIN), pp. 95–99 (2015)
4. AMC. The walking dead series (2015). http://www.amc.com/shows/the-walking-dead. Accessed 11 Nov 2015
5. Cano, P., Batlle, E., Kalker, T., Haitsma, J.: A review of audio fingerprinting. J. VLSI Sig. Process. Syst. Sig. Image Video Technol. **41**(3), 271–284 (2005). doi:10.1007/s11265-005-4151-3
6. Castells, M.: The Rise of the Network Society: The Information Age: Economy, Society, and Culture, vol. 1. Wiley, New York (2011)
7. Crunch, M.: Shazam pulls in $40 M from America Movil to Take on Latin America (2013). http://techcrunch.com/2013/07/07/shazam-pulls-in-40m-from-america-movil-to-take-on-latin-america/. Accessed 11 Nov 2015
8. Ducheneaut, N., Moore, R.J., Oehlberg, L., Thornton, J.D., Nickell, E., Ducheneaut, N., Thornton, J.D., Moore, R.J., Nickell, E.: Social TV: designing for distributed, sociable television viewing. Int. J. Hum. Comput. Interact. **24**, 136–154 (2006). https://doi.org/10.1080/10447310701821426
9. Encyclopædia Britannica. Media convergence (2017). https://www.britannica.com/topic/media-convergence%0A. Accessed 1 Jan 2017
10. Frank N. Magid Associates. Research: Shazam Extends Ad Engagement (2012). http://www.magid.com/node/239. Accessed 11 Nov 2015
11. Geerts, D., Leenheer, R., De Grooff, D., Negenman, J., Heijstraten, S.: In front of and behind the second screen - viewer and producer perspectives on a companion app. In: Proceedings of the 2014 ACM International Conference on Interactive Experiences for TV and Online Video - TVX 2014, pp. 95–102 (2014). https://doi.org/10.1145/2602299.2602312
12. Holmes, M.E., Josephson, S., Carney, R.E.: Visual attention to television programs with a second-screen application. In: Proceedings of the Symposium on Eye Tracking Research and Applications - ETRA 2012, p. 397 (2012). https://doi.org/10.1145/2168556.2168646
13. Howson, C., Gautier, E., Gilberton, P., Laurent, A., Legallais, Y.: Second screen TV synchronization. In: 2011 IEEE International Conference on Consumer Electronics - Berlin (ICCE-Berlin), pp. 361–365 (2011). https://doi.org/10.1109/ICCE-Berlin.2011.6031815
14. Iqbal, S.T., Bailey, B.P.: Oasis. ACM Trans. Comput. Hum. Interact. **17**(4), 1–28 (2010). doi:10.1145/1879831.1879833
15. Jenkins, H.: Convergence Culture: Where Old and New Media Collide (2006). https://doi.org/10.1017/CBO9781107415324.004
16. Lin, J.S., Sung, Y., Chen, K.J.: Social television: examining the antecedents and consequences of connected TV viewing. Comput. Hum. Behav. **58**, 171–178 (2016). https://doi.org/10.1016/j.chb.2015.12.025

17. Lochrie, M., Coulton, P.: Sharing the viewing experience through Second Screens. In: Proceedings of the 10th European Conference on Interactive TV and Video - EuroiTV 2012, pp. 199–202 (2012). https://doi.org/10.1145/2325616.2325655
18. Merkel, K.: HbbTV - a hybrid broadcast-broadband system for the living room. EBU technical review-2010 Q 1 (2010)
19. Mu, M., Knowles, W., Sani, Y., Mauthe, A., Race, N.: Improving interactive TV experience using second screen mobile applications. In: 2015 IEEE International Symposium on Multimedia (2016), Fig. 1, pp. 373–376. https://doi.org/10.1109/ISM.2015.19
20. Nagy, J., Midha, A.: The value of earned audiences: how social interactions amplify TV impact. J. Advertising Res. **54**(4), 448–453 (2014). https://doi.org/10.2501/JAR-54-4-448-453
21. Nielsen. Brain activity predicts social TV engagement (2015). http://www.nielsen.com/us/en/insights/reports/2015/brain-activity-predicts-social-tv-engagement.html. Accessed 7 July 2016
22. Nielsen. What's Empowering the New Digital Consumer? (2014). http://www.nielsen.com/us/en/insights/news/2014/whats-empowering-the-new-digital-consumer.html. Accessed 11 Nov 2015
23. Nielsen. Screen Wars - The battle for eye space in a TV-everywhere world (2015). http://www.nielsen.com/content/dam/corporate/us/en/reports-downloads/2015-reports/nielsen-global-digital-landscape-report-march-2015.pdf
24. Nielsen. The Total Audience Report: Q1 2016 (2016). http://www.nielsen.com/us/en/insights/reports/2016/the-total-audience-report-q1-2016.html. Accessed 10 Oct 2016
25. Reiss, S.: His Space. Wired Magazine 14(7) (2006). http://www.wired.com/2006/07/murdoch-2/
26. Scolari, C.A.: The grammar of hypertelevision: an identikit of convergence-age fiction television (or, how television simulates new interactive media). J. Vis. Literacy **28**(1), 28–49 (2009)
27. Scolari, C.A.: Narrativas Transmedia: Cuando todos los medios cuentan. Deusto, Barcelona (2013)
28. Shazam. Absolut, Gillette and Jaguar Increase Television Ad Recall & Likeability with Shazamable Ads (2014). http://news.shazam.com/pressreleases/absolut-gillette-and-jaguar-increase-television-ad-recall-likeability-with-shazamable-ads-1037055. Accessed 5 Apr 2016
29. Shazam. Shazam Announces New Digital Engagement Sales Solution "Resonate" to Support Television Industry (2015). http://news.shazam.com/pressreleases/shazam-announces-new-digital-engagement-sales-solution-resonate-to-support-television-industry-1037083. Accessed 5 Apr 2016
30. Shazam For TV. Shazam International - Youtube. https://www.youtube.com/user/shazamfortv/videos. Accessed 7 July 2016
31. Twitter. Best practices from the TVxTwitter Playbook (2015). http://bit.ly/22xUvpM
32. Ziegler, C.: Second screen for HbbTV—Automatic application launch and app-to-app communication enabling novel TV programme related second-screen scenarios. In: IEEE Third International Conference on Consumer Electronics Berlin (ICCE-Berlin). ICCEBerlin 2013, pp. 1–5 (2013)

Indagante: A Proposal for a Social Multiplatform Game to Motivate Interaction in the Living Room

Bernardo Cardoso$^{(\boxtimes)}$ and Jorge Ferraz de Abreu

University of Aveiro, Aveiro, Portugal
{bernardoc,jfa}@ua.pt

Abstract. Nowadays, the access to new personal and portable digital equipment capable to reproduce all kinds of media content is getting increasingly easy. However, the presence of these new devices in the living room resulted in family members sharing the same physical space but not talking to each other. In this article, we intend to highlight these observations, as well to present a proposal based on a digital game, associated with television content, which has the potential to create an effect of discussion and conversation between those present in the living room. We will also highlight the way this game and its dynamics were designed, with the Interaction Design process in mind, to allow the game to reach its full potential: be fun and breed discussion.

Keywords: Games · Living room · TV · Quiz · Interaction design

1 Introduction

The introduction of new screens, with the ability to view any kind of multimedia content, working as interactive and communicational devices, such as computers, smartphones and tablets, brought new challenges to the traditional family arrangement in the living room and to their conversational dynamics.

In the end of the last century, Lull [1] demonstrated the significant effects the introduction of television had caused on the families daily life. He was one of several authors that described how this "new" media become a regulator of the domestic dynamic, especially on the family activities, setting the timing of meals, bedtime and regular tasks. Television also changed the way family members started talking to each other. Just think about the way people watch TV, all focused on the device's screen, far away, rather than looking at each other.

This paper focus on how the introduction of new screens and their capabilities changed the status quo of activities within the family living room and how conversations and discussions are established, between people sharing the same physical space. In this way, in Sect. 2 we address the so-called "physically together but, virtually separated" phenomenon applied to the living room and present an outline on how this effect can lead to a reduction of the conversation levels between individuals that, in the opinion of some authors, partially results from the introduction of new devices. Taken in consideration this framework, Sect. 3 of the paper addresses the authors'

© Springer International Publishing AG 2017

M.J. Abásolo et al. (Eds.): jAUTI 2016, CCIS 689, pp. 105–116, 2017.

DOI: 10.1007/978-3-319-63321-3_8

vision on how the same technology can be used to counteract the problem that itself created, by presenting a proposal of a digital game that takes advantage of specific features of these new devices to try to increase conversations within the family. Besides the game description, its requirements and the basis for the authors' choices, this section will also describe the way the game is expected to be evaluated, in terms of usability of the interaction model and global user experience. Finally, in Sect. 4 the paper is wrapped up with some brief conclusions and proposals for future work taking in consideration a set of challenges already identified.

2   New Devices and the Living Room

2.1   Physically Together, but Virtually Separated

Sherry Turkle [2] dedicates his book "Alone Together" to the phenomenon where family and friends being together in a physical space do not interact or communicate with each other. On the contrary, they often use their digital equipment to talk to someone far away. This same effect also occurs on the family living room [3, 4], being caused by the massification of interactive screens with multimedia capabilities, mainly smartphones, tablets and portable personal computers, which now populates the families' daily lives.

Ironically, it was in part these recent technological developments that brought a new chance for family members to share the same physical space and be again in front of television [5]. This is corroborated by Ofcom's studies [6] in England, that revealed a reduction in the number of televisions in households. This greater physical approximation is due to an increased equipment mobility and to a rising simplicity in domestic Internet access allowed by wireless networks. Another factor that contributes to this physical approximation is the personal and private characteristics of these devices, making it possible to maintain a private activity, like read e-mail and Facebook activity, in a public space. However, this proximity does not imply an effective presence, with the simultaneous use of television and other devices indicating that there is hardly a great deal of conversation between users [7].

In this framework, it is very frequent to find families in which their members consume their favorite media contents in a shared physical space, but in distinct screens, each referring to their own world and often trying to avoid any kind of conversation. In his most recent book, "Reclaiming Conversation", Turkle [8] argues that this lack of communication, especially between adults and children, may be profoundly influencing their development. According to this author, a vicious cycle is being created in which children, not having parents present, focus on their devices and parents take this absorption as a kind of permission for themselves to focus on their smartphones. These issues of conversational difficulties within families are not new, but the author cites examples in which children found it easier to interrupt parents when they were reading the newspaper or actually watching TV than when they were absorbed by electronic devices.

2.2 Mitigation Proposals

To recover and improve conversation Turkle proposes the creation of "sacred spaces – the living room, the dining room, the kitchen, the car – that are device-free" and the promotion of ideas like the design of smartphones interfaces that promotes disengagement after a task completion, instead of encouraging the users to stay connected for as much time as possible [8]. These recommendations, however, are a fight against technology and appear to have little real life applicability. Others suggest that, since the new terminals are reducing face-to-face communication, perhaps they can be used to re-establish richer physical interactions. In this context, they propose the use of personal devices in a way that makes them a public space of interaction, describing a feature that mimics a common scenario in the past, where a group of friends shared and commented on a batch of paper photos, but transferred it to the digital world by splitting each photo into multiple parts and sending each part to a different smartphone. When the devices are physically joined in a kind of Lego, a larger viewing area is created, where all can focus simultaneously and comment on the photo [9].

There are also authors that have evaluated the sharing of the big television screen available in most living rooms [5]. In one instance, the TV is converted in a kind of mini screens, where each part of the screen can be taken by different individuals. This allow them, at any time, to share with the others what they are doing that can be public. That facilitates breaking the "digital bubble", but at the same time keeps each other privacy, because people only share what they want. The authors argue that the emphasis on the central equipment sharing and the consequent joint attention to the same device is fundamental to achieve more effective interactions. This is a result of a shared perception of all the activities being performed by the various people.

These proposals take advantage of existing devices to foster greater interpersonal interaction and are preferable to Turkle's proposals, since they integrate technology rather than trying to disconnect the user, but unfortunately do not show potential for regular use.

2.3 Game Shows

There is, therefore, a window of opportunity to try to find alternatives that promote the conversation using technology, not only with those who are far away (where technology is already excellent), but also with co-located people with shared family or proximity ties. However, to promote a frequent and continuous use, the effort of using the solution should not be significant, nor necessarily intentional. Currently, there are applications in the market to promote the most diverse activities between unacquainted people: hitchhiking, lodging, dating, etc. However, there are few that aim to make individuals who are close to each other, but who have different preferences in content or timing, to join and share not only the same space, but also the potential exchange of ideas resulting from a conversational process. It is precisely in this framework that this paper proposes an option that has the potential to take advantage of this gap.

Taking in consideration that one of the few television genres that is prone to generate discussion while being watched is 'game shows', especially those of trivia

[10], for example, "Who Wants to Be a Millionaire" or "Jeopardy", our proposal intends to evaluate if it is possible to put families back discussing and talking, by bringing this television 'game show' ambience and the challenge of answering trivia questions to the living room environment. This type of games enjoys some popularity, either in the board format with examples such as "Trivial Pursuit" and "Cranium", or in digital format, with games like "Buzz!" or "You Don't Know Jack". Some of the most striking television game shows, like the ones already mentioned, have also been implemented in domestic versions in either board or digital. An approach to this type of quiz game, using interactive television scenarios, was already tried with the "Wize" game [11]. However, since the game was a kind of hybrid and had a betting component associated with the quiz, it had serious constraints on a real test, because there were several law restrictions on gambling and betting in Portugal at the time.

In the education field there is also a large set of examples which, taking advantage of the fact that students bring to the classroom various digital devices, proposes to integrate them into a game that transforms a review activity into a kind of television competition, with several examples of such platforms: Kahoot!, Quizizz, Quizlet Live and Quizalize [12]. Particularly, in the case of Kahoot!, long-term studies identified a high propensity to maintain interest in the game, even after continued use [13], but unfortunately this platform is not geared to promote discussion around the questions, given the dynamics associated with the response speed. Quizlet Live works in a way that encourages discussion and even group work, but requires at least 3 players or groups of players and many possible answers to function.

On the television side, new formats are also emerging, joining the concepts of quizzes and engagement from viewers at home by using mobile devices. In the recent game show "Cue The Music", two teams of celebrities fight in a music themed quiz. On the 2nd screen play-along app, the smartphone or tablet synchronizes by audio fingerprinting, allowing the viewer to answer at home to the same question that appears on TV, both live or on-demand. Besides playing for fun, the viewers also have a chance to get their names inserted on the show by appearing on the game leaderboards [14].

3   Indagante - The Game

Inspired by these influences, our proposal is to develop a multiplatform quiz game, involving interactive television, computers, smartphones and tablets, whose mechanism will promote the discussion and interaction in the living room. For the development of our proposal we will follow the methodologies associated with Interaction Design, given its focus on human activities and relationships supported on digital interactive and communicational platforms, all relevant factors to the game that is being implemented. This methodology consists of four basic activities [15]: establishing functional and technical requirements, designing alternatives, prototyping and evaluating. Each of these activities aims to produce results that will be used as a starting point for the next one and continue to do so in an iterative and repeated way in several refinement cycles.

However, before listing the requirements and for sake of ease their understanding, we will start by characterizing three information architecture pillars [16]: context, content and users. For the Indagante game the main factor of the context attribute will be the space where the action will take place, in this case the family living room, while its members watch the television and simultaneously are also occupied with their digital devices. This context is fundamentally related to entertainment where the individuals involved are potentially relaxed at the end of a day of work or school.

The contents in this case will be the questions and corresponding answers on which the game will be supported. Although we plan to produce some pre-made question packages focusing on television themes (movies, series, sports, etc.), one of the goals of the game is to have an artificial intelligence (AI) algorithm that dynamically creates questions. To create them the AI will use the contents previously transmitted by the TV where the game takes place, therefore having a more personalized link to the household where it is taking place. Alternatively, it can also create questions on programs that are to be transmitted next, to raise interest in them, using sources such as the programming guide. This automatic generation of questions needs some further research but is already discussed in the literature [17] and is intended to provide a more dynamic gameplay than "Trivial Pursuit" that slightly loses the challenge over time, given the repetition of the questions. In a very basic way this type of solution was already used, for example, in the original iPod, with the game, "Music Quiz", which reproduced an excerpt from a song from the device and presents four different song titles as possible answers. This basically tested the knowledge that the user has about his own music library.

Finally, the users are members of a family or a group of friends who shares the same household where an interactive television is available (normally with a Set-top Box – STB), which has a variety of digital devices (iOS, Android and web browser), wishing to add some fun to their entertainment at night. If in a normal game it is expected that the participants are there of their own volition, in the case of Indagante this may not be a reality. Given that the game has two distinct levels of goals, on one hand, entertainment and on the other, the conversation promotion, it is expected that there may be a promoter for the game (a father who wants to add some debate to the family evening or a child which has the intent to draw attention from his parents) and other participants who are involved in the game with various levels of interest, from the very committed to the perfectly opposed. It should be noted that given the wide range of potential users of the game, young and old, parents and friends, a very large focus on human-centered design makes less sense than an activity-centered design because, as Norman refers, when the types of use are rather differentiated it is preferable to let the activity define the product and its structure [18]. In this case the main activities are play and conversation.

With the perception of who is the target audience and with its context and contents defined, the following subsections proceed with the description of how the four basic activities of Interaction Design apply to Indagante game.

3.1   Establishing Requirements

In this emergent phase of game design, the first batch of requirements was elaborated from a high level game concept built after the initial idea [19]. Emphasis has been placed on the main requirements with the potential to add value to a first evaluation phase, particularly those that raise concrete research questions. One of the first functional requirements for Indagante is that the television should function as the central screen of the quiz game, and as the only device where the questions will be prompted. The surrounding mobile devices, smartphones, tablets and laptops will work as the apparatuses to give the correspondent answers. This is deliberate, to force the players to take their eyes off the equipment they are using and to look at the television. In the evaluation stage for this requirement, it will be important to understand whether the users can spatially correlate the UI elements between the main device (the television) and the secondary device (the mobile equipment), particularly since they are in two different visual planes, the television at distance and the mobile equipment in the hand, both having very distinct features and capabilities (Fig. 1).

Fig. 1. Indagante game sequence

During the game at a random time, a question will be selected or generated and all the devices involved in the game will be notified that there is a question to be answered. The idea is that the notification will create a generalized but smooth disruption of the activities in the living room and produce a synchronization moment between the various members of the family. While the disruption is a factor deliberately designed onto the game, it is important that the number of notifications in each session is not exaggerated so the players do not see the notifications as an unwanted disturbance, but rather as an opportunity to score in the game. A previous study on notifications in secondary displays, found that a high rate of notifications can become tiresome for users, advising that they be spaced at least 30 seconds apart [20]. In the case of Indagante it will be important to realize the ideal number of questions to be launched per session, so that the players find the game attractive and not annoying.

In Indagante there will be a time limit to answer each question. The points will be assigned in the inverse proportion to the response time. Even before any prototype was developed, it was possible to do small trials using an adaptation of the Kahoot! [13, 21] on a Smart TV with an embedded web browser. With these small trials, it was possible to see that the game effectively disrupts normal activity and that the competitive ingredients associated with games were also present [22]. Indeed, the game created in the players the desire to play more, in order to be able to earn points and improve the classification. However, we have identified some typical situations of quiz games that do not fit the purpose of Indagante. In Kahoot! a great deal of attention is given to the response time - while this increases the competitive factor it does not promotes the discussion around the question, as each element tries to arrive at an answer as soon as possible to move on to the next question, and the room for discussion is reduced. There is time between questions to discuss why one answer was right and others are wrong, but it looks almost an off-game activity and did not feel competitive. The main purpose of Indagante is to get people to talk about a certain subject, to present their arguments and justify their response. To make the game more around the discussion, a variant was introduced to the normal quiz mechanics, by splitting the answer in two sequential but distinct parts. A first phase where the question is presented and each person responds as quickly as possible to have better scores. For instance, in the very simple question in Fig. 2, answering to "Who directed Pulp Fiction". Whereas in a second phase, participants can discuss the answers freely and eventually change their initial response losing some of their points. In the example, perhaps the discussing could be around the possible answer "John Travolta", who by coincidence appears on the screen and is very connected to the movie. This aims to create a space for discussion not limiting the game to the mere quiz effect, but still maintain the discussion inside the game. This factor may also mitigate in Indagante the lack of a common element present in the television game shows, that is the role of the TV presenter which gives tips and questions the competitor's confidence in his response. With the two answering phases, it is foreseen that the users will play this role.

Fig. 2. Mock-up of the Indagante interface

The game will operate in an open session format, which may run for several days and will only end at the end of a predetermined number of questions or at the end of a set of elapsed days, for example a week. So, in terms of the conceptual model, there is a need for an activation phase in the game. This stage will be used to indicate on the TV side that a game should start. At that moment, it will also be necessary to activate the players, validating from a technical point of view that they can participate. If the devices are iOS or Android, during the activation process it should be confirmed that they have the game application installed and that it has permissions to receive notifications. In the case of the web client, the functionality of receiving notifications and acting on them must be also validated. This will be a crucial phase in terms of the interaction model and one that may pose more difficulties and may represent the main obstacle to the adoption of the game. The expectation is that the use of a simple numerical code associated with QR Codes could minimize the issues to establish the association between the STB and the mobile device. Nevertheless, this will be one of the areas that, at the evaluation time, will need to be given a special focus. For example, it will be necessary to understand if the user realizes that after the activation, a random period will elapse until the first questions appear, and after that they will spaced in time and displayed at random moments.

3.2 Designing Alternatives

Following the model of Interaction Design, after some of the requirements are defined a phase to conceptualize and to design the system takes place. With this idea in mind and for the rapid development of prototypes, a simple mock-up of the desired interface, both for the television and the mobile devices, can be seen in Fig. 2 - as can be noticed the mobile interface has been reduced to the minimum elements.

Following the prompt of a notification in the surrounding mobile devices, the television presents in overlay to the TV content: the question, the answers proposed and a clock to indicate the time until the question is closed. On the side of mobile devices, the interface is reduced to only four buttons, which can be used to submit the desired response. At this stage of project development, the design was kept purposely simplistic and with a more functional characteristic, however, we have already chosen to introduce elements such as color in buttons, to help in the mapping between the television and the mobile devices, and also gave a letter to each button, to increase the accessibility of the solution.

The screens for game activation and finalization, among others, are being designed. Priority was given to the main game screens for faster user feedback. An interface element that also needs careful consideration will be the notifications for the mobile devices and the web browser. In recent versions, both Android and iOS push notifications have gained features, and it is technically feasible to have the buttons related to the responses integrated directly into the notification, at least on Android. This type of solution would have the advantage of creating a disruption that does not lead the player to leave the environment where he was before the notification. However, it would make the implementation of the second phase of the response process, where the player can correct their selection, complex from a cognitive point of view, so at this moment, in terms of conceptual design, the game will use standard native notifications.

It is worth to mention that the game will have a feedback screen to reveal the correct answer along with its score. Players can also have access to a ranking area, on the mobile device, with the current family scores and comparisons with other rankings organized by buddy list, geographical area, etc.

3.3   Prototypes

Prototypes are fundamental elements for discussing and evaluating ideas of each project with the stakeholders, since they allow to visualize in a tangible way concepts and ideas that are many times difficult to convey with a simple description. The very act of elaborating a prototype is sometimes sufficient to show the problems and mistakes associated with the previous phases. The prototyping phase of Indagante project is in its early stages, however, as previously mentioned, it was possible, through the use of an adapted form of the Kahoot! platform, perform a set of tests in a real scenario with members of a family. Although with some constraints, it was soon possible to identify some issues. For example, the Kahoot! competitive component does not have the potential to generate discussion and conversation, which is one of the main objectives of Indagante. It was also possible to verify that, given the wide range in terms of age groups that will be playing the game, it will be necessary to design a way to balance it between the various players, like the handicap in golf. For example, children read more slowly than adults, and adults thus have an undue competitive advantage. This balance can be achieved by detecting that a given player is a child and assigning him, for example, extra time to respond. Given the relative simplicity and the low fidelity, in terms of graphics, associated with the mockups already elaborated it is feasible to rely on a fast implementation of functional prototypes for the first rounds of evaluation, reducing the need to resort to tests with the Kahoot platform!

3.4   Evaluation

With some prototypes running, it will be possible to start a more accurate evaluation process, the results of which can give feedback to the whole process of Interaction Design. During the development of the Indagante game it is intended to make extensive use of assessments with real users, in this case families and groups of friends who share the same house, with the purpose of observing their activities, mainly to understand how the introduction of the game and its dynamics impact the normal daily proceedings. The two fundamental basic components that will be evaluated will always be if the game is fun to play, a fundamental condition for a game, and if it promotes conversations and discussions. Then, per some of the previously mentioned requirements, there will be a set of other topics to be evaluated. In terms of evaluation with users in controlled spaces, given that we have access to several scenarios of living labs [23], through a partnership with main IPTV operator in Portugal, we will gather a set of groups that meets the requirements for our target audience, families or group of friends, with access to interactive television and mobile devices, and we will carry out this type of evaluation in the operator facilities. The approach will be to make regular evaluations with different groups instead of a broad study and to refine and iterate in the development [24]. In this type of setting, living lab, we mainly intend to evaluate, in this initial phase, the questions related to the activation of the game, the issues associated with the input device being in one plane and the output device in another, completely different. It will also be an ideal scenario to carry out a study like the one in [20], in order to determine a balanced number of questions per event and extrapolate it to a session involving several days.

Another factor to evaluate will be the mechanics of having two distinct moments for answering each question. In this case, in addition to evaluating the format comprehension, it will also be very important to assess if this model induces a greater level of conversation than the most typical quiz format. In the living labs, we expect to have direct observation and, since the scenarios will always involve several family members simultaneously, we are studying the feasibility to record the sessions with a 360° camera, since in this way it will be possible to video record simultaneously all the actors. We anticipate to be able to see if the notifications effectively create the synchronous interruption and what are its effects in terms of the global user experience. At the same time, and in addition to direct observation, we will also use interviews and a triangulation of specific questionnaires to evaluate specific dimension of the user experience [25].

When the game will be more stable, and since we also have access via the IPTV operator partnership, with prior authorization, to a broad set of users with interactive television, identified in previous studies, we will select those who have more than two individuals with personal digital equipment in their households to do a set of field trials. In this case, we will not resort to direct observation, but only to questionnaires and occasional interviews.

In both scenarios, significant levels of logs will always be available, both from the television and from the mobile devices, which will be used in analytical evaluations. These data will have a greater preponderance in the field test case, since they will allow for analytical evaluation on the potential for a continued use of the game. It will be easy, for example, to obtain metrics such as the number of effectively answered questions, the number of sessions played and even determine the moment when the game will not be played anymore.

4 Conclusion

As we have seen in this paper, the introduction of a set of new equipment in the living room has ease the gathering of the family members in the same physical space, but to share little more than that, lacking in terms of social interaction, with the potential implications this can have. Taking advantage of the interactive features of the new personal digital equipment, and focusing on the fact that they are already present in the living room, we have seen several proposals and contributed with a suggestion that has the potential to promote conversations and healthy discussions in the living room. Our ongoing project aims to create a game, associated with television content, in a multiplatform and purposely disruptive context. To find out how much its concrete implementation in the field could have a significant effect on the way family members interact with each other, a field trial will be implemented. Meanwhile, various stages of establishing requirements, designing alternatives, prototyping and evaluating the game with several rounds of refinement will take place. The game will be designed to have the necessary elements to create a synchronized disruption, allowing for discussions and physical communication. Besides that, we are confident that the game will be able to function by itself, as pure entertainment.

References

1. Lull, J.: The social uses of television. Hum. Commun. Res. **6**, 197–209 (1980). doi:10.1111/j.1468-2958.1980.tb00140.x
2. Turkle, S.: Alone Together: Why We Expect More from Technology and Less from Each Other. Basic Books Inc., New York (2011)
3. Ley, B., Ogonowski, C., Hess, J., et al.: Impacts of new technologies on media usage and social behaviour in domestic environments. Behav. Inf. Technol. **33**, 815–828 (2014). doi:10.1080/0144929X.2013.832383
4. Wilson, S.: In the living room: second screens and TV audiences. Telev. New Media **17**, 174–191 (2015). doi:10.1177/1527476415593348
5. McGill, M., Williamson, J.H., Brewster, S.A.: A review of collocated multi-user TV: Examining the changing role of the TV in the multi-viewer, multi-screen home. Pers. Ubiquitous Comput. **19**, 743–759 (2015). doi:10.1007/s00779-015-0860-1
6. Ofcom: Communications Market Report (2013)
7. Deloitt: Digital Democracy Survey A multi-generational view of consumer technology, media and telecom trends (2015)
8. Turkle, S.: Reclaiming Conversation: The Power of Talk in a Digital Age. Penguin Publishing Group (2015)
9. Lucero, A., Jones, M., Jokela, T., Robinson, S.: Mobile collocated interactions: taking an offline break together. Interactions **20**, 26–32 (2013). doi:10.1145/2427076.2427083
10. Geerts, D., Cesar, P., Bulterman, D.: The implications of program genres for the design of social television systems. In: Proceedings of the 1st International Conference on Designing Interactive User Experiences for TV and Video (UXTV 2008), pp. 71–80 (2008). doi:10.1145/1453805.1453822
11. Almeida, P., Ferraz, J., Pinho, A., Costa, D.: Engaging viewers through social TV games. In: Proceedings of the 10th European Conference on Interactive TV and Video, EuroiTV 2012, pp. 175–183 (2012). doi:10.1145/2325616.2325651
12. Miller, M.: Game show classroom: Comparing Kahoot!, Quizizz, Quizlet Live and Quizalize. http://ditchthattextbook.com/2016/04/21/game-show-classroom-comparing-kahoot-quizizz-quizlet-live-and-quizalize/. Accessed 24 Jan 2017
13. Wang, A.I.: The wear out effect of a game-based student response system. Comput. Educ. **82**, 217–227 (2015). doi:10.1016/j.compedu.2014.11.004
14. Monterosa: TV proves its digital influence again as Monterosa's new Play-Along app for Cue The Music TV show hits the No. 1 App Store spot in Portugal (2017). https://www.monterosa.co/newslist/2017/1/18/cuethemusic-portugal. Accessed 10 Feb 2017
15. Preece, J., Sharp, H., Rogers, Y.: Interaction Design: Beyond Human-Computer Interaction, 4th edn. Wiley (2015)

16. Morville, P., Rosenfeld, L.: Information Architecture for the World Wide Web, 3rd edn. O'Reilly (2006)
17. Seyler, D., Yahya, M., Berberich, K.: Knowledge Questions from Knowledge Graphs. ArXiv e-prints (2016)
18. Norman, D.A.: The design of everyday things, Revised an. Basic Books (2013)
19. Adams, E.: Fundamentals of Game Design, 2nd edn. (2010)
20. Abreu, J., Almeida, P., Silva, T., Aresta, M.: Notifications efficiency, impact, and interference in second-screen scenarios. Int. J. Hum. Comput. Interact. (2016). doi:10.1080/10447318.2016.1210870
21. Wang, A.I., Øfsdahl, T., Mørch-Storstein, O.K.: An evaluation of a mobile game concept for lectures. Software Engineering Education Conference Proceedings, pp. 197–204 (2008). doi:10.1109/CSEET.2008.15
22. Salen, K., Zimmerman, E.: Rules of Play: Game Design Fundamentals (2004)
23. Følstad, A.: Living labs for innovation and development of information and communication technology: a literature review. Electron. J. Virtual Organ. Netw. 10, 99–131 (2008)
24. Nielsen, J.: Usability 101: Introduction to Usability (2012)
25. Abreu, J., Almeida, P., Silva, T.: A UX evaluation approach for second-screen applications. Commun. Comput. Inf. Sci. 605, 105–120 (2016). doi:10.1007/978-3-319-38907-3_9

From Live TV Events to Twitter Status Updates - a Study on Delays

Rita Oliveira$^{(\boxtimes)}$ ⓘ, Pedro Almeida ⓘ, and Jorge Ferraz de Abreu ⓘ

University of Aveiro-Digimedia, Aveiro, Portugal
{ritaoliveira,almeida,jfa}@ua.pt

Abstract. This paper reports on a preliminary study of a research project that proposes a new integration between the activity generated in social networks and television programs. The research team aimed to develop a tool that automatically creates summaries of popular TV programs based on the buzz (peaks of Twitter status updates) on Twitter, and, therefore, having as an editorial criterion the related status updates on Twitter.

In a preparatory stage of the project, in order to understand the best correlation between the sources of information and the foreseen narrative dynamics of the TV summaries, the research team analyzed four TV programs (two football matches and two entertainment programs) by means of manual observation and comparing it with the data gathered by a data mining Application Programming Interface (API) (being created by one of the research team partners), that would handle the detection and extraction of the activity on Twitter related to television TV programs, identifying the moments of greater buzz. The decision on these genres of TV programs was made based on Portuguese TV audience rankings (usually with higher audiences than other genres) and, also, in a previous analysis made through the data mining API, which confirmed the higher buzz on Twitter related to this kind of TV programs. This analysis provided important data to determine the elapsed time between the real events and the correlated comments on Twitter and the most optimized duration for a typical segment (a short video clip of an event) to be included in the automatically created summaries. This information provides support to better understand the time and narrative correlation between TV programs and related Twitter activity.

Keywords: TV highlights · Twitter updates · Delays · TV programs · TV summary

1 Introduction

The TV related activity on social networks is already recognized as an indicator of TV programs popularity [1–3]. Despite its use in the analysis of the most commented TV programs, namely via Twitter, the buzz on social networks has the potential to be capitalized as editorial criterion associated with the selection of most popular video excerpts (TV highlights). However, there is a lack of information regarding the time correlation between the peaks of the social buzz and the correspondent hot moments of the related TV show.

© Springer International Publishing AG 2017
M.J. Abásolo et al. (Eds.): jAUTI 2016, CCIS 689, pp. 117–128, 2017.
DOI: 10.1007/978-3-319-63321-3_9

This lack of information is special relevant as the authors of this paper aimed to use the Twitter activity as an input to an automatic engine able to automatically create summaries (based on a coherent sequence of highlights) of popular TV programs. With this objective in mind, the team of the nowUP project [4] developed a research to test and verify the validity and relevance of this approach as an identification criterion of the most popular moments of a television program. In addition, by proposing the automatic creation of summaries that connects user-generated content (tweets) with TV contents, a new narrative approach to summaries was suggested.

One of the initial tasks under this research was to understand the average elapsed time between the real events and the correlated comments on Twitter and to determine the most optimized duration of the segments for a specific event in the TV show in order to take this data in consideration in the narrative dynamics of the automatically created TV summaries. This paper aims to present this preliminary study, which was based on the analysis of four TV programs (two football matches and two talent shows) to determine the aforementioned correlation.

The paper is organized as follows. In the next section, a state of the art concerning detection methods of TV highlights based on the Twitter activity is presented. In Sect. 3, the analysis process of TV programs is described and its outcomes are also presented. The final section presents the most relevant conclusions and the work to be done in the future.

2 Related Work

In this section, a set of detection methods of TV highlights based on the Twitter activity is presented in two subsections: (i) studies that make use of the Twitter activity to create summaries of TV programs or to extract highlight scenes; and (ii) works that correlate the Twitter activity and TV highlights although without the purpose of generating videos.

Concerning the creation of videos based on the Twitter buzz, Marlow et al. [5] propose a simple method to generate summaries about sport TV programs. The method detects semantically important events, using scaling factors (mathematical relationships) in the MPEG bit stream audio files in order to generate an audio amplitude profile of the program. The scale factors applied to the bandwidth of audio information give a strong indication of the excitement level of the commentators or spectators. When periods of high audio amplitude are detected and classified, the corresponding video segments are concatenated to produce a summary of the program highlights. Sgarbi and Borges [6] also addressed football videos developing an automatic framework to implement a summarization of those videos using object- based features with the ability to detect shots towards the goal areas. Doman et al. [7] propose a detection method of TV sports events called "Twitter Enthusiasm Degrees (TED)", which is used to create highlight videos. This method is based on three variables: (i) frequency of exclamations on tweets; (ii) number of tweets using repeated expressions; and (iii) number of retweets. Also in sports, Kim et al. [8] work aim to detect highlights in baseball videos. The authors propose a method to extract important events detecting important plays from video. These are determined by a combination of audio and visual detection in real time.

Hayama [9] suggests a method for highlights scene detection in order to create summaries based on Twitter data classified by the user behavior. The user behavior is classified through the tweets metadata: heavy use of hashtags, parallel use of retweets and plain-tweets, heavy use of retweets and heavy use of plain-tweets. Once again, a football match was used to validate the method. Kobayashi et al. [10] suggests a method for detecting and extracting highlights in a Japanese baseball game according to what supporters said on Twitter. Consequently, the authors obtained two different sets of highlights scenes according the team viewers support.

Regarding works that correlate the Twitter activity and TV highlights without the purpose of creating videos, Hsieh et al. [11] collected a dataset of tweets from 18 sport games and correlated it with the corresponding video programs through a flexible threshold (according the global number of tweets). The authors consider that this method achieves high performance results. Nichols, Mahmud and Drews [12] created an algorithm in order to recognize TV program events using tweets. A sentence ranking method is used to extract relevant text from tweets, since the main goal of the algorithm is the creation of sports textual summaries. Marasanapalle et al. [13] analyzed tweets that were posted when a TV show was broadcasted using text- mining techniques. The authors selected a talk show to validate an experiment and concluded that the results were relevant for TV content producers because they can know what kind of viewers post tweets on the show and what viewers are saying about it. D'heer and Verdegem [14] studied the Twitter activity during a Belgian TV information program to understand how viewers talk about this TV program on Twitter and also to discuss the usefulness and value of this information for audience studies. Buschow, Schneider and Ueberheide [15] analyzed 30,000 tweets from various TV programs and found that different TV programs motivate different communication activities. Lochrie and Coulton [16] intended to study the use of mobile phone as a second screen for TV. For that, the authors analyzed a popular UK TV show and compared the tweets from this show with other shows from a different format. They concluded that audiences are creating their own narrative of the show through Twitter and this information has enormous potential for TV broadcasters and producers.

From this state of the art we may perceive that the correlation of the social networks activity, namely Twitter and TV shows is a hot topic. However, the studies are short in the discussion of the elapsed time between the real event and the correlated tweets but this information is crucial when creating an automatic sequence of highlights since it is important to detect the correspondent real events with time precision. On the other hand, viewers of short videos, like TV summaries, tend to look for short clips and therefore, an optimization of the clips duration is needed. In this scope, a tool for the automatic creation of summaries needs to use the best balance between the shortest duration of the clip and the need to include all the relevant narrative elements on a specific event. The answers for these goals were searched in this study and are now described.

3   TV Programs Analysis

As referred, the research team conducted an analysis of four TV programs (two football matches and two entertainment shows) to determine the elapsed time/delay between the actual event and the peak on twitter along with the duration of the video segments to be used in the summaries.

The selection of such programs was based on the high TV shares in Portugal [17] of these genres, namely sports programs and talent shows and also on its popularity in social networks, that is, the buzz generated on Twitter about this type of shows [18]. Some preliminary tests with data mining around Portuguese tweets also confirmed this trend.

3.1   The Problem Framework and the Information Analysis Approach

The data mining service that provides the needed information to create the TV summaries, implemented by the TV Pulse API (more information in [19]), detects the activity on Twitter related to TV programs, using as referenced data the Electronic Program Guide (EPG) of that program and other correlated information it fetches in the Internet, namely in Wikipedia (e.g. name of players or contestants). The API gathers the number of tweets generated during the broadcasting period of a specific television program and identifies the moments of greater buzz (peaks of Twitter status updates). In addition, the API has the ability to extract the text from tweets and their relevant information (user, location, number of followers and hashtags). To synchronize the tweets and the TV show, the timestamp (hh:mm:ss) of the tweets (retrieved from the Twitter API and related with the tweet publication time) and the timestamp (hh:mm:ss) of the TV show video/recording (retrieved from the EPG) are used.

In this framework, two main questions arise. First, what is the average time it takes for the Twitter community to react to a certain event, as an example, a football goal? Since viewers need some time to write and publish a related tweet what is the impact of such delay on the correlation between the TV show event and related tweets? Secondly, the average length of an event, or the main actions that make it an event, should also be determined. With this information the video creation engine could apply a delay when fetching the event mo ment and determine the length of each video clip to be extracted from the main video.

In order to get this information the team carried a manual task that comprised the visualization and inspection of the two TV shows of each genre (sports and entertainment), previously recorded on a streaming server from one of the nowUP project partners. It is worth to say that the team followed the generic editorial criteria found in official summaries of TV programs to identify the start and end point of an event (e.g. for a goal, the event started in the beginning of the play that led to the goal and finished after the first celebrations). Accordingly, TV moments like a contestant performance or the judge opinion about a performance (in talent shows) were considered.

For the first task, the elapsed time to an event, the team first looked at the information retrieved by the TV Pulse API, that is, the peaks of tweets, the timestamp of each peak and the text of tweets. This information was synthetized in a table and was then complemented with the manually obtained information, gathered from observing the correspondent TV show. The complete comparison table was compounded by the following items: the timestamp of the event gathered in Twitter (the peak timestamp) (hh:mm:ss); the event description (assigned by the nowUP team); the event starting time (hh:mm:ss) and the event ending time (hh:mm:ss) - both gathered from direct observation - watching the show; the total number of tweets; the number of tweets with related content to the event ("Related" column), and; the number of tweets with unrelated content to the event ("Unrelated" column). This content correlation task was verified manually by the team reading through every of the tweets selected by the data mining engine to confirm if it contained related or unrelated content to events. Then, comparing the obtained information, the elapsed time between the actual event (determined by the average timestamp between its start and end point) and the peak on twitter was registered in the "Delay" column and duration of the event (the time difference between the event ending and starting) was stored in the "Duration" column.

3.2   Characterization of the TV Shows

As previously mentioned, the analyzed TV programs were of two different genres: sports/football matches and entertainment programs. Specifically, the following TV shows were used: (i) 'SLBenfica vs VitoriaFC' football match; 'FCPorto vs FCBayern Munich' football match; (iii) an episode of the Portuguese 'Idols" talent show; and (iv) an episode of the Portuguese "Dancing with the Stars" talent show. The results of the analysis of each TV show are represented in the graphs (Figs. 1 to 4). In the y axis the number of tweets is represented (in the black line the detected events and in color the verified related tweets). In the x axis the timeline of events with the occurrence time is shown. Also in the x axis, the delay of each event is identified (with the same color of the event). The list of events is included in the right of each graph.

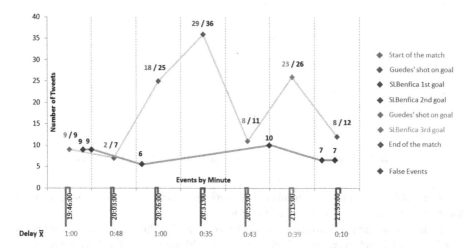

Fig. 1. Highlights of the 'SLBenfica vs VitoriaFC' football match

The Football Matches

In the 'SLBenfica vs VitoriaFC' football match (Fig. 1), 7 true events and 6 false events were identified by the API. Besides the start and end of the football match that were commented on Twitter, the three and only goals of the match and some dangerous plays of 'SLBenfica' were also commented by Twitter users. The event with more tweets was the 2nd goal of 'SLBenfica' with 29 related tweets (in the figure, the number of related tweets is in the same color of the event). The delay of the events was not higher than 1 min and the duration of them was also not higher than 1 min. Regarding the "false events" it is important to notice that these were not expressive peaks. Therefore, increasing the threshold that determines the peaks it would be easy to configure the system to ignore such events without losing a major relevant event (only the start of the match and 2 missed shots could be ignored due to the threshold increase).

It should be noted that the delay can have more than one value (which is not the case), because two or more peaks can belong to the same event. In this case, a mean of the event delays was calculated.

In the 'FCPorto vs FCBayern Munich' football match (Fig. 2), 4 true events and 1 false event were identified. The four goals of the match were only the events detected by the TV Pulse API. The first detected event was a penalty that originated the 1st goal of 'FCPorto' and for that reason was the event with longer duration. The event with more tweets was the 3rd goal of 'FCPorto' with 337 related tweets. The delay of the events was not higher than 1 min and 40 s and the duration of the events was not higher than 2 min and 30 s. Once again, the "false event" was clearly bellow any of the "true events" so an adjusted threshold (that takes in consideration the gap between the majority of the tweet clusters and other clusters) would remove the false positives with no impact.

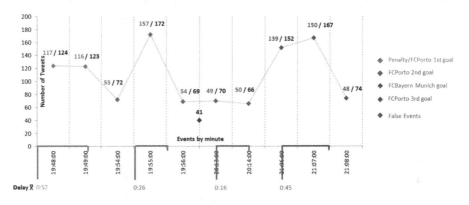

Fig. 2. Highlights of the 'FCPorto vs FCBayern Munich' football match

The Table 1 presents the number of tweets and events that were found in each football match and also the mean of these values.

In the 'SLBenfica vs VitoriaFC' football match, the TV Pulse API found 174 tweets in total, 97 of which were related with the events, 29 were not related with the events and 48 were not associated with any TV highlight, creating 6 false events.

Table 1. Number of tweets and events in the analyzed football matches

	No. of tweets	Related		Unrelated		No events		True events		False events	
	#	#	%	#	%	#	%	#	tw/e	#	tw/e
Match 1 Overall	174	97	55,7	29	16,7	48	27,6	7	18	6	8
Match 2 Overall	1130	933	82,6	156	13,8	41	3,6	4	272	1	41
MEAN	652	515	69,2	93	15,2	45	15,6	6	145	4	25

The 'FCPorto vs FCBayern Munich' football match involved much more tweets then the first analyzed football match, 1130 in total. The tweets related with the events were in greater number (933) and the unrelated represented only 156 of them 41 tweets were not associated with any event, creating only 1 false event.

Comparing the two football matches, the mean elapsed time between the TV moment and the buzz on Twitter was of 38 s (Table 2). The mean duration of the events was 1 min and 11 s (Table 2).

Talent Shows

In the Portuguese 'Idols' talent show (Fig. 3), 12 true events and no false events were

Table 2. Mean of the delay and duration obtained in the two analyzed football matches (separately and jointly)

	Duration	Delay
Match 1 Mean	00:00:56	00:00:42
Match 2 Mean	00:01:22	00:00:36
Global	00:01:11	00:00:38

identified. Most of the detected events were contestants' performances. The events with more tweets were the *Pedro Cau's Performance* and the *Kizomba Moment* with 68 related tweets. The delay of the events was not higher than 3 min and 22 s and the duration of the events was not higher than 3 min and 20 s.

In the Portuguese 'Dancing with the stars' talent show (Fig. 4), 16 true events and 8 false events were identified. In the same way as the first analyzed talent show, most of the detected events were contestants' performances. The event with more tweets was the 2nd performance of the invitees with 13 related tweets. The delay of the events was not higher than 5 min and 50 s and the duration of the events was not higher than 5 min and 35 s. The "false events" were once again on the bottom section of the activity allowing for an increase of the threshold without losing the most relevant true events.

The number of tweets and events that were found in each talent show and also the mean of these values are presented in Table 3.

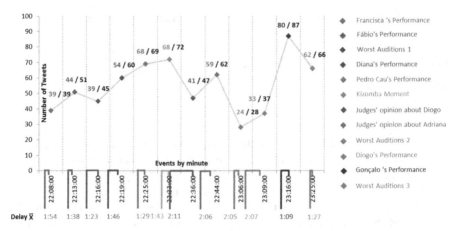

Fig. 3. Highlights of the Portuguese 'Idols' talent show

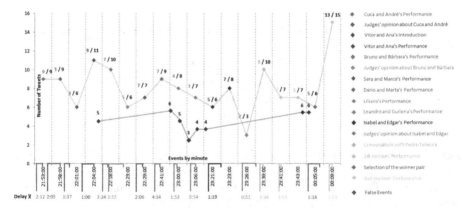

Fig. 4. Highlights of the Portuguese 'Dancing with the stars' talent show

Table 3. Number of tweets and events in the analyzed talent shows

	No. of tweets	Related		Unrelated		No events		True events		False events	
	#	#	%	#	%	#	%	#	tw/e	#	tw/e
Show 1 Overall	663	611	92,2	52	7,8	0	0,0	12	55	0	0
Show 2 Overall	183	104	56,8	40	21,9	39	21,3	16	9	8	5
MEAN	423	358	74,5	46	14,9	20	10,7	14	32	4	2

In the Portuguese 'Idols' talent show, the TV Pulse API found 663 tweets in total, 611 of which were related with the events and only 52 were not related with the events. Tweets without events were not detected and consequently there were no false events.

The Portuguese 'Dancing with the stars' talent show involved much less tweets then the Portuguese 'Idols' talent show, 183 in total. 104 of the tweets were related with the events, 40 were not related with the events and 39 tweets were not associated with any event, creating 8 false events.

Concerning the delay and duration of the two entertainment programs (Table 4), it was found that both the delay between the TV moment and the Twitter buzz and the duration of the TV moment are considerably larger than in football matches: a delay of 1 min and 41 s and a duration of 2 min and 17 s.

Table 4. Mean of the delay and duration obtained in the two analyzed talent shows (separately and jointly)

	Duration	Delay
Show 1 Mean	00:01:35	00:01:44
Show 2 Mean	00:02:39	00:01:38
Global	00:02:13	00:01:41

3.3 Outcomes

The results of this study have shown that the TV genre influences the reaction time of Twitter's users about TV moments and the length of those moments.

Comparing the two TV genres, it was possible to verify that the duration of the segments is twice longer in summaries of entertainment programs, namely talent shows, than summaries of sports programs (Fig. 5). Regarding the delay between the actual event and the peak on Twitter, it is possible to note that this variable is two and a half times longer in summaries of entertainment programs than summaries of sports programs. This fact may be due to the longer duration of events and a less precise reference moment for the peak. While in sports events the trigger to post in Twitter is

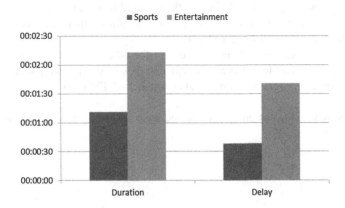

Fig. 5. Comparison of the duration and delay between the two TV genres

typically a goal or another well determined action, in an entertainment show, the trigger is less precise and spectators may take longer to react to a more emotional event.

With this information, the segments duration and time correlation with Twitter events were defined for each genre. The results concerning the creation of nowUP summaries are detailed in another publication [4].

4   Conclusions and Future Work

Although this preliminary study integrates a limited number of TV shows, it was possible to perceive the average duration of the delay that has to be considered before automatically fetching the video segment that will integrate the summary. For the nowUP solution this was crucial information, along with the average duration of those segments. Through these results, it was possible to conclude that the automatic creation of the summaries has to take into account the genre of television program establishing different values for each genre. In football matches, the buzz on Twitter related to the TV highlights has a shorter delay as compared to entertainment programs, namely talent shows. Thus, both the delay and the duration of the video clips tend to be shorter in football matches and longer in entertainment programs.

Another important issue is the total duration of the summaries. With the use and application of the obtained results, the TV summaries could easily exceed well over 5 min, reaching up to 15 min. But, as it was noticed, the API threshold could be adjusted by means of an increase of the threshold which would have two positive results: reduce the total amount of events, and therefore the overall length of the summary, and; discard the false events and increase the quality of the summary. However it is important to refer that the entertainment TV shows have a tendency to generate more events and therefore, the summaries will get longer any way.

With all this information the team followed the work in order to fine-tune some of the API features and develop the video engine taking these results in consideration. Despite this data, such an automatic system may produce false events or get segments not perfectly adjusted to each event. The team foresees functionalities that may allow the community of users to comment or react to a certain summary. For that to happen, a mechanism that allows the users to inform the editorial team that there is a clip which is not correctly adjusted (e.g. in a football match: the clip needs to start earlier and end later to show a goal) could be introduced.

Finally, the gathered results may be useful for other works that use Twitter as a source of correlated data to TV events. Further studies may apply similar approaches to other genres of TV programs or to a higher number of TV shows.

Acknowledgements. Authors are grateful to the project partners: Altice Labs and Telecommunications Institute.

References

1. Nielsen Social, TV Season in Review: Biggest Moments on Twitter (2015). http://www. nielsensocial.com/tv-season-in-review-biggest-moments-on-twitter/. Accessed 01 Mar 2017
2. Kantar Media, Who's Tweeting about TV in the UK? (2015). http://www.kantarmedia.com/ uk/thinking-resources/latest-thinking/who-is-tweeting-about-tv-in-the-uk. Accessed 01 Mar 2017
3. Viacom, When Networks Network - TV Gets Social (2013). http://vimninsights.viacom. com/post/61773538381/when-networks-network-tv-gets-social-in-our. Accessed 01 Mar 2017
4. Almeida, P., Abreu, J., Oliveira, R.: nowUP: a system that automatically creates TV summaries based on Twitter activity. In: Abásolo, M.J., et al. (eds.) jAUTI 2016. CCIS, vol. 689, pp. 18–31 (2017). Springer, Cham (2017)
5. Marlow, S., et al.: Audio processing for automatic TV sports program highlights detection. In: Proceedings of Irish Signals and Systems Conference (ISSC 2002), pp. 25–26. CIT, Ireland (2002). http://doras.dcu.ie/326/
6. Sgarbi, E., Borges, D.L.: Structure in soccer videos: detecting and classifying highlights for automatic summarization. In: Sanfeliu, A., Cortés, M.L. (eds.) CIARP 2005. LNCS, vol. 3773, pp. 691–700. Springer, Heidelberg (2005). doi:10.1007/11578079_72
7. Doman, K., et al.: Event detection based on twitter enthusiasm degree for generating a sports highlight video. In: Proceedings of 22nd ACM International Conference on Multimedia, pp. 949–952. ACM, New York (2014). doi:10.1145/2647868.2654973
8. Kim, H.G., et al.: Real-time highlight detection in baseball video for TVs with time- shift function. IEEE Trans. Consum. Electron. **54**(2), 831–838 (2008). doi:10.1109/TCE.2008. 4560167
9. Hayama, T.: Detecting TV program highlight scenes using twitter data classified by Twitter user behavior. In: 10th International Conference on Knowledge Information and Creativity Support Systems (KICSS), pp. 164–175. SIIT-TU, Thailand (2015). http://aiat.in.th/ kicss2015/app/webroot/downloads/Proceedings-KICSS2015.pdf
10. Kobayashi, T., Takahashi, T., Deguchi, D., Ide, I., Murase, H.: Detection of biased broadcast sports video highlights by attribute-based tweets analysis. In: Li, S., Saddik, A., Wang, M., Mei, T., Sebe, N., Yan, S., Hong, R., Gurrin, C. (eds.) MMM 2013. LNCS, vol. 7733, pp. 364–373. Springer, Heidelberg (2013). doi:10.1007/978-3-642-35728-2_35
11. Hsieh, L.C.: Live semantic sport highlight detection based on analyzing Tweets of Twitter. In: IEEE International Conference on Multimedia and Expo (ICME) 2012, pp. 949–954. IEEE, California (2012). doi:10.1109/ICME.2012.135
12. Nichols, J., Mahmud, J., Drews, C.: Summarizing sporting events using Twitter. In: Proceedings of the 2012 ACM International Conference on Intelligent User Interfaces, pp. 189–198. ACM, New York (2012). doi:10.1145/2166966.2166999
13. Marasanapalle, J., et al.: Business intelligence from Twitter for the television media: a case study. In: 2010 IEEE International Workshop on Business Applications of Social Network Analysis (BASNA). IEEE, California (2010). doi:10.1109/BASNA.2010.5730304
14. D'heer, E., Verdegem, P.: What social media data mean for audience studies: a multidimensional investigation of Twitter use during a current affairs TV programme. Inf. Commun. Soc. **18**(2), 221–234 (2015). doi:10.1080/1369118X.2014.952318
15. Buschow, C., Schneider, B., Ueberheide, S.: Tweeting television: exploring communication activities on Twitter while watching TV. communications. Euro. J. Commun. Res. **39**, 129–149 (2014). doi:10.1515/commun-2014-0009

16. Lochrie, M., Coulton, P.: Sharing the viewing experience through second screens. In: Proceedings of the 10th European Conference on Interactive TV and Video (EuroiTV 2012), pp. 199–202. ACM, New York (2012). doi:10.1145/2325616.2325655
17. M&P: A TV que os portugueses viram em 2016, M&P (2017). http://www.meiosepub licidade.pt/2017/01/a-tv-que-os-portugueses-viram-em-2016/. Accessed 01 Mar 2017
18. Maglyo, T.: Nielsen Reveals 10 Biggest Fall TV Shows on Twitter and Facebook. The wrap (2017). http://www.thewrap.com/nielsen-fall-tv-shows-twitter-facebook/. Accessed 01 Mar 2017
19. Vilaça, A., Antunes, M., Gomes, D.: TV-Pulse: Improvements on detecting TV highlights in Social Networks using metadata and semantic similarity. In: Proceedings of 14th Conferência sobre Redes de Computadores, Évora, Portugal (2015)

IDTV Interaction Techniques

Design and Usability Evaluation
of a Multi-input Interface
in an idTV Environment

Juan Felipe Téllez$^{(\boxtimes)}$ ⓘ , Juan Carlos Montoya ⓘ ,
and Helmuth Trefftz ⓘ

EAFIT University, Medellín, Colombia
{jtellez,jcmontoy,htrefftz}@eafit.edu.co

Abstract. In recent years, and considering the rise of Interactive Digital Television (idTV), it has been great interest in the design of applications and services for this platform. However, the success of these applications largely depends on the ease of use and how users interact with them. For this reason, we have explored different interfaces and modes of interaction to improve the user experience with these applications in comparison with the traditional Remote-Control (RC). This article presents an interaction with idTV applications using multiple input control interfaces with different modes of interaction such as touch buttons, gesture recognition, voice recognition, and recognition of movements. These modes of interaction were validated through usability testing using a model of quasi-experimental evaluation of three dimensions, where each dimension represents respectively: users, tasks and control interfaces. As a result of the qualitative and quantitative assessments, we performed an analysis of possible improvements in the usability of a particular application of idTV. The results showed few differences between one multi-input control interface and one RC in tasks the user was familiar with, on the opposite, significant differences were found in performing tasks involving greater user interaction, such as the text input or navigation between menus.

Keywords: Interactive digital television · Usability · User experience · Multimodality · Mobile devices

1 Introduction

Interactive Digital Television (idTV) offers the possibility of a new range of applications and services such as: electronic programming guide (EPG), video recording, video on demand (VoD), games, e-commerce, information services, among other. This new set of applications and services allow operators and producers of content to increase and enrich the range of products available to users, but in turn, increase the complexity in the way they access and interact with such content [1]. In this context, and as mentioned by some authors in [2, 3], challenges have arisen for the design of idTV applications and in particular emphasis is given to the problems that occur with the experience of using interfaces and control devices. In particular, the authors highlight the existing differences and relative user experience when comparing idTV

© Springer International Publishing AG 2017
M.J. Abásolo et al. (Eds.): jAUTI 2016, CCIS 689, pp. 131–148, 2017.
DOI: 10.1007/978-3-319-63321-3_10

applications with applications developed for PC or other devices. In [4], an analysis of the differences is made and classified mainly in four areas: (i) the users, (ii) the purposes/tasks of the users, (iii) the equipment and (iv) the environment. In this sense, the idTV brings new challenges in the area of Human-Computer Interaction (HCI), which are related to the way in which the interaction between the user and the content.

According to Kunert's analysis [4], the user should be the center in designing applications for idTV. As a consequence, it suggests that usability in the context of idTV is the most important criterion when compared to accessibility or emotional appeal. Kunert understands usability as the "quality of the user experience when interacting with something". In this way, you can achieve: ease of use, satisfaction, efficiency of use and prevention of errors when working with an interactive application. From the above, it can be inferred that improving usability allows users a better understanding of the interface, as well as the control device and a better understanding of how to interact with a specific application through the device. Better usability also leads users to know how they want to use the platform, knowing how to do it in the best way. On the other hand, Kunert [4] in his proposal focuses on the performance of the graphical interface and the application, leaving aside other important attributes for the control device that are part of the UX user experience, as proposed Hassenzahl in [5] and ISO 9241-210: 2010 in [6], which include both pragmatic and hedonic attributes. Even the definition of ISO user experience is even broader and more general, since it asserts that it is "the perception and response of a person resulting from the use or prior to the use of a product, system or service", such Form that is intended to group a greater amount of perceptions on the part of the user and not only to take into account the functionality of the system.

The pragmatic attributes are consistent with Kunert's concept of usability [4], with respect to product functionality and access functionality. On the other hand, hedonic attributes describe the qualities and ability of the product to evoke the emotional appeal, pleasure and comfort in the user. In [5], it is proposed to divide the hedonic attributes into three categories: attributes that produce stimulation, identification and recall.

Summarizing the above, it can be inferred that improving the user experience in the context of the idTV is achieved by means of a better perception of these when interacting with an idTV application through a control device, in the accomplishment of objectives Specific and in a context of particular use. It should be ensured that the user achieves greater efficiency, efficacy and satisfaction, which has traditionally been known as usability, while perceiving an attraction, pleasure and comfort from the interface. The relationship of these aspects that are part of the user experience is shown in Fig. 1. All elements that affect the user experience should be considered in an evaluation. However, studies as cited in [1, 7–9], focus on the analysis of equipment and coincide in concluding that the RC severely limits the possibilities of interaction. These studies suggest that the remote control has the following limitations: (i) it does not support the direct manipulation interaction style, (ii) does not support text input, (iii) requires line of sight with the TV or STB (Digital Decoder Set Top Box), (iv) has many unfamiliar buttons, (v) in some cases, are very large devices, (vi) response to commands is generally slow; Among other functional limitations, these observations are similar to those made by Jakob Nielsen [10].

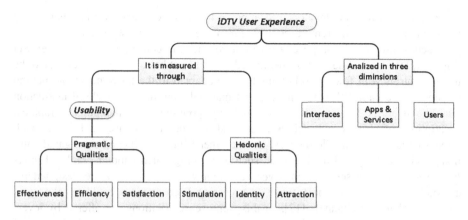

Fig. 1. User experience and usability variables.

The proposed work focuses on the part of the means of control and interaction, specifically the remote control and the interaction with the users according to tasks and very specific applications of entertainment and information and a model of interaction is proposed using several modes of input: voice, gestures, movement and buttons, in order to build a multi-input interface. A training design model is proposed, using an evaluation of usability and user perception in an iterative way. An iterative evaluation of usability allows a more rigorous monitoring of the user's response to the interaction modes of the device, even when it is in the early stages and provides useful information for the development of a new control interface with multiple modes of interaction.

The article is organized as follows: In the section related works, a summary of the different works done in the HCI area for idTV applications is presented. The proposed work section shows the development of the study and describes its three stages of evaluation, with all its considerations. The results section presents the statistical analysis with all the data obtained from the user studies, including the comparison between the interfaces and tasks. Finally, in the conclusion section, we present the future debate and the challenges that remain to be addressed.

2 Related Works

The problem of user interaction and control means for idTV applications has been analyzed and studied in different works. In particular, we have tried to develop interfaces that make use of different modes of interaction for idTV. Researchers have essentially worked on several lines of work: voice recognition, gesture recognition, interface customization, touch screens, keyboards, pointing devices and multi-input/multi-output interfaces on mobile devices. In particular, this last line of work stands out because it brings together the works of the previous lines under the premise of offering the best of different modes of interaction, in such a way that the user is given several modes of control.

Proposals have been developed to improve the user experience without neglecting the original idea of the remote control. From the point of view of the device it is proposed to use a multi-purpose remote control that can control all TV Receiver, Set Top Box, DVD, DVR devices as mentioned in [1, 11]. It has also been investigated the use of controls with few or no buttons that are adapted to the movements and natural gestures of the hand [9], which have direct manipulation, this is a style of interaction that allows users to complete their tasks by pointing and manipulate graphical descriptions of objects and actions of interest, as does the mouse on PCs or touch screens of tablets or mobile devices. On the other hand, have been investigated solutions from the design of applications, such as creating much simpler graphical interfaces for interactive services, in a very different way to how they are designed for computing, so browsing the Internet or accessing Web services could be almost as simple as changing channels [12]. In this same sense solutions are offered by leveraging the convergence of services and existing devices in the market, as is the case of Amazon and Apple companies that making use of the capabilities of mobile devices is working in conjunction with hardware manufacturers in an application that uses it as a remote control either through its wireless 802.11b/g or Bluetooth module, it is possible to control its own TV platform from anywhere [13]. In this way, many applications are being developed to take advantage of the multitude of options offered by mobile devices and tablets, and thus have much more sophisticated controls, with new capabilities and features that go beyond what conventional remote offers. Solano et al. have proposed a number of heuristics to be used when evaluating Interactive Digital TV applications [14]. This shows the growing importance of these types of interaction given the current growth of Digital TV.

2.1 Interfaces with Multiple Modes of Interaction

The use of interfaces with multiple modes of interaction has been possible thanks to the growth in the speed of the processors and the capacity of the embedded devices, both advances are the basis to implement new devices that serve as means of interaction, with a greater capacity of communication with other equipment and in turn with the user.

Among the multi-input and multi-output interfaces that have been investigated, we have worked with dual-screen interfaces. These are based on a model of interaction with two devices, each with a different screen to display audiovisual information or additional support information either for entertainment or learning as mentioned [15, 16]. In this model, the main screen is usually the TV screen and the secondary screen can be a tablet, a Mobile device or a laptop, among others. The great advantage of these devices is that the information displayed on the main screen can be complemented by the second screen where users can select preferences and interests. In this interaction model one can take advantage of the resources available on the Internet and that can be accessed through the second device, in such a way that the return channel is established by means of this second device. The weak point of this form of interaction is the distraction that is caused to the user, insofar as this must be attentive to two screens to interact and this can lead the user to lose interest in the content offered on the main screen.

Studies such as [9] suggest an interaction model that resorts to different senses of sight and hearing, specifically focusing on physical contact between the user and the control interface, in such a way that they implement haptic interfaces as a mode Intuitive interaction. These types of interfaces are usually complementary to others that are oriented to the use of the view, so the intention of the designers of haptic interfaces is to create a more immersive environment for the user, creating scenarios where you can feel what is heard and what it looks. In [17], it is proposed the use of an embedded device to replace the RC through gestures created by the movements of the hand, using an accelerometer and neural network algorithms to recognize the patterns of users.

2.2   Mobile Device Based Interfaces

Some of the most studied modes of interaction are the interfaces based on mobile devices. The proposals of [8, 11, 18–21] explore the possibility of using the hardware resources of these devices, be they PDA's, tablets or Mobile devices. These mobile devices are embedded systems very close to a computer, but characteristics such as size, mobility, access to communication networks, sensors, low power consumption, low cost, among others, make them very interesting as tools of interaction in idTV. Because of the wide acceptance of mobile devices, it is not difficult to think of its use as a supplement or replacement of the remote, but on the other hand involves some change in the form of traditional interaction. Application designers can use many of the tools that mobile devices have, applying what is most useful to them as the case may be: they can be used as a second screen, as a simple control, as a touch keyboard, as a support web browser, as Pad tactile, among other uses. One difficulty that arises is that they are complex devices for many users and use them to replace something as simple as the remote control may be unattractive to some users.

These interfaces are highly complementary with the recognition of gestures and images, as demonstrated in the studies [22, 23], which present a non-intrusive interface for users in order to share television in a group. In open television, [24] presents a complex interaction model that uses tactile devices for users to interact with television content in a personalized way, either with a learning objective, which gives the user the possibility of Being more immersed in an event or situation, or even interacting with an object that appears on the screen.

Mobile devices have also increased research on the use of the touch screen and interfaces have been proposed with pencils and finger gestures. The pencils allow you to create symbols similar to the marks and signs that are made in the physical world, like making a cross on a word to remove something, or marking a circle around a paragraph and then drawing a line to move the paragraph to a new site. Interfaces that are designed with a stylus must decide whether to process commands as a symbol or as a written form. A common solution is to implement the two options separately and use a menu in a toolbar next to the screen to change the functions according to the need, the only drawback is that you have to make constant changes between the menu Options, which means a waste of time if the screen is large. This can be improved with the use of functions that allow the use of both hands [25].

3 Proposed Work

It is proposed the development of a multi-input control interface that substantially improves the experience of idTV users, through an iterative design methodology, where the study of the users is the center of the project and in turn serves as feedback for the construction of the same. In each phase the users validated the pragmatic qualities and the hedonic qualities in the context of the idTV according to the chosen model.

All modes of input of commands and data evaluated are available on the current mobile devices, because the purpose of the study is to use the features of current Mobile devices to create an alternative interface that exceeds the usability of RC. The modes of input commands evaluated were: Voice recognition, Recognition of tactile gestures, use of the touch screen like keyboard (tactile buttons), Recognition of movements of the hand using the device accelerometer.

3.1 Iterative Evaluation

To develop the multi-input interface, an iterative design and evaluation model was established, which was divided into three phases. Each phase was characterized by the selection of the interfaces to be evaluated, the selection of the user group and the characterization of the tasks to be developed. This three-dimensional evaluation methodology seeks to evaluate the 3 most important aspects in the context of idTV usability as suggested [11].

The first phase evaluated the RC and a mobile application called BOXEE App [18] to control multimedia content through a Mobile device, in order to find and confirm the problems and limitations that arise with the use of the remote control in an interactive environment. The second phase explored the performance of users through 4 mobile device interfaces created exclusively to take advantage of each of the input modes of selected commands and everything in the context of idTV, with tasks typical of this environment. The third phase took the results of the second phase and proposed a multi-input interface with the union of several data input modes evaluated; This integration of modes of interaction was tested against the RC and the same tasks of the second phase were used in order to follow up and a statistical evaluation that allowed conclusions to be drawn.

3.2 First User Study

The objective of this first user study was to determine the user perception about the use of idTV with the RC, as well as to find the difficulties that users have when using the remote control. In addition, the evaluation suggested a tactile interface as a first approximation to an alternative option for the control of interactive digital television.

In the first user study, two input methods were evaluated: a common remote control and a mobile device with a touch screen application. The application runs on Android devices and uses the tactile button approach, in an attempt to emulate the RC functionality. The mobile application BOXEE App [18] was used. This application requires the additional installation of a client on a computer, which allows video playback, access to menus and interactive television applications such as games. The system was tested with the computer attached to a 42" TV, creating in an environment that looked like a living room. This assembly emulated an STB or decoder and a common television, so the user did not realize that he was actually interacting with a computer.

A performance measurement type study was applied with 6 users, according with Nielsen usability studies [26]. Each individual user was evaluated with two interfaces in random order: one RC and one button-based control application on a mobile device equipped with a touch screen. The study evaluated the usability of the interfaces, in particular the measured variables were: the user efficiency with the interface, the efficiency to perform a task with the interface and the satisfaction perceived by the users through a questionnaire after the test.

The study contemplated the accomplishment of two specific tasks on the part of each user. The assignments for all were the same and consisted of: Searching for a video in an EPG through the introduction of the text "Digital Television" to reach several videos and select one of them. The second task was to play one of the videos that were suggested by the EPG, and once the video ended, they had to exit the playback application, return to the EPG and then return to the main menu. Both tasks must be performed with each interface in the same order. Therefore, in order for the remote control and the touch interface to be evaluated under equal conditions and to mitigate external factors influencing the experiment, the same graphical interface was presented to the users. Once the users finished all the tasks, they continued with a questionnaire. The questions were designed to explore the background of the user: knowledge and experience with mobile devices, age of the user and general perception of the test performed. In addition, the questions were designed to determine which of the interfaces they preferred because of practical factors such as ease of use or understanding of the interface and which one they felt most comfortable with.

The results of this first phase corroborated what studies as [27] had already raised regarding the problem of introducing text through the RC, while a viable alternative was seen on the touchpad.

3.3   Second User Study

For the second user study, an evaluation of 5 control modes for idTV was performed: the RC, voice recognition, touch gesture recognition, tactile buttons and recognition of hand movements; These last 4 modes of interaction were implemented in a tablet with Android operating system. To achieve each mode of interaction, a unique application was developed for each one, so that it was fully operational and had all the basic control functions for the idTV, as well as a method of entering text and navigating through the same interaction mode.

The four applications developed had as a medium of transmission between the tablet and the STB of idTV the Bluetooth protocol, which passed through a module developed on an Arduino system, which served as a Bluetooth gateway to IR signals that were sent directly to the STB. This functionality allowed the integration of the tablet directly into the STB so that the control interfaces with the RC can be tested under the same conditions and in a real idTV environment.

The participants of the study were recruited from several local universities and other institutions. A total of 10 people participated in the study, 5 were men and 5 were women. Their ages ranged from 18 to 31 years with an average age of 24 years. Participants were asked to complete a questionnaire before the experiment to know their basic data, previous experience in idTV and with mobile devices. All sessions were recorded using a video camera and the performance of the users was measured by the project team in the same scenario used in the first phase of the project.

Before performing the actual tasks, each user received a short introduction on the mechanics of each interaction device. Each introduction took between two to five minutes. Users were required to finish a simple task as training. Training tasks included, for instance: changing a channel, turning the TV on or off or access a specific menu on the STB.

During the study, the following three tasks were proposed for users:

- Task 1: Search for a particular channel, which was given by name and not by its number, so the user should go to the channel guide to find it and select it. Then he had to go back to the previous channel.
- Task 2: Through the menu of available applications, find and use a content recommendation application, then find the list of most viewed programs and select one of these.
- Task 3: Through the available application menu, find and use the Twitter application to send a tweet of a defined phrase (the phrase is the same for all users) and then return to the main screen (Fig. 2).

After users completed all tasks with all input methods at random, they were asked to complete a short survey asking them about the ease of use and functionality of the devices they had been assigned. All of the questions followed a 5-point Likert scale, where 1 meant they strongly agreed and 5 meant they strongly disagreed. The questionnaire not only inquired about satisfaction in the traditional way, but included questions related to the stimulation, identity and attraction that make up the hedonic aspects of the interfaces. See Annex 1 for the questionnaire used in the user study.

3.4 Third User Study

In the third user study two control means were evaluated: a first version of a multi-input application and a RC. For this third phase, a new application was developed based on the different modes of interaction evaluated in the second phase. Based on the results obtained, we selected the interaction modes that had better results in the second phase and with the functionalities which users had a better perception, thus in this proposal of multi-input control the users can choose the mode of interaction with which they feel more comfortable; i.e. a user could change a channel through a voice command, enter the text through the touchpad and choose an application by means of tactile gestures. All these modes of interaction could be combined as the user felt more comfortable. The architecture of the proposed interface is presented in Fig. 3.

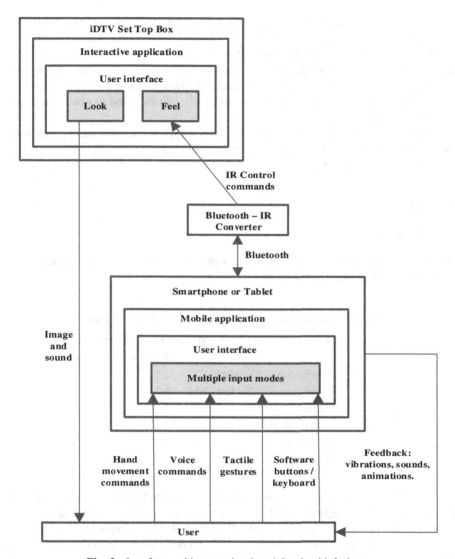

Fig. 2. Interface architecture developed for the third phase.

For the study the participants were recruited from local institutions and there were 10 participants with the same characteristic as those of the second user study. These users were completely different to the users of the first two phases, with the aim of having statistical independence and avoid having users with some experience in the interfaces and modes of interaction evaluated.

Before the experiment participants completed a questionnaire similar to the one in the second phase of the project. Each participant was shown the two interfaces that were to be tested and the order of use of the interfaces was assigned at random. The test scenario and the evaluation methodology were the same as the previous phases of the experiment.

The tasks proposed for users were the same as the second user study. After each user completed each task using all randomly assigned interfaces, they were asked to complete a short survey asking them about the ease of learning, ease of use and functionality of the devices that had been assigned. All questions followed a 5-point Likert scale, 1 meant completely in agreement and 5 meant strongly disagree. The same questionnaire used in the second phase of the study was included to obtain an evaluation of the hedonic aspects.

After users completed all tasks with the two control interfaces at random, they were asked to complete a brief survey asking them about functionality and subjective perception of assigned interfaces.

4   Results

4.1   First Phase

After the experiment with users of the first phase, the measurements and responses shown in Table 1 were consolidated.

Table 1. Measurements of the study of users of the first phase.

Factors	Levels		Mean of response variables	
			RC	Touch-screen control
Measure	Time (seconds)	1st task	1,5	1,2
		2nd task	10,1	6,2
	Errors		0,45	3,5
Perception	Easiness of use		42,9%	57,1%
	Navigation		28,6%	71,4%
	Text entry		57,1%	42,9%

This first user study required performing the activities that are most difficult with the RC: navigate through the graphical interface of the screen and enter text respectively. For the first task, it was observed a mean time in the accomplishment of the task very similar for both interfaces, with a very uniform performance in all the users, only a slight decrease in the time of the touch interface on the traditional interface.

For the second task, the average users took a shorter time with the touch control interface than the traditional interface, however, it was not the same case for all users. Those users who took longer time to achieve the task later expressed their lack of experience with mobile devices, but being familiar with the RC. The number of errors was significantly higher in the touch interface compared to the remote control. One difficulty that the users expressed was the small size of the buttons on the touch interface, which led them to make mistakes, very often involuntary. There was also a lack of a quick response from the interface, so users got positive or negative responses in their actions, which caused delays or errors.

In this first study, in addition to the measurements obtained, it was possible to observe behaviors that should be taken into account in the design of a control interface, some of these were:

- With the RC, the interaction of the users was made in a more relaxed position.
- Users when using the Mobile device were distracted when looking at the device and stopped watching the TV screen, especially when they were writing the text.
- The direct command buttons customized for the application were more intuitive in the Mobile device.
- Most users were using both hands on the test, a hand to support the control and the hand of pressing the buttons or touching the screen, but on the Mobile device, they used both hands to type on the keyboard in a similar way as text messaging users do, whereas with the RC it was more common to use one hand to hold the device and push the buttons.
- Users with both control interfaces pointed the device towards the screen and did not realize that with the Mobile device there was no need to do so.
- The size of the mobile device touch screen buttons turned out to be a relevant factor in the mistakes made by most users. The size of the buttons on a touch interface depends largely on the size of the screen and the design of the interface. For this first study, the equipment used was a HTC Dream that had a screen of 3.2″.

4.2 Second Phase

The objective of the experiment was to study the usability of the interfaces proposed specifically for this project, which were compared with the RC. This evaluation of the usability was obtained from a measurement of 3 variables: perceived satisfaction, number of errors and the time of execution of the task. These three variables are subject to the variation of two factors: the type of interfaces and the task to be performed. Since it is a multi-factorial experiment, the analysis must be cross-referenced, so the results should be seen from the influence of all factors. The results obtained were computed and validated through the statistical software Statgraphics Centurion, version XVI from Statpoint Inc. (Herndon, Virginia, USA), which determined the statistical validity of the experiment. The means obtained in the study are summarized in Table 2; for simplicity only the 3 control interfaces that showed better performance in each one of the tasks and for each of the evaluated variables were presented.

The results of tasks 1 and 2 in execution time and number of errors are not statistically different between the RC and the Tactile Buttons interface in spite of the numerical differences, this is because their differences are within the limits of Fisher least significant difference (LSD). In the case of the execution time are considered different values that had a mean whose difference was statistically greater than 86.71 s, for the number of errors, only the values whose difference was greater than 1.84 were considered different, and in the same way only the values were considered statistically different Obtained for satisfaction when the measured difference was greater than 0.43.

According to the measurements and the statistical validations, only in task 3 the three response variables were statistically different, with superior performance in all

Table 2. Means obtained for the variables measured in the second experiment.

Factor	Levels	Mean of response variables		
		Execution time (seconds)	Number of errors	Satisfaction
Task	1	RC 66.87	Tactile buttons control 1.66	RC 4.71
		Tactile buttons control 96.59	RC 1.92	Tactile buttons control 4.63
		Voice control 189.47	Voice control 3.57	Voice control 4.30
	2	RC 55.73	RC 1.21	RC 4.88
		Tactile buttons control 78.02	Tactile buttons control 1.28	Gestures control 4.77
		Gestures control 152.32	Gestures control 3.14	Tactile buttons control 4.77
	3	Tactile buttons control 215.48	Tactile buttons control 5.18	Tactile buttons control 4.75
		RC 364.09	Voice control 7.43	RC 3.97
		Gestures control 557.27	RC 10.44	Voice control 3.90

cases for the interface based on the touchpad. In tasks 1 and 2, statistically the same results were obtained for the RC and the interface of tactile keyboard and only in the satisfaction of the task 2 the interface of tactile gestures obtained a result statistically equal to the first two modes of control. In neither case did the voice and motion control interfaces perform better than the others.

On the other hand, during the experiment were observed behaviors that should be taken into account for the development of the multi-interface interface. The use of control interfaces that had very different modes of interaction than traditional ones such as voice commands, the use of tactile gestures and the control by movements had low performances in all the tasks, with only some exceptions as the case of the Channel search, in which the use of the voice got a positive response and although it did not achieve the results of the RC or tactile keyboard, if it obtained good comments from the users, some of whom considered that this mode of interaction could be useful for basic tasks such as finding channels, finding an application, or turning on/off.

In the development of task 2, the gesture interaction mode did not perform well in terms of execution time and number of errors committed, but it had a good perception by the users, with results statistically equal to RC and the interface of tactile buttons, in particular to the people it seemed very novel to them the way of navigation through short cuts realizing basic symbols and affirmed that with practice they could have a similar performance to the one obtained with the other modes of interaction.

In task 3, the results followed the trend of other studies, with a clear advantage in performance and preference for the interface with touch buttons. The case of the control interface through the voice had a particularity in this task, because it obtained a performance superior to the RC in number of errors, but the users did not manifest feel better with this type of interaction for a task of introduction of Text regarding the RC, they even showed discomfort when having to dictate a very extensive text through the tablet. They also expressed the need to implement a feedback medium in the control device, since it was always necessary to visualize both screens to verify that the actions performed were correct.

The results obtained were consistent with other studies and showed that a single mode of interaction, with the exception of touch button control, was not sufficient to overcome RC in performance and only in text input tasks was clearly overcome by the interface that had an explicit keyboard. In the construction of the multi-input interface, the results obtained in the second phase of the project were an input to determine what types of interaction should be included in the final version of the prototype. It was also determined that modes of interaction were not appropriate for some tasks and therefore their use should be restricted to avoid confusing users.

4.3 Third Phase

With the data obtained from the measurements and the questionnaires, the results were validated in order to verify their statistical independence. The results are presented in Table 3. The results of tasks 1 and 2 in execution time and number of errors are not statistically different in spite of the numerical differences, this is because their differences are within the confidence interval of the experiment. In the case of the execution time only relevant values are considered those that have a statistically greater difference to 18,1 s, the number of errors for the values whose difference is greater to 0,93 and for the satisfaction when the difference is greater to 0.34. The method used to discriminate between means is Fisher least significant difference (DMS) method. With this method, there is a 5.0% risk of saying that two means are significantly different when the real difference is equal to 0.

Table 3 shows that only in task 3 the three response variables were statistically different, with superior performance in all cases for the multi-input interface. There was

Table 3. Means obtained for the variables measured in the second experiment.

Factor	Levels	Mean of response variables		
		Execution time (seconds)	Errors	Satisfaction
Task	1	RC 60.73	Multi-input interface 2.10	Multi-input interface 4.45
		Multi-input Interface 71.48	RC 2.20	RC 4.11
	2	RC 38.01	RC 1.00	Multi-input interface 4.7
		Multi-input interface 54.27	Multi-input interface 1.30	RC 4.32
	3	Multi-input interface 156.20	Multi-input interface 3.60	Multi-input interface 4.64
		RC 275.32	RC 6.60	RC 2.96

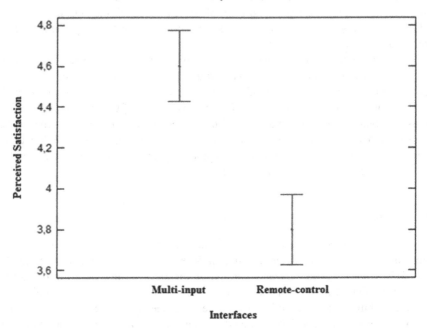

Fig. 3. Means and intervals of confidence obtained for the satisfaction perceived by the users.

also a significant difference in the perception of users in all three tasks, showing a preference in all cases for the multi-input control interface. In the tasks with more focus in the navigation and in actions common of a user of television did not find significant differences in the performance. From the results, the perception of the users on the evaluated interfaces is highlighted, see Fig. 5 and, showing a clear preference for the multi-input interface even though tasks 1 and 2 did not gain a clear advantage over RC. These results show a difference with respect to what was obtained in the second experiment with users, where they had superior perception results for the traditional remote control in the first 2 tasks.

Users stated that the multi-input control interface could perform better if navigation options were improved and more practical with them, since the use of gestures and movements are not intuitive enough, despite the improvements introduced in this version of the prototype. On the other hand, users rated very well the fact of having a visual and haptic feedback of the actions performed, since this prevented them having to visualize the screen of the tablet and the screen of the television at the same time.

5   Conclusions and Future Work

A multi-input control interface for idTV applications was proposed and developed from an iterative study with users and the combination of four input modes: voice commands, hand movements, tactile gestures and a tactile keyboard on the screen of a tablet. This mode of interaction was subjected to a usability study with the RC, as in previous phases of the project.

In the first two phases of the project, users were evaluated to determine how they responded to unimodal modes of interaction and in particular to different interaction options available on current mobile devices. These studies corroborated user's preference for the RC in tasks that were normal in non-interactive television use, but they always showed performance and satisfaction deficiencies when dealing with idTV own tasks. In spite of this, none of the proposed unimodal control interfaces was constant in all the tests and could surpass the RC, only the tactile buttons interface matched the performance of the RC, but failed to gain a better perception by users. Finally, a third user study was carried out, testing the RC with the new multi-input interface proposal. The results of the studies showed that for simple tasks in the context of television there were no significant differences in the performance of the proposed interface and RC, as well as in tasks related to navigation and resource searching for the case of idTV. Only one significant advantage of the multi-input interface was presented in the perception of user satisfaction during the test when both tasks were performed. By contrast, for the task that was related to text input, an improvement was found in the performance of users that can be considered as statistically valid. These results indicated that the tasks that the users performed in the context of idTV have a great effect on the results obtained, and should not be neglected in a usability evaluation and the design of new interfaces.

According to the results of the evaluation, the multi-input interface largely solved the problem of text entry in the tasks that required it, demonstrating that, for this type of tasks, it represents a performance improvement over RC. However, the problem of menu navigation and the search for resources still does not solve it completely and only allows to improve the user perception, or so-called hedonic attributes. It is necessary to make new adjustments to the interface and use the information obtained to improve the performance of the same, which in turn translates into an improvement in the practical performance of users.

An iterative design must be followed, in which a complete cycle of development and evaluation of the results with the users is carried out. Further development of the interface is still needed to achieve results that can improve usability in all its components and for all tasks in the context of idTV. It is clear that a multi-input interface with a blend of entries only at low level, does not allow to complement the strengths of the modalities. This can be one of the reasons why performance is not better. The development of a multi-input control device must include a bidirectional communication with the STB of idTV, this would enable the development of an interface that fuses the modalities at the semantic level. Bidirectional communication would give a feedback between all the components of the interface and not only a response that can be given to the user through the image and sound. This type of interaction would give developers a useful tool when creating a fully multimodal interface. Based on the work done, it is proposed that the 3-dimensional evaluation: users, tasks and interfaces could be extended to an additional factor such as the usage environment, which can give complementary information, and a context that could change or confirm results obtained in the studies. In addition to the environment, a greater number of levels in each of the evaluated factors could also be useful, especially in the number and type of tasks that the users can perform with the interfaces.

Given the rather small number of users in this user study, and the specific age group (18 to 31) it is not possible to conclude that one interface is better than other for all tasks at hand nor for all group ages. Further user studies should be conducted in order to produce more conclusive results.

Annex 1

Questionnaire: Final Perception of Control Interfaces
Please answer the following questions by choosing one of the answers presented.

The scale is as follows:
1 .... 2 .... 3 .... 4 .... 5.............
Where:
1. Strongly Disagree
2. Partially Disagree
3. Neutral
4. Partially agree
5. Strongly Agree

Please do not think too much about your answer, try to respond spontaneously. Answer all the questions so do not have a clear opinion about it. Keep in mind that there are no right or wrong answers, it is your opinion what really matters to us!

1. The behavior of the interface is predictable and logical.
1 .... 2 .... 3 .... 4 .... 5.............
2. Performing the task through the interface is clear and does not create confusion.
1 .... 2 .... 3 .... 4 .... 5.............
3. The management of the interface is simple.
1 .... 2 .... 3 .... 4 .... 5.............
4. The interface is practical to perform the proposed task.
1 .... 2 .... 3 .... 4 .... 5.............
5. The interface is easy to master to perform the proposed task.
1 ... 2 ... 3 ... 4 ...... 5.............
6. I learned to use the interface quickly to perform the proposed task.
1 .... 2 .... 3 .... 4 .... 5.............
7. I am satisfied with the interface to perform the proposed task.
1 .... 2 .... 3 .... 4 .... 5.............
8. The interface responds the way I want it to respond when performing the task.
1 .... 2 .... 3 .... 4 .... 5.............
9. It is fun and enjoyable to use the interface to perform the task.
1 .... 2 .... 3 .... 4 .... 5.............
10. Other comments or suggestions:

References

1. Darnell, M.J.: Making digital TV easier for less-technically-inclined people. In: Proceeding of the 1st International Conference on Designing Interactive User Experiences for TV and Video - uxtv 2008, p. 27 (2008)
2. Chorianopoulos, K.: The digital set-top box as a virtual channel provider. In: CHI 2003 Extended Abstracts on Human Factors in Computing Systems, New York (2003)
3. Collazos, C.A., Rusu, C., Arciniegas, J.L., Roncagliolo, S.: Designing and evaluating interactive television from a usability perspective. In: Second International Conferences on Advances in Computer-Human Interactions (2009)
4. Kunert, T.: User-Centered Interaction Design Patterns for Interactive Digital Television Applications. Springer, New York (2009)
5. Hassenzahl, M., Tractinsky, N.: User experience - a research agenda. Behav. Inf. Technol. 25(2), 91–97 (2006)
6. ISO (International Organization for Standardization), ISO 9241-210:2010 Ergonomics of human-system interaction, part 210: Human-centred design for interactive systems, p. 32 (2010)
7. Pemberton, L., Griffiths, R.N.: Usability evaluation techniques for interactive television. In: Proceedings of HCI International, vol. 4, pp. 882–886 (2003)
8. Riecke, R., Juers, A., Chorianopoulos, K.: Interaction design in television voting: a usability study on music TV and input devices. In: Tscheligi, M., Obrist, M., Lugmayr, A. (eds.) EuroITV 2008. LNCS, vol. 5066, pp. 268–272. Springer, Heidelberg (2008). doi:10.1007/ 978-3-540-69478-6_36
9. Ferscha, A., Vogl, S.V., Emsenhuber, B., Wally, B.: Physical shortcuts for media remote controls. In: Proceedings of the 2nd International Conference on INtelligent TEchnologies for Interactive enterTAINment, Cancun, Mexico (2008)
10. Nielsen, J.: Nielsen Norman Group, June 2004. https://www.nngroup.com/articles/remote-control-anarchy/
11. de Melo, J.C.P., Azevedo, S., Leite, L.E.C., Burlamaqui, A.M.F., Dantas, R., Goncalves, L. M.G.: ITV-telearch an architecture for enabling device telecontrol and sensor data access over IDTV systems. In: 2010 IEEE International Conference on Virtual Environments Human-Computer Interfaces and Measurement Systems (VECIMS) (2010)
12. Shin, S., Yim, J., Song, S.: Mu: channel UI to optimize the widget control in internet TV. In: Proceeding of the 1st International Conference on Designing Interactive User Experiences for TV and Video (2008)
13. Apple Inc., iTunes Preview, Apple Inc. (2016). https://itunes.apple.com/us/app/amazon-fire-tv-remote/id947984433?mt=8&ign-mpt=uo%3D4
14. Solano, A., Rusu, C., Collazos, C.A., Arciniegas, J.: Evaluating interactive digital television applications through usability heuristics. Ingeniare. Rev. Chil. Ing. 21(1), 16–29 (2013). Cited 2017-05-31
15. Cesar, P., Bulterman, D.C.A., Jansen, A.J.: Usages of the secondary screen in an interactive television environment: control, enrich, share, and transfer television content. In: Tscheligi, M., Obrist, M., Lugmayr, A. (eds.) EuroITV 2008. LNCS, vol. 5066, pp. 168–177. Springer, Heidelberg (2008). doi:10.1007/978-3-540-69478-6_22
16. Tsekleves, E., Cruickshank, L., Hill, A., Kondo, K., Whitham, R.: Interacting with digital media at home via a second screen. In: Ninth IEEE International Symposium on Multimedia Workshops (ISMW 2007) (2007)

17. Ducloux, J., Petrashin, P., Lancioni, W., Toledo, L.: Remote control with accelerometer-based hand gesture recognition for interaction in digital TV. In: Argentine School of Micro-Nanoelectronics, Technology and Applications, pp. 29–34 (2014)

18. Gil, A., Fraile, F., Ramos, M., de Fez, I., Guerri, J.C.: Personalized multimedia touristic services for hybrid broadcast/broadband mobile receivers. In: 2010 Digest of Technical Papers International Conference on Consumer Electronics (ICCE) (2010)

19. Blanco-Fernández, Y., Pazos-Arias, J.J., Gil-Solla, A., Ramos-Cabrer, M., López-Nores, M.: ZapTV: personalized user-generated content for handheld devices in DVB-H mobile networks. In: Tscheligi, M., Obrist, M., Lugmayr, A. (eds.) EuroITV 2008. LNCS, vol. 5066, pp. 193–203. Springer, Heidelberg (2008). doi:10.1007/978-3-540-69478-6_26

20. Fallahkhair, S., Pemberton, L., Griffiths, R.: Dual device user interface design for ubiquitous language learning: mobile phone and interactive television (iTV). In: IEEE International Workshop on Wireless and Mobile Technologies in Education (WMTE 2005) (2005)

21. Teixeira, C.A.C., Melo, E.L., Cattelan, R.G., Pimentel, M.G.C.: Taking advantage of contextualized interactions while users watch TV. Multimedia Tools Appl. 50(3), 587–607 (2010)

22. Lorenz, A., Jentsch, M., Concolato, C., Rukzio, E.: A formative analysis of mobile devices and gestures to control a multimedia application from the distance. In: Melecon 2010 - 2010 15th IEEE Mediterranean Electrotechnical Conference (2010)

23. Cesar, P., Bulterman, D., Obrenovic, Z., Ducret, J., Cruz-Lara, S.: An architecture for non-intrusive user interfaces for interactive digital television. In: Interactive TV: a Shared Experience (2007)

24. Cha, J., Ho, Y.S., Kim, Y., Ryu, J., Oakley, I.: A framework for haptic broadcasting. IEEE Multimedia 3(16), 16–27 (2009)

25. Lawrence Erlbaum Associates, Input Technologies and Techniques (2008)

26. Nielsen, J.: How Many Test Users in a Usability Study? (2012). https://www.nngroup.com/articles/how-many-test-users/

27. Barrero, A., Melendi, D., Pañeda, X.G., García, R., Pozueco, L., Arciniegas, J.L.: A research on typing methods for interactive digital television applications. IEEE Latin Am. Trans. 13(11), 3612–3620 (2015)

Usable Control System for Interaction with Ubiquitous Television

Enrique García[1(✉)], Juan Carlos Torres[2], and Carlos de Castro[1]

[1] Department of Computer Science and Numerical Analysis,
Universidad de Córdoba, Leonardo da Vinci Building, Rabanales Campus,
14014 Córdoba, Spain
egsalcines@uco.es, carlos@cpmti.es
[2] Department of Electronics and Computer Science,
Universidad Tecnica Particular de Loja, Loja, Ecuador
jctorres@utpl.edu.ec

Abstract. This paper, proposes a new interaction model for virtual remote controls, using a second screen through smart phones and tablets. The model follows an intuitive, user-centered design that allows transparent communication between the user and the television in a double-screen environment. To measure the degree of usability, real tests were performed with users in a relaxed time context. Those sessions were recorded to generate qualitative indicators through empirical observations, surveys and interviews.

Keywords: Interaction · Usefulness · Smart TV · Online · TDI · IPTV · Ubiquitous TV

1 Introduction

In recent years, there has been a steady increase in the networking capabilities of electronic devices. This applies to multi-purpose devices such as computers, as well as to devices targeting specific applications such as: televisions and mobile devices like smartphones or tablets. Nowadays, most of this devices can consume multimedia content based on Internet Protocol (IP): video on demand, IPTV with smart-TV's, video-conference, video-games, among others.

Wireless access networks such as WLAN, WMAN, 3G, and Bluetooth already guarantee a continuous connectivity of portable devices introducing a new challenge in the form of interaction, taking into account the mobility [1]. In this sense, it is especially important to create new scenarios of ubiquitous computing [2] in which the user can interact in a simple and intuitive way with two or more devices at the same time, being able to transfer information from one to another. This into the field of television has created a new concept called "ubiquitous television" [3], which suggests a set of scenarios in which multimedia content is not localized in a specific device or limited by time. We can imagine smartphones and tablets connected to televisions to control the content and also to move it from one screen to another. This is known as "session mobility" [4, 5].

© Springer International Publishing AG 2017
M.J. Abásolo et al. (Eds.): jAUTI 2016, CCIS 689, pp. 149–160, 2017.
DOI: 10.1007/978-3-319-63321-3_11

On the other hand, the remote control has been the most common way of inter-action with television. For many years, the usability of remote controls has been in continuous debate. In our homes there are as many controls as electronic devices. The truth is: in most of the cases, users usually use do not use more than 33% of the buttons [6]. The rest of the buttons only manage to confuse the users.

2 Background

For many years, the usability of remote controls has been and continues be into a huge debate. In our homes, there are as many controls as electronic devices. In the living room of a common family you can find several appliances: TV-set, DVD, stereo, satellite, set-top box, video game console, etc. Most of these remote controls follows the same pattern: lots of buttons with similar shapes, small sizes and difficult to read the small letters or understand signs that confuse the user. A clear example are three buttons that can appear in a television remote control: "guide", "info" and "help" [6] (Fig. 1).

Fig. 1. Typical remote control models

So, it is becoming necessary to create a new, more intuitive form of interaction. There are some approaches that try to improve interactivity with the user, although they have a big limitation for the user. The need to purchase additional products. These solutions are valid only for the product in question. There is no a standard product that anyone can use without the need to purchase an additional device or software.

This is the case of the Nintendo's Wii video game console remote control. Its charm lies in the ability to detect movement in space and the ability to point to objects on the screen. A heuristic study conducted in 2010 qualifies this user-friendly remote as perfect for people of all ages and types [7]. The minimalist design stands out. It overcomes each of the 10 heuristic rules [8].

In other cases, this gadgets provides full body motion capture in 3D, face recognition, voice recognition, and so on. Products that offers this technology are Kinect [9], Wii Motion-Plus [10] or Smart Interaction [11]. In this type of remote controls, the remote is the person himself, who can communicate directly with the television (Fig. 2).

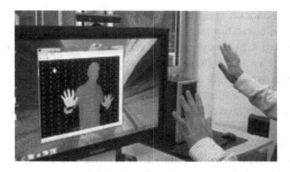

Fig. 2. Interaction using Kinect and Smart-TV

By the way, in recent years, there are a proliferation of devices called "set-top box" that can be connected to a compatible TV or even, that come already "built-in" them, increasing the possibilities of interaction, connectivity and entertainment. These devices come with a software that turns the TV-set into a media center allowing the user to navigate and stay connected to the Internet using broadband connections over the IP protocol (IPTV). In addition, with the appropiate software, the user could share multimedia content and video signals among TV and different smart devices such as smart phones and tablets.

Mobile devices such as smartphones and tablets have "capacitive touch-sensitive displays". These screens capture the interaction of the user's fingers with the device. The new language specifications have a series of events that allows to open a web application on a mobile device and capture that interaction as if it was a native application. It is possible, among many other things, to capture the position of one or several fingers at one/any time [12].

Although many of these technologies represent a revolution for the user experience in their interaction with Smart-TV's systems, new mobile technologies are not being exploited for this purpose. Smartphones and tablets are, already, globally accepted and can play an important role in the world of ubiquitous television. In addition, many of the control devices mentioned, have sophisticated and complex controls, with a low usability, causing the average users to have problems to understand and to handle the television.

On the other hand, another limitations into the existing systems lies in their closed infrastructure. Subscriptions are needed, devices have to be purchased and mobile applications have to be installed for virtual control.

Regarding software, the new HTML version 5, contains dedicated elements to improve the user experience in web pages, making it easier for the designer to be add audio and video elements. HTML5 offers new tags and APIs, creating a much more powerful language with native functions, for which you previously needed plugins or external libraries. Additionally, the specification defines an event-based mechanism under a JavaScript API for drag-and-drop functions. This system allows marking any type of elements to be draggable [13].

These new features represent a breakthrough in HTML5 in the mobile world, improving the possibilities of web development and user experience in this type of devices. The WebSocket specification defines an API that establishes a socket-like connection between a web browser and a server. This means, a persistent client/server connection is created, where any party can start a communication [14].

This technology is a considerable improvement from the predecessor AJAX, in which is the client who sends a request to the server and then awaits a response. Websockets can become a solid standard in web development, supported by most of the browsers and with guarantees to create bi-directional channels for real-time communication.

Considering the problems described in the previous section, the present work tries to approach them from the usability point of view, remarking the end user like center of the analysis design and development of the prototype. The project focuses on the context of ubiquitous television and how new technologies can be useful to users.

3   Architecture of the Proposed System

The developed system consists of several functional prototypes in the ubiquitous television environment. It is composed of two main subsystems: television and remote control. Figure 3 shows the different actions that can be performed from the remote control subsystem (smart phones and tablets) to interact with the television subsystem through the following controls: (A) playback; (B) information; (C) opinion; (D) session.

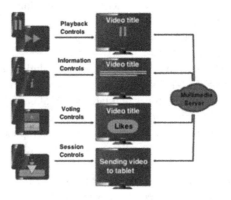

Fig. 3. Dual interactive system

The mentioned capabilities generate a new interactive dual system that allows to watch and control the television from a tactile device with screen, through tactile gestures, with movements to avoid losing the attention on the content.

The main subsystems are described below.

3.1   Television Subsystem

This subsystem provides content and receives the orders from the remote control, visualizing at all times what the user is doing, in a visual layer above the content itself. The television is constantly "listening" until a new remote control device is linked to it.

3.2   Remote Control Subsystem

This subsystem is linked to a television to load the content into and control it. The remote control is used as a remote control that brings together some controls.

Following, the description of some basic controls for content reproduction.

- **Play/Pause:** Plays and pause the video.
- **Forward/backward video:** possibility to fast forward or rewind a video.
- **Navigate through the list of videos:** possibility to view the playlist and navigate through it
- **Change video while is playback:** possibility to select a video from the playlist and play it.

Information management controls:

- **View information:** Show relevant information of a video. Title, author, duration, description, etc.
- **Social Controls:** Opinion: Possibility to evaluate a video according to your tastes and preferences.
- **Controls "session transfer":** Transfer Video: possibility of transferring the session from the television to the device with which it is being controlled so that it can continue to visualize the content from the screen of the remote control device.
- **Extend video:** possibility to transfer the session from the remote control device to a TV-set, connected to the system, to view the contents on it and control them remotely from a mobile device.

4   Development Methodology

Very often, a poor focus on the development of engineering projects produces products with little or no usability. A clear example in relation to this is common remote controls. Given that television is so widely spread that the end users of this product can be engineers, plumbers, housewives and people of any age, including children and the elderly. It is logical to think, that the most important and at the same time, the most complicated variable to deal with, is the final user. Therefore, is necessary to use a different, user-centered project methodology.

The "usability engineering process" is a method that encompasses the classical process of software engineering as a further step in a cyclical process, where, in each

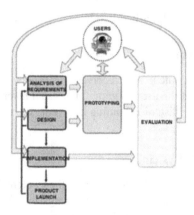

Fig. 4. Usability engineering process

iteration, a prototype is produced. Each prototype is evaluated with users and they are who set the guidelines to redefine the requirements to be analyzed (Fig. 4)

With the prototypes created in each different iteration, the evaluations have a similar importance in this project. The goal is to bring together a different set of end users for each iteration and make decisions that will affect the next phase. Evaluations will consider the formal usability standards ISO 9241, 13407, 9126 and 14598, process and product oriented. With them we will be able to carry out objective quality measures in terms of efficiency, satisfaction, easy to learn, attractiveness, productivity, user experience, etc. These standards provide a framework to evaluate the quality of all software product types and show us measurement requirements, parameters and the evaluation process [15].

Therefore, it is very important the generation of a set of prototypes to study them extensively in order to arrive to conclusions from the first to final iterations in the development process of the product. This process is widely studied and follows guidelines that have as their ultimate goal generate usable products. These prototypes will aim to be a system that allows the visualization and control of audiovisual content.

The test of the hardware environment is summarized in a series of tactile devices to be linked to the TV-set according to the different scenarios under study. Specifically, the use of a smartphone and a tablet. The rise of these devices in modern society makes essential the analysis of their impact into the environment of ubiquitous television.

For the software, a web application was developed based on HTML5 technology. The remote control interface will be designed with base on mobile phone patterns, trying to give a visual look close to a desktop application. "The Sencha Touch" framework will be used [16] for the final prototype views, although in the process of the project it will be necessary the use of applications for the design of low and medium fidelity sketches and prototypes, such as "Balsamiq Mockups software" [17]. The Node.js framework [18] will be used as server. It aims to achieve a visually attractive interface, intuitive, easy to learn and usable. Figure 5 shows the set of technologies used.

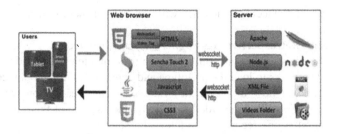

Fig. 5. Technologies used in the system

The development process consisted of 10 cycles or iterations, what began as an idea, evolves and acquire more complexity. Each cycle produces a prototype that is evaluated. After evaluating the prototype, the results analized serve as an input to the next iteration.

Starts with a simple prototype paper drawing, with few requirements, ending with a fully functional software prototype that goes to an evaluation. The project does not have, in its last iteration, the end of the development process, since the methodology used allows to extend the route as the developers can consider. In any case, the objectives defined at the beginning of the work have marked the completion requirements of the process, resulting in 10 cycles (prototypes).

The figure shows the evolution of the different iterations (Fig. 6).

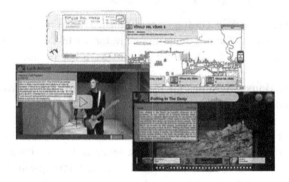

Fig. 6. Evolution of TV subsystem prototypes

5   Evaluation

A group of 10 people were selected, they didn't know anything about the system. One by one, they went through each one of the evaluation processes. According to the evaluation methodology, the following tests were performed:

- **Preliminary form:** Users, once given their consent to perform the tests, filled out a previous form answering questions about their training, age, occupation and their relationship with the technologies they will use: state-of-the-art touchscreen mobiles and tablets.

- **Logging and Retrospective Testing:** Users are then recorded while using the prototype. In this test, users sit comfortably in front of a television and are provided with portable devices to load the prototype and begin using it without receiving any prior indication of how it works, they only knew the description written in the consent report. This test is recorded with two cameras. One of them in front of the user and the other one recording the television screen.

  To perform this test, they had two devices: iPod Touch and iPad 3. Each user performs 2 test.

- **Test 1:** The user tests the prototype using the iPad for the remote control. The test begins solving the interactive tutorial and automatically moves to a real device management. The test takes about 15 min.

- **Test 2:** The same user, after a reasonable time, 20 to 30 min, performs the same test with the iPod Touch device. This time the interactive tutorial is not considered, and the user goes directly to the normal prototype management.

The performance of the two tests, by each user, provides useful information on the differences in the handling of the devices, the sensations with each one and if it's easy to learn, since the second test has no tutorial. It is important to note that the iPod Touch has the option of retracting and extending videos inactive, which is used only as a remote control. This way, is compared reactions in both devices.

After the evaluation sessions finished, the recordings should be reviewed to analyze the behavior of the users and to draw conclusions.

- **Questionnaire:** Once the recording time is finished, users receive a questionnaire to be filled that moment. There is a questionnaire for the test with the smartphone and another one for the tablet. The questionnaires have been made with two types of questions.
  - **Scalar questions:** Questions the user can answer by scaling from 1 (not agree) to 5 (completely agree).
  - **Open-ended questions:** are questions for the user, to write personal impressions on different issues. The questions are about: the degree of comfort, if it's easy to use, the user experience or the attention level to the television.
- **Interview:** Interviews complete the questionnaire. Some questions are done personally, and the user was asked about doubts related with the prototype.

6   Results

To carry out the tests, we selected a set of people of different ages, occupations and studies, different for each iteration. First, users log in with the tablet device and then with the smartphone. Each session lasts 15 min. Previously we explained to each user, the different tactile gestures for the control of the interactive system.

Figure 7 shows how the learning times evolved with respect to each iteration using the retrospective test. In general, a downward curve can be observed at times indicating

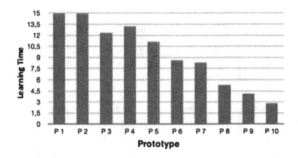

Fig. 7. Evolution of the learning times with respect to each iteration

that as development progressed, usability improved. However, the results of prototype 4 show a decrease in learning time. This coincided with the use of the prototype 4, of multi-touch gestures with more than one finger caused some confusion in the final user. Therefore, prototype 4, was a turning point in the redesign of the interfaces, replacing the multitouch gestures by a new design based on simple gestures with a single finger scroll.

Below are also the results of the questionnaire in iteration 10 (Fig. 8).

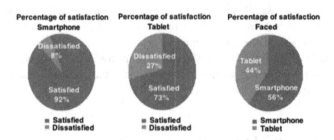

Fig. 8. Evaluation of the iteration number 10

The results showed that the level of satisfaction is higher in the smartphone. This is because the differences in size and manageability of the phone compared with the tablet. Users prefers to operate the television with one hand and a lighter device like the phone.

The tactile gestures have been modified and improved in each iteration, resulting in iteration 10, the next set of tactile gestures and that constitutes one of the main contributions of this article (Fig. 9).

The following are the resulting gestures and their representation:

- **Play/Pause:** is represented by a single star. Means that the user can pause or play touching any point on the screen.
- **Forward/Backward:** the user can go forward or backward a video by holding the finger on the left or right edge respectively.

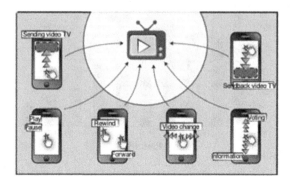

Fig. 9. Representation of the gestures for the most important interactions between the mobile system and the TV

- **Change Video:** the user can browse the list of videos by swiping left or right to select the video in question.
- **Information/Opinion:** User shows additional information of the video by sliding the finger down or up to vote or comment on the current video.
- **"Session Transfer" Controls:** These are performed by holding the finger on the screen until the icon shows up.
  - **Bring Video:** Possibility to transfer the session from the television to the device with which it is being controlled in order to continue visualizing the content from the screen of the remote control device.
  - **Send video:** Possibility to transfer the session from the remote control device to a television connected to the system to view the contents and control them remotely from the mobile device.

7 Conclusions and Future Improvements

The conclusions of the retrospective test, revealed the problems some users had with some of the gestures. Once learned, they were retained without problems but the learning process was expensive.

Doing an analysis of the videos, you can see the learning curve of the users and how they finish the test with the tablet, knowing how to use the prototype perfectly. When the time comes for the second test, with the smartphone, they know how to use it. They enjoy more and are more relaxed. Also, we can see that they hardly look at the mobile device and, being able to use it with one hand, do not lose the attention to the television screen.

The model of remote control is the classic of remote controls. In the questionnaires, the control of the tablet have a high score, but is surpassed by the smartphone use. Everyone is more familiar with smartphones and how to use it with the one-hand style. It is logical that users feel more relaxed with this device.

The software developed was based on the engineering of usability and focused at all times on the user, in order to create a system for content control and interaction of interfaces for the ubiquitous TV. Also, the system was successfully tested with people who had never used a touch device or even a desktop computer.

After performing 10 iterations in the usability process model, a stable prototype has been obtained and of a certain magnitude. Evaluations have been a relentless source of data and ideas; although the evolutionary design philosophy has marked the way changes in systems have been made. Defective modules have been modified as well as little usable designs and have been added, little by little new functionalities without breaking the molds of the process.

Through the development of the project, ideas and functionalities have been accumulated from a prototype perspective. This project intention is not to launch a user application, installable or accessible in the market. The objective of the prototypes has been the continuous evaluation and improvement of the user experience. Once a stable prototype has been achieved, it can open the range of applications, and can be tightened in the integration of this idea into other systems.

In terms of user interaction functionalities, the following can be noted:

- A volume control mechanism, either using the device's own controls, or some kind of gesture. Among others, a circular gesture is proposed with any finger, a vertical gesture with two fingers or some playable area of the reproduction view. This last option is the least attractive, since it would break with the idea of not having to look at the remote control.
- For the list of videos, new improvements are proposed to expedite the selection of videos. For example, a fast forward. This could be according to the acceleration of the gesture with the finger in the moment of passing through the videos. This solution was already tested and have usability problems. Another option is considered, such as holding down the remote control for a second until a new scrolling control appears that moves the video list quicker.
- Also a circular list is proposed, to move from the last video to the first one.

Acknowledgments. Our appreciation to Raúl Román, for the work done, who collaborated with the authors in the preparation of the tests in his final project, as well as the Ibero-American Program of Science and Technology for Development (CYTED) for the funding provided, to RedAUTI that has allowed the accomplishment of this work.

References

1. Mangialardi, S., Rapuzzi, R., Reppeto, M.: Streaming multimedia contents to nomadic users in ubiquitous computing environments. In: INFOCOM Workshops 2009, pp. 1–6. IEEE (2009)
2. Mattern, F., Sturm, P.: From distributed systems to ubiquitous computing - the state of the art, trends, and prospects of future networked systems. In: Proceedings of the Symposium on Trends in der Informations technologie am Beginn des 21. Jahrhunderts, pp. 109–134 (2002)

3. Burón, F.J., de Castro, C., García, E., Sainz, B., Ramirez, J., Chorianopoulos, K.: New approaches on iTV: usability and mobility issues. In: Advances in Dynamic and Static Media for Interactive Systems: Communicability, Computer Science and Design. HandBook (2011). ISBN: 978-88-96471-08-1
4. Más, I., Berggren, V., Jana, R., Murray, J., Rice, C.: IPTV session mobility. In: Communications and Networking in China, ChinaCom 2008, pp. 903–909 (2008)
5. Hutchings, D.R., Smith, G., Meyers, B., Czerwinski, M., Robertson, G.: Display space usage and window management operation comparisons between single monitor and multiple monitor users. In: Proceedings of the Working Conference on Advanced. Visual interfaces, AVI 2004. ACM, New York, NY, pp. 32–39 (2004)
6. Nielsen, J.: Remote Control Anarchy. Jakob Nielsen's Alertbox. http://www.useit.com/alertbox/20040607.html. Accessed June 2017
7. Troy, J.: Wii Remote Usability Heuristics (2010)
8. Nielsen, J.: Ten Usability Heuristics. Useit. http://www.useit.com/papers/heuristic/heuristic_list.html. Accessed Nov 2012
9. Kinect. http://www.xbox.com/es-ES/Kinect. Accessed Nov 2016
10. Wii Motion Plus. http://www.nintendo.es/NOE/es_ES/games/wii/. Accessed Nov 2012
11. Smart Interaction. http://www.samsung.com/es/article/. Accessed Nov 2016
12. Smus, B.: Multi-Touch Web Development (2011). HTML5Rocks. http://www.html5rocks.com/en/mobile/touch/. Accessed Nov 2012
13. Scmitt, C., Simpson, K.: HTML5 Cookbook. Solutions & Examples for HTML5 Developers Ed., p. 284. O'Reilly Media, November 2011
14. Ubl, M., Kitamura, E.: Websockets introduction. Sockets Incorporation to the web. HTML5Rocks. http://www.html5rocks.com/es/tutorials/websockets/basics/. Accessed Nov 2016
15. Granollers, T., Lorés, J.: The Usability and Accessibility Engineering Applied to the Website Design and Development. Departament Informàtica, Universitat de Lleida, Campus de Cappont (2004)
16. Sencha Touch. http://www.sencha.com/products/touch. Accessed Nov 2016
17. Balsamiq Mockups. http://www.balsamiq.com/products/mockups. Accessed Nov 2016
18. Node.js. http://nodejs.org/. Accessed Nov 2016

IDTV User Experience

InApp Questions – an Approach for Contextual Evaluation of Applications

Jorge Ferraz de Abreu$^{(\boxtimes)}$ ⓘ, Pedro Almeida ⓘ, and Pedro Beça ⓘ

University of Aveiro DigiMedia, Aveiro, Portugal
{jfa,almeida,pedrobeca}@ua.pt

Abstract. The growing success of second-screen devices is changing the way users relate and interact with the television bringing a new dimension to the TV ecosystem. Nevertheless, the specificities of mobile devices are creating numerous and significant challenges in the field of usability and user experience (UX). In addition, the evaluation of applications of the TV ecosystem should not be restricted to the measurement of its instrumental qualities typically belonging to the usability dimension, since it is also important to consider dimensions related to the UX. This paper focuses on the evaluation of a second screen application - the TV content discovery App GUIDER. Two data collection strategies for the evaluation of the App were used: a methodology based on InApp questions (that allows to measure momentary UX) and a more conventional evaluation based on an online questionnaire answered at the end of evaluation sessions (episodic UX). The use of both data collection strategies was intended to get comparative insights to validate if the InApp questions approach could get similar results when compared with those from traditional surveys. The results showed that the response deviation was very low reinforcing the suitability of such alternative data gathering method. The results indicate that triggering InApp questions while users are interacting is a promising method for evaluating applications, namely for UX dimensions, either for functional prototypes or final products. Nevertheless, the validation of such hypothesis requires further and dedicated research.

Keywords: User experience · Usability · Evaluation methodologies · Interactive television

1 Introduction

The specificities of mobile devices created numerous and significant challenges in the field of usability and user experience (UX). Mobile context, multimodality, connectivity, small screen size, different display resolutions and power emerged as factors to be taken into consideration when designing interfaces for mobile devices [1]. Interacting with these devices implies a different look at usability and UX. User's hand is no longer over a mouse but directly interacting with the interface through multi-touch gestures such as swipe, pinch, press and hold [2, 3], creating the need for bigger buttons (to solve the "fat-finger" problem), wider distance between icons and new navigation paradigms.

M.J. Abásolo et al. (Eds.): jAUTI 2016, CCIS 689, pp. 163–175, 2017.
DOI: 10.1007/978-3-319-63321-3_12

In addition, mobile usability models often focus on the effectiveness, efficiency and satisfaction, disregarding the cognitive load and the emotional impact of interacting with applications in no-longer defined time and place. However, when developing second-screen applications designed to enhance the TV viewing experience, it is even more relevant to take into account the cognitive capacity and attention selectiveness as well as other UX dimensions.

Following the work on TV Discovery & Enjoy (TDE) project that lead to the development of an IPTV application to assist the user in finding the content to watch on his/her TV set [4], this paper addresses the evaluation of a second screen approach, a tablet application as an alternative to traditional EPGs, to support the discovery of content and to assess how second screens, interconnected with an iTV platform, can improve the residential TV ecosystem. The application, implemented for iOS, was branded GUIDER and allows users to discover TV content from unified sources.

While addressing the evaluation of the App, the paper main focus is on the comparative results of the two adopted strategies for data collection: a methodology based on InApp questions triggered upon users' interaction and a more conventional evaluation based on an online questionnaire delivered to participants after a lab session evaluation. Taking in consideration the Roto [5] model of time spans of User Experience, one can say that the InApp questions give us an interesting opportunity to measure the momentary UX, while final questionnaire evaluation allows to measure the episodic UX.

Taking this main objective in consideration, the paper is structured as follows. The next section presents the state of the art addressing the second-screen applications domain and its integration in the TV ecosystem; the specificities of the evaluation processes of applications belonging to the current TV ecosystem, namely when UX dimensions are at stake; and the need for new and dynamic data gathering mechanisms. In order to contextualize the main issue of the paper, Sect. 3 presents the GUIDER Application, opening the floor to Sect. 4 ("Evaluation procedure") where the two adopted strategies for data collection are described. Section 5 presents a comparison of the results based on the average results gathered from the two mechanisms highlighting that the deviation is rather small. Finally, the paper concludes by reporting on the possible advantages of the InApp data collection method.

2 State of the Art

2.1 Second-Screen Applications

The growing success of second-screen devices is changing the way users relate and interact with the television bringing a new dimension to the TV ecosystem. Using second-screen devices while watching TV is an increasingly common activity: according to recent numbers of Nielsen Company [6], 62% of North Americans and 44% of European consumers use second-screen devices while watching TV. In this sense, consumers are increasingly adopting a lean forward approach to the television experience, using connected devices as extensions of the program they are watching [6].

Secondary Screen applications are, according to the description of Red Bee Media [7], those that provide a companion experience, aiming to increase and synchronously improve the viewer experience with content related to what is being displayed in the TV.

When considering TV recommendation systems (with a scope in line with the goals of this research), many research projects have been developed over the past few years. In 2007 the "AIMED" system [8], which uses as indicators for recommendations information based in the activities, interests, mood, experience and demographics, was created. It is a hybrid recommendation system as it combines two different techniques: content-based recommendation (based on the user's television footprint) and collaborative recommendation (based on the tastes of users with similar profile). In addition, the AIMED system stores the viewing behaviours of each user (e.g. channel, time and length of viewing session), comparing it with the different moods of users (manually inputted via a remote control which includes 3 coloured buttons: "Happy", "Bored" and "Unhappy") [8]. The "Sybil Recommender System", an experimental prototype for the web, funded by BBC Research & Development, introduces a model for the evaluation and recommendation of TV programs. The system displays a set of recommendations that can be filtered by gender (e.g. children, comedy or drama). For that, users drag and drop the recommendations to "Like" or "Dislike" boxes. Each time a content is drawn into one of the boxes, the list of is updated with new content, increasingly closer to the tastes of the user [9]. The Fraunhofer FOKUS has also introduced an application for the recommendation of TV content called "TV Predictor". This system analyses the viewing habits and the evaluations of users to determine, among other things, channels, genres, directors or favourite actors, as well as preferred viewing times [10].

2.2   TV Apps Evaluation Process

The evaluation processes of applications belonging to the current TV ecosystem are shaped by its specific characteristics, which derive from several contextual factors (spatial, temporal, social and personal) as well as technological [11]. In addition to the challenges brought by these factors, the evaluation of this kind of applications (namely when UX dimensions are at stake) presents an additional complexity due to the multiple devices present in the living room: the TV set (often used as the main display for the most varied audio-visual contents); the common Set-Top Box (STB); the likely sound system; the remote controls; and ultimately the omnipresent mobile devices (which often play the role of secondary screens or even primary screens - depending on the generation who uses it).

There is also another factor that adds to this already complex equation - the purpose (based on the uses and gratifications theory [12]) with which the user uses the TV ecosystem: informational clarification; strengthening of personal identity; integration and social interaction; or simple entertainment.

2.3   The User Experience

According to what was previously mentioned, the evaluation of applications of the TV ecosystem should not be restricted to the measurement of its instrumental qualities (such as control, effectiveness and ease of learning) typical belonging to the usability dimension, since it is also important to consider dimensions related to the UX. This issue is of decisive importance for the TV industry and operators, since the overall UX is one of the central aspects that influence the choice of customers by one or another pay-TV solution.

UX Definition Currently, it is not possible to find a unique understanding of the concept of UX and, consequently, of the methods that can be applied in the evaluation of applications belonging to the TV ecosystem. The difficulty in finding a single, global definition of UX derives from its self-nature being associated with different concepts and meanings:

"User Experience (UX) is a catchy as well as tricky research topic, given its broad applications in a diversity of interactive systems and its deep root in various conceptual frameworks, for instance, psychological theories of emotion." Law et al. [13, p. 1].

There is an ISO (9241-110:2010 - clause 2.15) definition for UX: "A person's perceptions and responses that result from the use and/or anticipated use of a product, system or service" [14], but even this approach allows for distinct interpretations, namely others less formal like: "User experience explores how a person feels about using a product, i.e., the experiential, affective, meaningful and valuable aspects of product use" [15].

In this framework, one can observe that the interest on the UX topic by the industry and the scientific community is reflected in a profusion of methods, for the conception and global appreciation of the UX, whose systematization and organization in application domains has been attempted by some authors [16, 17].

UX Dimensions Taken in consideration the reported (in)definition, a possible approach to better analyse the UX concept is to consider its various dimensions (namely the ones more relevant for the applications of the TV ecosystem) as proposed by Bernhaupt and Pirker [18]:

- Stimulation – which "describes to what extent a product can support the human need for innovative and interesting functions, interactions and contents."
- Identification – that "indicates to what extent a certain product allows the user to identify with it."
- Emotional – which includes the feelings and emotions brought about during the course of the experience, such as satisfaction, motivation and control;
- Visual/aesthetics – which is related to the pleasure and attractiveness translated by sensory perceptions.

2.4   A UX Evaluation Approach for Second-Screen Applications

Despite the existence of methods valid to specific application domains, the authors of this paper noticed a considerable lack of free access contributions specifically adapted to the evaluation of applications of the TV ecosystem [18] [19], allowing to quantify variations of UX between the original version and the corrected version of a same prototype/product. Taking this in consideration and in order to contribute with an open methodology, the authors present in [20] a UX evaluation approach for second-screen applications (also adaptable to other applications of the TV ecosystem). This approach was specified to assess users' perspectives on the instrumental and non-instrumental qualities of the application, as well as the emotional reactions triggered by episodic UX. The proposed methodology is based on validated questionnaires articulated as follows.

In order to evaluate the instrumental qualities of the application (which is useful for analysing how the perception of usability of the application relates to its UX), the SUS - System Usability Scale [21] and the Pragmatic Dimension of the questionnaire AttrakDiff ("PQ") [22] are used.

In order to evaluate the non-instrumental qualities of the application (stimulation and identification), the AttrakDiff Hedonic Quality component is used (sub dimensions "HQ-S" and "HQ-I").

To evaluate the emotional reactions (satisfaction, motivation and control) the approach make use of the SAM questionnaire [9] and the attractiveness value obtained from Attrakdiff ("ATT") that indicates a global value of the product based on the quality perception.

All these questionnaires were designed to be applied immediately at the end of an experience cycle (guided or free) in the following order: SAM, SUS and, finally, Attrakdiff.

2.5 Dynamic Data Gathering Processes

In the development of software applications, the User Interface (UI) is a fundamental element. To ensure that the UI is easy to use and meets the users' expectations usability and UX evaluations during and even after de development cycle are needed [23].

In this context, laboratory usability evaluation tests are the most common [23] method. However, despite being useful for the UI design phase, this type of evaluation procedures loose its relevance when trying to measure the satisfaction in using a product [24] since the use of such technique is unlikely to reproduce the natural usage environment or context.

On the other end, field trials that allow researchers to test their prototypes or products in real conditions appear as an ideal alternative. However, these methods are very demanding in what relates to the needed resources for its implementation and techniques for data gathering operations. It is however important to notice, that the use of different evaluation techniques allows to identify different problems. For example, the use of questionnaires to report critical incidents or other relevant information allows the users to provide different feedback about the product or application being evaluated [25].

One of the most relevant aspects in the usability of mobile devices is the ubiquitous context in which they are used. Since these devices are idealized to be used in movement, some of their characteristics, such as small screen sizes, limited connectivity, high power consumption rates and limited input modalities, may condition their use in different contexts. Another factor that has great relevance in usability and UX is the cognitive overload, mainly due to multitasking use and device size limitations [26].

To overcome these issues, it is possible to make use of automated usability evaluation processes, as for example in-app user feedback tools that allows gathering users' opinions in a contextualized way straight from the App being evaluated. This is by far a much more promising method than gathering opinions from external surveys or even reviews carried at App stores. A recent research shows that the users' app reviews allow analysts and app designers to know about the users' requirements, to detect bugs, get requests for new features, and the overall UX with a specific app [27]. However, the analysis of such (qualitative) information (user reviews) is highly demanding, and may suffer from bias resulting from the diversity of the quality and relevance of reviews. On the other hand, the utility of star ratings (quantitative and therefore easy to process data) is very limited [27]. Another limitation of this information, is that it is generated after the use of the App, not allowing to gather the UX right while using it. Thus, in mobile usability studies the hands-on measurements are one of the most used evaluation methodologies [28]. The use of these methodologies makes it possible to test the applications in real-life contexts without the need for observer/researcher intervention (as is typical of the final questionnaire evaluations), allowing to segment the evaluation by very specific functionalities, synchronizing the "question/answer" with the moment of its use.

3 The GUIDER Application

The current television ecosystem has been going through very significant changes, one being the huge increase in the existing TV content, either live or on demand, which is available to users with access to pay-TV solutions. In several countries, this offer has been increased because, in addition to over a hundred of linear-TV channels and thousands of contents available on the Video On Demand (VoD) service provided by most of the TV operators, they also offer Catch-up TV services (based in automatic cloud recordings) of the TV programs aired in the last 7 days. In this context, the viewer has constant access to a huge TV offer that may exceed 20,000 different TV programs.

Considering that many times when viewers sit in front of the TV they don't know in advance what to see, this huge offer of content means that they may feel "lost" with such offering. This may lead to a typical "mindless zapping" behaviour to find something matching their preferences; possibly missing a specific TV content that would be of their real interest. It is precisely to assist the user in this context that the authors had been focused on developing technological solutions to assist the user in discovering the TV content most suitable for his/her actual situation.

As referred, the first steps of development of the GUIDER iOS App started in the TDE research project [29], whose main objectives were to understand and identify the cognitive processes associated with deciding what to watch and, based on this study, to develop a prototype of an IPTV application that supports viewers in the search and selection of a TV program to watch. At the time, the research team also wanted to identify implementation strategies and opportunities for having a similar approach based on TV companion devices. Therefore, a medium fidelity prototype was developed, being the genesis for the development of the fully functional GUIDER application now presented.

3.1   System Architecture

Considering the system architecture, the GUIDER App is supported by a client and server approach. The client side includes, besides an iOS device (typically an iPad), a set-top-box (for a fully functional usage, namely allowing to start playing the program that was discovered/selected in the GUIDER app on the TV set).

The application connects to the home network via Wi-Fi and finds existing set-top boxes on the same network to have access to. If the App is used in a different TV operator from the one it was developed to, this control of the set-top-box is not available (it is worth to say that to maintain the same evaluation scenario between Brazil and Portugal this feature was disabled). At server side, the SearchEngine is responsible for the classification of TV contents and the search and discover features. In parallel, a module ©Parse is used to store all the information related with the use of the application, namely the answers to in App evaluation forms (later described).

3.2   Main Features

GUIDER includes some social features (namely profiling and social networks interaction) that require users to login in the app, which can be made through Facebook or Twitter. To achieve a complete integration with the TV ecosystem, the user has the ability to connect, if he/she is a client from the partner operator, to his/her set-top box. This association allows starting TV programs from the App. The main GUIDER area is the discovery screen (Fig. 1).

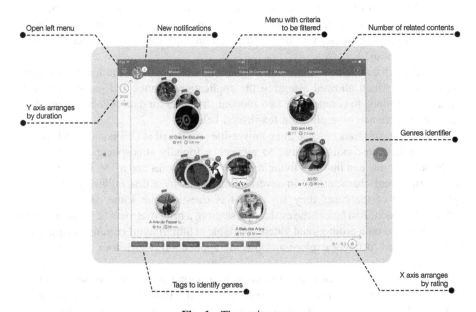

Fig. 1. The main screen

This area is structured as a multidimensional graphic presenting TV programs according to the criteria defined by the user. Programs are represented as circles and spatially distributed according to its classification (IMDB) (x axis) and duration (y axis). The user can easily change these values. The size of the circles varies accordingly to the popularity of the programs, which is determined by its reputation in the Catch-up TV of the operator (when possible) and the VOD viewers' evaluations.

According to what could be found on the IPTV application of the TDE project users may define other filters like program categories; content source (e.g. TV, VOD); age rating, and; starring decade.

The details panel about a program consists of general information of the program, such as genre, year, length and a brief synopsis and score (the IMDB rating and GUIDER users rating). Through this panel, users can also add programs to their favourites, watch a trailer, share or recommend it to friends in social networks, evaluate the program and, if in a compatible TV ecosystem, play it in the TV set. For a full list of features check [29].

4   Evaluation Procedure

Although the GUIDER App was designed to be used by clients of a Portuguese IPTV provider the research team decided to open the scope of the evaluation to try to predict if it had the potential to be adopted in other markets, namely by Brazilian users. To accomplish this, it was decided to evaluate the application in both countries with a sample of 20 participants in Brazil (herein referred as BR) and other 20 in Portugal (herein referred as PT). The number of evaluators in each country was decided in order to make the best usage of the Attrackdiff tool [30] that complemented the evaluation of the UX. Along with UX objectives, the evaluation goals were related to: determining the level of interest in the several features of the application, filtering criteria and future features; identifying usability issues; and predicting the future uses of GUIDER in domestic scenarios.

The research team chose to carry an evaluation in both countries following the same methodology, which allowed assessing the application features and particularities. It was also envisioned to compare the two adopted strategies for data collection regarding the usage experience of application (explained below).

The lab sessions took place at three universities (in Brazil at UFPE and UFPB and in Portugal at UA) in rooms prepared to recreate a friendly atmosphere, in some way similar to what one can find in a living room with some sofas and a TV. Participants of both groups were characterized in several dimensions by a first online questionnaire (Q1). In most of the cases they answered this questionnaire some days before the evaluation session. Just before the evaluation session, a brief overview of the application was made based on a promotional video (available at http://tinyurl.com/ns5dbdp). Then they were asked to freely explore and use the application, which took an average of 20 min per session.

In order to ensure a complete data collection during the evaluation sessions (and during a future regular use of the application) to allow future improvement of GUIDER, the team chose to use two complementary data gathering methods:

QInApp (InApp questions): The first method consists of an internal rating system, based on closed queries that appear contextualized while users interact with the app. These InApp questions are triggered when a specific GUIDER feature is used a certain number of times – being the related threshold (that was configured in an associated platform - at the time the ©Parse platform was used) dependent of the probability of use of each functionality at stake (i.e. for the features with a high probability of use the InApp question appeared after a higher number of interactions than the ones needed to trigger an InApp question for a feature with an expected lower probability of use).

For each functionality two questions are triggered (see Fig. 2), one concerning the level of interest in that specific feature and another about usability related issues. Participants were not obliged to answer the InApp questions.

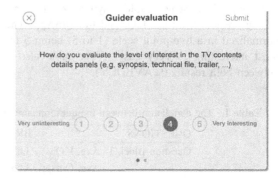

Fig. 2. A user getting an InApp question (left) and the details of the InApp interface.

F.Q. (Final questionnaire): The second data collection method involved an online final questionnaire (F.Q.) that participants answered at the end of the evaluation sessions. Questions of the Attrackdiff tool were included as an optional final section of the questionnaire. All participants were able to answer, allowing the research team to subsequently enter these answers on the online platform of the Attrakdiff tool (Fig. 3).

2.2 Please point out your level of interest in each of the following features that you have experienced: *
Rate from 1 (very uninteresting) to 5 (very interesting)

	1	2	3	4	5
TV contents detailed information (e.g. synopsis, technical file, trailer, etc.)	○	○	○	○	○

Fig. 3. A question table from the final questionnaire (translated from the original Portuguese version).

5 Results from the InApp Questions Versus Final Questionnaire

Considering the main objective of the paper the results from both data collection mechanisms were treated and the answers (both from Likert scales) were processed.

Despite the difference in the data gathering process, it was attempted that the data collected in QInApp and F.Q. were similar. As the questionnaires were applied in different mediums, the questions that compose them were also different and the F.Q. included other questions not addressed in InApp questions. So, it was necessary to create a matching table between the questions of QInApp and of the F.Q in 7 different blocks.

After doing this match, the results gathered in the questions from both methods were then analyzed. It is important to refer that both type of questions addressed a five-point Likert scale. Table 1 synthetizes the answers with the presentation of the average results from the F.Q. and the QInApp. The results from the Likert scale are normalized in a five-point scale (1 to 5) being 5 the most positive answer (e.g. "The most interesting", "Very easy"). The table also includes the deviation percentage between both results (%AVEDEV).

Table 1. The correlation between the questionnaire questions and questions in the app

QUESTIONS		BR	PT	ALL
Question Block 1	Avg. F.Q.	3,65	3,50	3,58
	Avg. Qinapp	3,65	3,50	3,60
	% AVEDEV	0,00%	0,00%	0,35%
Question Block 2	Avg. F.Q.	4,55	4,45	4,50
	Avg. Qinapp	4,40	4,00	4,22
	% AVEDEV	1,68%	5,33%	3,26%
Question Block 3	Avg. F.Q.	4,45	3,90	4,18
	Avg. Qinapp	5,00	4,67	4,90
	% AVEDEV	5,82%	8,95%	7,99%
Question Block 4	Avg. F.Q.	4,35	4,03	4,15
	Avg. Qinapp	4,60	4,75	4,19
	% AVEDEV	2,79%	8,26%	5,41%
Question Block 5	Avg. F.Q.	4,80	4,35	4,58
	Avg. Qinapp	4,73	4,33	4,59
	% AVEDEV	0,76%	0,19%	0,14%
Question Block 6	Avg. F.Q.	4,31	3,95	4,13
	Avg. Qinapp	4,11	4,40	4,21
	% AVEDEV	2,36%	5,39%	1,01%
Question Block 7	Avg. F.Q.	4,03	4,05	4,04
	Avg. Qinapp	4,20	4,33	4,25
	% AVEDEV	2,13%	3,38%	2,56%

As can be noticed, the results show a close correlation between the answers on both instruments. Only Question Block 3 (7,99%) and 4 (5,41%) got an overall percentage of deviation higher than 5%. Question Block 3 asked users about their willingness to be able to share program recommendations on social networks. It is interesting to notice that users graded that question with very high responses in the InApp questions (e.g. 5 in 5 from the BR users) but with lower results on the F.Q. One possible reason could be that this feature refers to a reaction behavior. An action that typically is driven by immediate willing to share. This may reinforce the relevance of getting the answers right after using such a feature, and shows that the momentary UX evaluation can have different results from the episodic UX evaluation. Regarding Question Block 4, that is related with the level of interest to rate the audiovisual content (providing a score and a potential target audience), the reason for the inherent deviation is not clear. It is mainly verified within PT participants (8,26%) - the deviation on BR users was only 2,79%, but despite the potential differences between momentary and episodic UX no clear reason for that could be perceived.

It is important to notice that although the deviations are globally very small (see Fig. 4), the higher numbers are associated with the Portuguese participants, probably due to a lower number of InApp questions answered (as referred, participants had the chance to skip these questions).

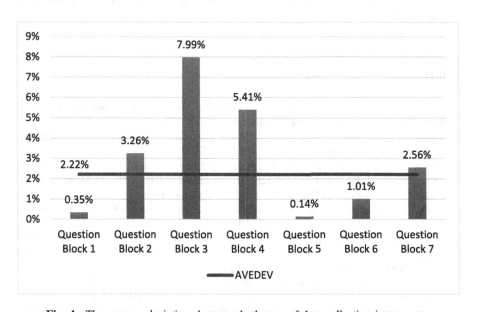

Fig. 4. The average deviations between both type of data collection instruments.

6   Conclusions

The reported evaluation allowed to get complementary information useful to improve the GUIDER application. With the use of both data collection strategies it was also expected to get comparative insights to validate if the InApp questions approach could get similar results when compared with those from traditional surveys. The results showed that the response deviation was very low reinforcing the suitability of such alternative data gathering method. The results from one of the questions can even let us perceive a possible higher accuracy in certain InApp questions, due to its immediate time correlation with the specific feature in analysis. The validation of such hypothesis requires further and dedicated research.

From these results, it was also possible to highlight the particular advantages of the InApp questions as a suitable method for evaluating applications, namely for UX dimensions, either for functional prototypes or final products, because they can be triggered at any time, based or accordingly to the users' activity, without the need for the researchers to be around and allowing to get the results in real time.

Triggering InApp questions also allows to evaluate the addition of new features to already established products, making it easier and faster for companies to decide if such features were appreciated or should be removed. Such methodology will be used in future UX evaluations of other TV related Apps to further confirm the suitability of such approach.

References

1. Zhang, D., Adipat, B.: Challenges, methodologies, and issues in the usability testing of mobile applications. Int. J. Hum. Comput. Interact. **18**, 293–308 (2005)
2. Treder, M., Pachucki, A., Zielonko, A., Lukasiewicz, K.: Mobile Book of Trends (2014)
3. Bank, C., Zuberi, W.: Mobile UI Design Patterns (2014)
4. Abreu, J., Almeida, P., Teles, B.: TV discovery & enjoy: a new approach to help users finding the right TV program to watch. In: Proceedings of the 2014 ACM International Conference on Interactive Experiences for TV and Online Video, pp. 63–70 (2014)
5. Roto, V., Law, E., Vermeeren, A., Hoonhout, J.: User experience white paper. In: Bringing Clarity to Concept User Exp., pp. 1–12 (2011)
6. T.N. Company: Screen wars: the battle for eye space in a TV-everywhere world (2015). http://www.nielsen.com/us/en/insights/reports/2015/screen-wars-the-battle-for-eye-space-in-a-tv-everywhere-world.html, Accessed: 13 June 2015
7. R. B. Media, Second Screen Series - Paper 1: Setting The Scene, vol. 1 (2012)
8. Hsu, S.H., Wen, M.-H., Lin, H.-C., Lee, C.-C., Lee, C.-H.: AIMED-A personalized TV recommendation system. In: European Conference on Interactive Television, pp. 166–174 (2007)
9. BBC Research & Development, "Sibyl Recommender System" (2012). http://sibyl.prototyping.bbc.co.uk/. Accessed: 26 Dec 2013
10. Krauss, C., George, L., Arbanowski, S.: New Systems Programming. TV predictor: personalized program recommendations to be displayed on SmartTVs. In: Proceedings of the 2nd Int. Work. Big Data Streams Heterog. Source Min. Algorithms Appl. BigMine 2013. Vol. 23, pp. 63–70. ACM, New York (2013)

11. Obrist, M., Bernhaupt, R., Tscheligi, M.: Interactive television for the home: An ethnographic study on users' requirements and experiences. Int. J. HCI **24**(2) (2008)
12. Gauntlett, D., Hill, A.: TV living: Television, culture and everyday life. Routledge (2002)
13. Law, E.: The measurability and predictability of user experience. In: Proceedings of EICS, pp. 1–10. ACM, New York (2011)
14. I.S.O. (ISO), Ergonomics of Human–System Interaction – Part 210: Human-centred Design for Interactive Systems (formerly known as 13407) (2010)
15. User Experience. https://en.wikipedia.org/wiki/User_experience. Accessed 13 Jan 2017
16. Vermeeren, A.P.O.S., Law, E.L.-C., Roto, V., Obrist, M., Hoonhout, J., Vananen-Vainio-Mattila, K.: User experience evaluation methods: current state and development needs. In: Proceedings of the 6th Nord. Conf. Human Computer Interact. Extending Boundaries, pp. 521–530. ACM (2010)
17. All about UX (2017). http://www.allaboutux.org/. Accessed 13 Jan 2017
18. Bernhaupt, R., Pirker, M.: Evaluating user experience for interactive television: towards the development of a domain-specific user experience questionnaire. In: Kotzé, P., Marsden, G., Lindgaard, G., Wesson, J., Winckler, M. (eds.) INTERACT 2013. LNCS, vol. 8118, pp. 642–659. Springer, Heidelberg (2013). doi:10.1007/978-3-642-40480-1_45
19. Drouet, D., Bernhaupt, R.: User experience evaluation methods: lessons learned from an interactive TV case-study. In: Bogdan, C., Gulliksen, J., Sauer, S., Forbrig, P., Winckler, M., Johnson, C., Palanque, P., Bernhaupt, R., Kis, F. (eds.) HCSE/HESSD -2016. LNCS, vol. 9856, pp. 351–358. Springer, Cham (2016). doi:10.1007/978-3-319-44902-9_22
20. Abreu, J., Almeida, P., Silva, T.: A UX evaluation approach for second-screen applications. In: Abásolo, M.J., Perales, Francisco J., Bibiloni, A. (eds.) jAUTI/CTVDI -2015. CCIS, vol. 605, pp. 105–120. Springer, Cham (2016). doi:10.1007/978-3-319-38907-3_9
21. Brooke, J., et al.: SUS-A quick and dirty usability scale. Usability Eval. Ind. **189**(194), 4–7 (1996)
22. Attrakdiff (2017). http://www.attrakdiff.de/, Accessed 13 Jan 2017
23. Jenny Preece, H.S., Rogers, Y.: Interaction Design: Beyond Human-Computer Interaction (2015)
24. Benedek, J., Miner, T.: Measuring Desirability: New methods for evaluating desirability in a usability lab setting. Proc. Usability Prof. Assoc. **2003**(8–12), 57 (2002)
25. Burzacca, P., Paternò, F.: Remote usability evaluation of mobile web applications. In: Kurosu, M. (ed.) HCI 2013. LNCS, vol. 8004, pp. 241–248. Springer, Heidelberg (2013). doi:10.1007/978-3-642-39232-0_27
26. Harrison, R., Flood, D., Duce, D.: Usability of mobile applications: literature review and rationale for a new usability model. J. Interact. Sci. **1**(1), 1 (2013)
27. Pagano, D., Maalej, W.: User feedback in the appstore: an empirical study. In: 2013 21st IEEE International Requirements Engineering Conference (RE), pp. 125–134 (2013)
28. Nayebi, F., Desharnais, J.-M., Abran, A.: The state of the art of mobile application usability evaluation. 2012 25th IEEE *Canadian* Conference *on* Electrical *and* Computer Engineering, pp. 1–4, May 2012
29. Abreu, J., Almeida, P., Silva, T., Oliveira, R.: Discovering in a second screen app: perspectives from portuguese and brazilian markets. Procedia Comput. Sci. **64**, 1240–1247 (2015)
30. Hassenzahl, M.: The interplay of beauty, goodness, and usability in interactive products. Hum.-Comput. Interact. **19**(4), 319–349 (2004)

Author Index

Printed in the United States
By Bookmasters